Tell Us

Tell Us a Story

An African American Family in the Heartland

Shirley Motley Portwood

Southern Illinois University Press

Carbondale and Edwardsville

An earlier version of parts of the present work appeared in
the author's article "In Search of My Great, Great Grandparents:
Mapping Seven Generations of Family History," *Journal of the
Illinois State Historical Society*, 92 (summer 1999): 95–118.

Frontispiece: Shirley Portwood's maternal grandparents, Lee Gene
Jones Sr. and Bessie Jones (*background*), with their children,
Leora "Toots" Jones and Lee Gene "Billy" Jones, ca. 1942.

Library of Congress Cataloging-in-Publication Data

Portwood, Shirley Motley, 1946–
Tell us a story : an African American family in the heartland
/ Shirley Motley Portwood.
    p.   cm.
    1. Afro-American families—Illinois—Springfield Region—
Biography—Anecdotes. 2. Afro-American families—Middle
West—Biography—Anecdotes. 3. Motley family— Anec-
dotes. 4. Springfield Region (Ill.)—Biography—Anecdotes.
5. Middle West—Biography—Anecdotes. 6. Springfield Re-
gion (Ill.)—Race relations—Anecdotes. 7. Middle West—
Race relations—Anecdotes. 8. Portwood, Shirley Motley,
1946– 9. Oral history. I. Title.
E549.S7 P67   2000   99-040182
977'.00496073 21—dc21
ISBN 0-8093-2313-3 (cloth: alk. paper)
ISBN 0-8093-2314-1 (pbk.: alk. paper)

To Daddy and Mudeah

Contents

Illustrations

Motley Family Genealogy

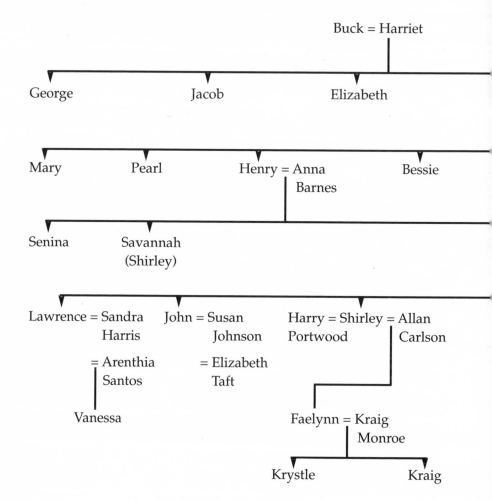

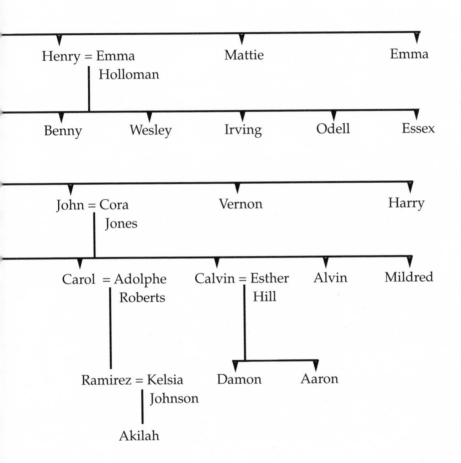

Henry = Emma Holloman   Mattie   Emma

Benny   Wesley   Irving   Odell   Essex

John = Cora Jones   Vernon   Harry

Carol = Adolphe Roberts   Calvin = Esther Hill   Alvin   Mildred

Ramirez = Kelsia Johnson   Damon   Aaron

Akilah

Introduction

Grandma, tell us a story," Krystle and Kraig urge as they have done since they were scarcely more than babies. I readily oblige, happy that my granddaughter and grandson enjoy tales of family history just as I did when I was their ages. Krystle and Kraig, clad in the adult-sized T-shirts that are their favorite sleepwear, snuggle beside me as we prepare for our bedtime ritual of storytelling. They remind me of their favorite stories:

"Tell us about when you were little."

"Yeah, about when you did something bad and got into trouble."

"Tell us about when Mom picked all the lady's flowers."

"And you got mad."

"Tell us about when we were little and did something funny."

"Tell us about . . ."

Their words call to mind countless evenings in rural Mounds, Illinois, during the 1940s and 1950s when my family gathered around the old wood-burning stove and my siblings and I begged our parents to tell us stories. Mudeah, as we called our mother, rarely shared memories of her past, but Daddy often obliged. Meanwhile, Mudeah prepared fresh roasted peanuts, baked sweet potatoes, or hot buttered popcorn—all grown on our own farm. We'd grin happily as Daddy began to talk about what we called "the olden days." He'd tell about his childhood during the Great Depression of the 1920s and 1930s when the rabbits and squirrels he and his brothers, Harry and Vernon, had hunted and trapped and the blackberries and nuts they'd gathered had become staples of their meager diet. Or he might tell about when he and his two

1

buddies had walked to Lincoln University—a historically black college in Jefferson City, Missouri—from their homes in Charleston, Missouri. As Daddy talked, I'd try to picture him wearing what he called a "stupid-looking green beanie" that freshmen had sported at Lincoln and many other colleges and universities.

Sometimes Daddy told stories about his experiences as deputy sheriff of Pulaski County, Illinois, like when he'd helped to capture two men who had robbed the bank in Mounds. We'd been a little disappointed that he hadn't had occasion to "wing" at least one of them, like Wyatt Earp or Matt Dillon might have done in the western movies and on television, but Daddy's photograph had been in the newspaper when bank officials had given him and the others involved in the apprehension a cash reward.

At other times the entire family got into the act and told stories about incidents that we all could recall. The time that Daddy had run—literally—a white man off our farm was a real favorite. Or we'd talk about how shocked we had been, as had the entire town and all of Pulaski County, when one local teenager had killed another teenager after basketball practice at Douglass High School in Mounds. All of us had known both of these young men, who had been about the same ages as my two older brothers, Larry (Lawrence) and June (John Jr.). Or perhaps we'd tease my younger sister, Carol, about how Preacher Brown always wanted her to "sit on Preacher's lap" and to "hug Preacher's neck." Mudeah usually made an excuse for Carol to leave the room then. She didn't go for all that physical contact with Preacher.

At still other times we recalled various neighbors. Mrs. King, who had a reputation for being very industrious and frugal, was one very interesting figure we liked to discuss. She was a widow who had run her small farm entirely alone for many years. A thin, wiry woman, she walked virtually everywhere she went, often selling both the produce she grew on her farm and the beautiful handmade quilts that she created. Several times each week, Mrs. King slowly made her way past our house, sometimes stopping for a visit.

We speculated about when Grampa, our paternal grandfather, might make his next visit from Peoria. We could count on him to be very indulgent, taking us to buy ice cream and other treats. "I'm going into town. If you want to go with me, you'd better get ready!" he'd say. We also talked about Papa and Grandma Bessie, our maternal grandparents, and the summers we had spent with them in Lansing, Arkansas, about fifteen or twenty miles west of Memphis, Tennessee. We fondly recalled Miss Mary Ella Miller—whom virtually everyone called Miss *May* Ella, rather than Miss Mary Ella. She was a teacher, now retired, who always let us attend her little one-room country schoolhouse in Lansing whenever we were there. We also reminisced about going to Sunday school and church with Grandma Bessie. We really thought it was funny when one or two of the "good sisters" would jump up and shout, each swinging her purse perilously as she danced up and down the aisles. Some church members explained to us that these women had felt the Holy Spirit. Grandma Bessie, who was very outspoken and didn't put up with a bunch of foolishness, generally held to the opinion that they were "just showing out!"

Reminiscences about Lansing sometimes reminded me about the lynching of a black man, a neighbor and acquaintance of my grandparents, which had occurred when we were there. This terrifying experience had made me afraid to remain at my grandparents' home. Further, it had made me keenly aware of the tremendous power of southern whites and the ways in which they sometimes wielded that power against their black neighbors.

With the family gathered beside the hot stove, we talked about our plans for the future: short-term plans for blackberry picking and gathering black walnuts and pecans, or for picking cotton and string beans for our neighbor Everett Meeks during the summer and fall, or for butchering hogs, cutting our own Christmas tree, and making snow ice cream during the winter. I'd think about skating on the ice at the pond across the road, although I didn't dare mention that around Mudeah and Daddy because they'd warned that this was very dangerous. I'd glance stealthily at Larry and June, wondering if they were anticipating this, too. Carol and the babies, Calvin and Alvin, were too young to be included in these daring escapades. That Carol was such a little tattletale that I might never include her. Mildred, the youngest of my brothers and sisters, was born in 1960, after we had left Mounds.

Inevitably, the conversation turned to long-term plans. "When you go to college" was a common theme. At that point Mudeah and Daddy would tell us about schools we might attend, like Southern Illinois University (SIU) in Carbondale, which was about thirty miles north of Mounds and was where many of our schoolteachers had studied. And they'd talk about Lincoln University in Jefferson City, where Daddy had gone, or Shorter College in Little Rock, Arkansas, which Aunt Theresa and Uncle Billy had attended. Daddy and Mudeah often bragged about how smart we all were and said that we'd probably get scholarships, but that we'd also have to work part-time to help pay our expenses. After each of us graduated, we'd help the younger ones. We'd all be doctors, lawyers, engineers, or whatever we chose.

Later, when our parents weren't around, my siblings and I talked about the new cars and the big house we would buy for them after we graduated from college. We would get a Mercury for Mudeah and an Oldsmobile for Daddy. The house would have indoor plumbing, fancy carpeting, and all the amenities. And we'd buy them lots of new clothes, so that Mudeah wouldn't have to turn the collars on Daddy's shirts and her own dresses, and they wouldn't have to put cardboard in the bottoms of their shoes to cover the holes. We imagined their surprise and joy when they saw all the things we would buy for them.

This book includes many of these and other stories that the Motley family has shared for close to fifty years. In addition to my own memories, interviews with my father, three brothers, two sisters, and other relatives, together with notes and recollections from our annual family reunion, have helped me to piece together a composite view of the Motley family. This colorful mosaic of African American family life is set in rural southern Illinois, Missouri, and Arkansas from the Great Depression through the 1950s and is accented with recollections from the present era. It includes oral history from five generations, going back to my grandparents who were born more than one hundred years ago. Information about two additional generations—those of my great-grandparents and great-great-grandparents—is based upon historical research into primary data from state archives, county and local records, plantation sources, and manuscript censuses.

My brother John Henry Motley Jr.—called "June" in his early years—and I conducted historical research on our family in the fall of 1982. He and I met in Memphis and then went on a whirlwind data-collecting tour of three states—Arkansas, Mississippi, and Tennessee. We first interviewed Grandma Bessie, our maternal grandmother, in Earle, Arkansas. From there we visited our great-uncle Odell Motley, our paternal grandfather's younger brother, Uncle Odell's wife and daughter, and other relatives in Colt, Arkansas. We went to Little Rock, Arkansas, to study assorted state records and federal census materials. Next we proceeded to Humboldt and Trenton, Tennessee, about eighty-five miles northeast of Memphis, the area where our paternal great-great-grandparents, Harriet and Buck Motley, and our paternal great-grandfather, Henry Motley, had been slaves more than 130 years ago. We subsequently went to the small Delta town of Hernando, Mississippi, an hour's drive from Memphis, near our maternal grandparents' childhood homes. Finally we returned to Memphis, where we stayed at the historic Peabody House, noted as much for the ducks that live on its roof as for its elegant decor and excellent service.

I made a second family history research trip in May 1997. Harry Michael Portwood Sr., my husband since March 14, 1992, was my companion and research assistant. We returned to Humboldt and Trenton, where we found a few additional bits of historical data about the Motleys. Then we went to Corinth, in northeast Mississippi, where Buck Motley and other family members had migrated in the post-Civil War era. Here we found numerous crucial pieces to the jigsaw puzzle that is the Motley family history. We concluded this trip with a visit to Lansing to talk to Uncle Lee Gene "Billy" Jones Jr., my mother's brother, who provided photographs and other useful information about the Jones family.

Leora Jones Hughes, my mother's younger sister, and Phyllis Benton, my cousin, shared their collections of family photographs, official documents, letters, and personal papers with me during a summer 1998 trip to Portland, Oregon, where they both live. Phyllis, who is the daughter of my mother's older sister, Theresa Jones Benton, and William "Bill" Benton Sr., has inherited her mother's carefully maintained scrapbooks and other memorabilia and has also done extensive research in family history. My cousins Bill Jr. and Irma Benton and their daughter Mercedes provided gracious hospitality during this visit and research venture. Gregory, the youngest of Theresa and William Sr.'s four children, also contributed to this very warm welcome.

Vignettes from the annual Motley family reunion introduce most sections of this family history. Four generations have attended these family retreats since 1987. Fifteen to twenty-four of us spend an entire week each year on a joint vacation. The first reunions were held either at my brother John's house in Connecticut or at my own in southwestern Illinois. Since 1996, we have met in other locations, including the Missouri Ozarks in 1996, Kissimmee, Florida, in 1997, and San Diego, California, in 1998 and 1999. We often gather around the kitchen table or in the family room, talking, eating, laughing, playing cards, and teasing one another. We also tell stories, reveling in sharing recollections, much as we have done for some fifty years. We add new stories regularly as we recount the escapades of assorted family members, past and present. We urge our children and grandchildren to share their treasured remembrances, too. We are all storytellers; we are all included in the Motley family history.

The tales in this book range from the humorous to the poignant and reveal much about culture and history that is universal among African Americans, especially those from rural cultures: a rich and often joyful family life and community with cultural traditions reaching back to the slave past and beyond; the harsh poverty that made life a difficult struggle to provide even the basic necessities; racial issues that divided blacks and whites during the era of "Jim Crow" segregation and inequality; and tremendous emphasis upon self-improvement through hard work and education. Other aspects of the Motley family history are less commonplace: a father who earned two college degrees in midlife, after fathering seven children, one of whom died in infancy; and six siblings who became very well educated and highly successful—two university professors, two attorneys, and two businessmen. African Americans also share a culture and a history with many white Americans, especially those from rural backgrounds. As William Edward Burghardt Du Bois, the highly acclaimed African American historian and sociologist, noted in a 1903 essay entitled "Of Our Spiritual Strivings," which is included in *The Souls of Black Folk*, African Americans imbibe of two cultures—American and Negro (to use Du Bois's terminology).

Much of this book focuses upon Pulaski and Alexander Counties in extreme southern Illinois, the home of three generations of Motleys, from about 1920 until 1978. Henry and Anna Motley, my paternal grandparents, and their two children, Senina and John, moved to Future City in Alexander County, of which Cairo is the county seat, in the early 1920s. John Motley, my father, recalls Future City as an impoverished, predominantly black community. The Motleys were included in the second wave of blacks who migrated to southern Illinois in the post–World War I era. Blacks first migrated to Pulaski and Alexander Counties in large numbers during the Civil War and postwar era. In the late nineteenth century, the black population of the tri-county area at the southern tip of Illinois, which includes Pulaski, Alexander, and Massac Counties, was proportionately the largest outside the South. Most black migrants were former slaves or descendants of slaves who came to southern Illinois from the South for economic, social, and political reasons. Many hoped to purchase farmland or to establish a business. Area blacks owned many small shops in the post–Civil War era, and a few of these businesses survived into the mid-twentieth century and later. Further, the incidence of blacks owning farmland, especially in Pulaski County, was well above that of most other areas of the United States.

Grampa Henry Motley, who was named after his father, worked at a lumber mill when he and his family lived in Future City. Earlier, according to his recollections, he had been a brakeman on the railroad. While riding the rails through southern Illinois, he had admired the families that labored together on their small farms and had vowed to join their ranks. Strongly committed to his extended family, Grampa temporarily abandoned his own hopes of becoming an independent landowner and moved to the Charleston, Missouri, area in the boot-heel of the state at his mother's behest. The Henry and Anna Motley family remained there during the Great Depression. Meanwhile, John Motley and Cora Jones met, attended high school together, and married. During the 1940s, John and Cora Motley and Henry and Anna Motley moved to Mounds in Pulaski County, where they purchased the small farm that provides the setting for much of this book. After brief stays in Chicago and Springfield, Illinois, John and Cora and their family returned to Pulaski County in 1952, where they remained until 1959 when they returned to Springfield.

In Pulaski County most blacks were farmers or worked in farm-related occupations. Many lived on small farms that they owned, rented, or sharecropped, usually at or near the subsistence level. Only a few black farmers, such as Everett Meeks, regularly produced for the market. Black men also found employment, usually as unskilled laborers, at the sawmills in Pulaski and Alexander Counties or on the railroads. Black women in Pulaski County rarely worked outside their own households, because the few places that hired women usually employed only whites. The sewing factory, retail shops, newspapers, banks, and the telephone company pursued this whites-only employment policy.

The rural, northern setting of this work is an unusual one for an African American autobiography, most of which usually focus on either the South or the urban North. Rural Mounds, located near Cairo at the confluence of the Mississippi and Ohio Rivers, shares much with the rural South. Indeed, two southern states, Missouri and Kentucky, are just across the rivers. The southern culture, the racial segregation and discrimination, and the character of the black community all bespeak the southern origins of its population—both black and white. In other respects, Mounds is northern. Very significantly, blacks in Illinois gained the right to vote in 1870 and retained it even after black southerners had lost the franchise. Pulaski County blacks immediately became a substantial part of the electorate in 1870 when they first acquired the vote. In that year, they represented over 27 percent of the total population. By the end of the nineteenth century, they composed over 40 percent. During World War I, the black population of Pulaski County declined significantly, but even so, blacks remained a substantial minority of the population. Well-educated, politically sophisticated black leaders in the county, with the support of a strong African American community, many of them propertied, were able to translate these large numbers of black voters into limited political power. Their participation in electoral politics assured that blacks would wrest some concessions from whites, although total equality remained elusive.

This current work, while not neglecting the struggles of black life, focuses heavily on the many strengths and triumphs within the black community. It looks at a community that often was able to insulate its members against the harsher realities of a larger society filled with racial animosity and riddled with discrimination. A rigid system of *de facto* segregation permeated Pulaski County and southern Illinois until the mid-1960s, when the Civil Rights movement finally ushered in a few changes. Meanwhile, the Jim Crow system caused tremendous disadvantages for blacks and conferred privileges upon whites. Blacks and whites had very limited social contacts with each other. Blacks attended separate and unequal schools, sat in the balcony of the movie theater, and ate only in black-owned restaurants. Although blacks attended SIU in Carbondale, they could not live in campus housing until the 1950s. Larry, my oldest brother, who entered the college in 1959, recalls that this barrier had been eliminated shortly before his matriculation there. Nor could we count on being taught by African American faculty at that college or most others in the United States, except for the traditionally black schools. We knew also that even medical care at the hospital in Cairo was separate for blacks and whites. When Alvin, my youngest brother, was gravely ill with pneumonia in 1959, he was placed in a segregated ward in the Cairo hospital.

Introduction

African Americans in Mounds, in southern Illinois, and throughout the country established their own support networks in order to address their own and their children's needs and to combat the debilitating impact of the Jim Crow system. The black community included various institutions, such as churches, clubs, and small businesses. The black schools, although publicly supported and controlled by a predominantly white board of education and a preponderance of white administrators, played an important role within the black community. African American teachers took the concept of *in loco parentis* seriously, reinforcing the same values and aspirations in children as did the children's own families. Despite class divisions among blacks, we all intermingled within this community. Everyone knew virtually everyone else. As my siblings and I grew up, we were personally acquainted with blacks whose status ran the gamut from doctors, dentists, landowners, schoolteachers, and businessmen to skilled and semi-skilled laborers, to subsistence farmers and sharecroppers, to common laborers. We all knew that Hugo Chambliss, a black businessman, reportedly was one of the wealthiest people in southern Illinois. His Front Street real estate office was one of several black businesses in Mounds. That we knew blacks who were very economically secure and well educated reinforced our parents' and teachers' promises that we, too, could become successful.

A major theme of this work is the self-empowerment of the Motley family. Many African American autobiographers have told of the pain and self-doubt that black children suffered as they witnessed the powerlessness and humiliation of their parents and other respected black adults who shrank from confrontations with whites. In contrast, I write of adults—both male and female—who commanded respect both within the African American community and in the larger society. This black self-empowerment, in turn, helped the Motley children to envision ourselves in positions not commonly held by black people. Thus, we saw our future selves as the independent, self-assured, and outspoken adults that we have all become.

My interest in family history, which goes back to my own childhood experiences of the oral tradition, combined with my professional interest as a university history professor, prompted me to do research on the Motleys. Yet it took the entreaties of various family members to induce me to write a book on the subject. Krystle Lauren Monroe and Kraig Tyrone Monroe Jr., the children of my daughter, Faelynn Carlson Monroe, and her husband, Kraig Tyrone Monroe Sr., provided the inspiration for me to write this book. Krystle, born on January 16, 1985, and Kraig, born on January 9, 1986, have enjoyed listening to stories about family history since they were only two or three years old, often preferring them to the usual children's classics. Several years ago, they urged me to write the stories down so that they could share them with others, including during show-and-tell at their school. "Do you have pictures, too?" they asked. Thus, in May 1994, I began to write a collection of stories based upon the Motley family's oral tradition, planning to complete eight or ten stories to share at the annual family reunion in August of that year. But soon I began to spend virtually every available moment working at the computer, often alternately laughing and crying as I recalled the past. Later I incorporated the historical data from the aforementioned research trips. After I had written a few stories, I asked Harry, my husband, to read them. His profuse compliments prompted me to write others.

Among the first stories that I wrote were some that Daddy had told for many years. Even as I wrote them, I wondered whether I could properly tell his stories. Indeed, can one person tell another's stories? Would I inadvertently transform them in the process, making them mine rather than his? During my father's next visit, I asked him to read several pieces, and I sent another to him for Father's Day 1995. He was enormously pleased with these vignettes. Daddy, normally very emotionally reserved, even confessed that some had "caused him to get emotional." He also told me additional tales I either had not heard previously or simply did not recall, thus providing still more family history. His observation that he had been unaware of the tremendous impact of his storytelling upon his children until he read these stories further encouraged my writing, because I wanted him and others who had shaped my siblings' lives and my own to be aware of their very positive influence. Because my mother had died several years before I began this manuscript, I was unable to incorporate the perspective that she would have offered.

When my sisters and brothers and their families found that I had begun to write a family history, they, too, shared stories with me. Old stories, new stories. "Shirl, did you write about the time that . . ." they asked. Indeed, an avalanche of information followed. Sometimes I felt quite overwhelmed, as though my family now expected me to write about everything of significance in all of our lives. What will I include? How can I possibly bring any order to this maze of information? Will my attempts to impose organization reshape the stories? I wondered.

As this volume took shape, it encompassed much more than the Motley family history. It became the story of a larger African American and American past. I now wish to share this work with a broader audience. It is my hope that others will see in these stories a part of our shared experience.

1

The Cast of Characters

Daddy Runs the White Man off Our Property

Git off my property! Go on! Git!" Daddy is yelling at someone.

"I'm going," comes the nervous reply.

Two figures appear—Daddy and a white man. Both are walking fast. Daddy is agitated. He increases his pace, and now he is almost running in pursuit of the white man who has come to look at our pigs. The two of them are coming down the hillside by our modest farmhouse. They are followed at some distance by another white man, Orville Campbell, who had brought the first man by our farm. No longer obscured by the honey locust trees between the house and the hill, they come into full view now.

Daddy is angry because the white man has insulted him, first by offering a very low price for the pigs, and second by saying that the pigs were scrawny and therefore not worth much. Daddy had countered that the man was under no obligation to buy the pigs if he found them so unsatisfactory. But the man persisted, continuing to argue about how puny the pigs looked. Daddy grew impatient, then angry, and finally ordered the man off his property, and upbraided Campbell, an acquaintance of long standing, for bringing such a person to his farm. This same man had attempted earlier to cheat Daddy by offering him a low price for a cow that Daddy had just purchased. The man had contended that the cow was not with calf, but Daddy knew that she was because that was much of the reason he had bought her in the first place. Now the guy was trying to swindle Daddy again.

"Go on, git! You son of a bitch!" Things are escalating. Daddy reaches down, picking up a stick and flailing it wildly, as though he means to hit the man. I am watching from the backyard, having emerged from the outhouse. I am eight years old, skinny, with long braids. My two older brothers, Larry and June, twelve and eleven years old respectively, are coming in from working in the fields, and they witness the scene also. The three of us are transfixed with surprise. We are fascinated. And we are very, very proud. Daddy is running a white man off our property! Daddy has real nerve! The year is 1954. We are in Pulaski County, Illinois, perilously close to the South. White people have most of the power; black people have very little. We have even heard about blacks being lynched "across the rivers" in Kentucky and Missouri. And yet Daddy is unmindful of the inherent danger of the situation. At this moment, his only concern is to drive from his property someone who is trying to cheat him for the second time.

"I'm going as fast as I can," shouts the white man. He has abandoned earlier attempts to maintain his dignity. Clearly he recognizes that he is in real danger of being struck by the huge stick Daddy continues to wave. No longer simply walking fast, the man has broken into a full-fledged run. Daddy is in hot pursuit.

"Well, you're not moving fast enough!" Daddy continues to chase the man. Daddy is wearing his big, black galoshes, with several buckles. The top three buckles are unfastened, and now that he is running, they make a lot of noise. We hear the "Whoom! Whoom!" of the boots hitting the ground and the "Jangle, jangle," of the buckles as Daddy pursues the white man. The sound effects add to the comedy of the scenario. They also make Daddy sound more fearsome as he runs. Hearing the commotion, my mother comes out of the house. As she evaluates the situation, she stifles the sound of her laughter with a hand over her mouth.

The two white men finally reach the truck parked on the road. Daddy makes a final admonition to Campbell. "Don't ever bring this son of a bitch on my property again!"

Daddy turns around, aware for the first time that his family is

14

watching. He breaks into laughter and throws the stick on the ground. We all gather around him. He is our hero. We talk in excited tones about how "Daddy didn't take nothing off that white man!" We each talk about where we were and what we were doing when we heard Daddy's words—and his galoshes. We each recount our own version of how he cursed at the man, omitting the exact words because we aren't permitted to swear. We talk about how afraid the man was. How he ran when Daddy picked up the stick. How Orville Campbell stayed out of the whole affair, offering no comfort or assistance to his companion.

And we are not afraid, because we know that Daddy will protect us.

Family Reunions: The Motley Crew

The Motley family, gathered for its annual one-week reunion, sits around the kitchen table and tells this and other stories about our history. The current one has been a favorite since it occurred forty years ago. During each retelling, those who were there the first time relive it, savoring every detail. This is a story of pride, principle, and self-empowerment. It is also a story about the impact of race upon our lives.

We laugh heartily and make jokes as we talk about Daddy's running the white man off the farm. We punctuate the story, especially the ending, with our comments.

"Yeah, that was one scared white man!"

"Daddy sure scared him!"

"I thought he was going to hit him!"

"Daddy never did take anything off anybody!"

"That white boy turned red as a motherfucker. I've never seen a motherfucker's face as red as his!" Larry declares empathically. We all turn and stare at him for a moment before bursting into laughter. Despite the levity, what we are really saying is very serious: We are and have always been a strong, proud black family. We have always been willing to stand up for our principles, regardless of the risks inherent in challenging a society fraught with institutionalized racism. This story embodies our collective self-image as a family, and so we love it and we tell it again and again. This tale is often the prelude to a full-fledged storytelling session.

Other stories follow. The premier storyteller is Daddy, the family patriarch. Daddy is the one who first fostered our interest in oral family history. Years ago, before we had a television, we would gather around, grinning and entreating him, "Daddy, tell us a story."

After protesting that he couldn't think of a new one, he would say, "Well, there was this time when . . . " And another story had begun. Or maybe an old one would be retold. Even now, we still gather around, smiling and encouraging Daddy to tell us a story. One sees the pride on his face, hears it in his voice as he recognizes the impact that his storytelling and his own experiences have had upon his family. "Well, I'll swundle," he'll say. "I didn't know you remembered that. Why you were just a baby when that happened."

The Motley family reunion has been a tradition since 1987. We six siblings—Larry, John, Carol, Calvin, Mildred, and me—and our families have spent one week together since that first reunion at John and Susan's vacation home in West Goshen, Connecticut. We held the first four there. In 1990 John and Susan moved into a new house a few miles away in Burlington, Connecticut, the site of the 1991, 1993, and 1995 reunions. In 1995 John married Elizabeth "Liz" Taft; he and Susan had divorced two years earlier. The 1992 and 1994 get-togethers were hosted by my husband, Harry, and me in Godfrey, Illinois. Subsequent reunions have been held at various vacation venues, rather than at private homes.

The sites of the reunions, as well as our experiences there, have also become enshrined in family lore. We cannot resist the temptation to compare our current houses with the ones of our childhood. We also compare them to those in Lansing, Arkansas, where our maternal grandparents lived. A picture of one of their homes shows our grandparents and the two youngest of their five children—Billy (Lee Gene Jr.) and Toots (Leora)—in front of a crude, unpainted sharecropper's shanty, similar to the one in which they lived when we visited them during the summers.

"I thought it was nice then. It had three bedrooms," someone says.

"Yes, Billy and Toots each had their own room," someone else notes.

"And there was a dining room."

"Yeah, the house was a lot bigger than ours!"

The West Goshen house, where our first family reunions were held, was an A-frame on a large, heavily wooded lot, with a little stream running past. The farm in Mounds had a stream also. Maybe "ditch" would be a more appropriate term. It wasn't a place where one might go to contemplate the meaning of life, as one might in West Goshen. But sitting beside the stream in West Goshen and listening to the gentle gurgle of the water, one might recall the similarly peaceful sounds of the water that flowed behind our old home. One could almost hear the children's laughter as we jumped from stone to stone on our way to the pasture to bring the cows home for the evening milking. "Hurry! Hurry! Mudeah's making a blackberry cobbler for dinner!"

And perhaps, too, one would recollect how difficult life was in that time and place where children's labor was necessary for the family's survival. "Go down to the spring and wash the greens for dinner! Hurry up! We don't have all day." Both the laughter and the tears were important parts of life in Mounds, Illinois, during the 1940s and 1950s.

We also discuss the house that John and Susan built in Burlington. It is a two-story frame, Connecticut-country home. We all had watched it emerge. The first time we saw the homesite, we thought it was the perfect pastoral setting for the house of our childhood dreams: a peaceful, secluded area, surrounded by white birch trees; a latticework of blackberry canes; birds and other wildlife hidden by lush vegetation. John kept saying, "Should I build a white picket fence? I've always dreamed of having a house with a white picket fence." Two years later, the house was completed, and we were able to have the family reunion at this lovely place. We picked wild blackberries for jams and cobblers, further recapturing our nostalgia for home. And we had the modern amenities that our house in Mounds had lacked.

Harry and I live on bluffs overlooking the Mississippi River in a two-story brick French Provincial, which we built in 1991 and 1992. We moved into it only days before the 1992 family reunion was held there. It too has a large, heavily wooded lot, much of which we allow to remain in its natural state. In order to preserve its pristine appearance, I had to fight with my city-boy husband who wanted to cut up to one-third of the trees and plant grass among those that remained.

"Why buy a heavily wooded lot if you're going to cut down the trees?" I argued.

"To have a better view of the river. During the summer we'll hardly be able to see it," he reasoned.

"Anyone who has trouble seeing the river can go out and stand on the edge of the bluff and see it!" was my rejoinder. I thought that we had resolved the matter, but shortly thereafter the landscaper was busily cutting down trees. I ran out and demanded that he stop immediately under penalty of both his own and my husband's demise. Although I anticipated that Harry and I would have an ongoing conflict over this issue, he soon changed his mind. In fact, Harry has said repeatedly that he is very pleased that I insisted on retaining the trees.

The children like the house's secret closet best. When Kraig and Krystle, my grandchildren, visited prior to the family reunion, they had been really excited about it. As we entered the closet of the master suite, they had anxiously looked around, as though expecting something to leap out at them.

"Grandma, where is the secret closet?" they asked.

"Secret closet? There is no secret closet," I had responded, puzzled. This merely confirmed for them that there was a secret closet. I mean, who would expect that someone would actually admit to having a secret closet, just because someone asks to see it?

They exchanged knowing looks and smiled approvingly. This was like their secret password at home, which only they and their parents were to know. "Um huh! Come on, Grandma. We won't tell anyone about it," they had reassured me. Finally it dawned on me: they had heard me say that there is a cedar closet; they thought I'd said *secret* closet.

"Oh, you mean the cedar closet?" I had said, showing them to it. They were both very disappointed, but ultimately Krystle was persuaded that there had been a misunderstanding. Kraig wasn't. Just as Krystle and I had convinced him that there was no secret closet, Harry had come into the room. Having overheard the discussion, he decided to have a little fun at my expense.

"Did your Grandma show you the secret closet?" he asked conspiratorially.

"We knew it! We knew it!" They were delighted that we did have a secret closet, even though we wouldn't show it to them.

When Vanessa, my niece, visited for the family reunion a few days later, we went through the same scenario upon entering the master suite. "Aunt Shirley, where is the secret closet?" she asked. So all the kids think we have a secret closet.

Our house and farm in rural Mounds, where we lived in the 1940s and 1950s, is a favorite topic at the family reunion. We reminisce about our last trip to look at "the old place" in October 1978, long after we had moved away from the area. Larry, John, Carol, and I had gone to Grampa Henry Motley's funeral, held a few miles away at Bethel AME Church. On the way to the house, we had talked of our childhood memories, including those of Bethel, our old church. We recalled the many times we children had walked to church, which was several miles from our home. Sometimes we got a ride with Mrs. Mary Belle Robinson, whom everyone called Miss May Belle and who lived about a mile from us. Miss May Belle had no children of her own, but all the children of Bethel became her charges as she prepared for the Sunday school Easter and Christmas programs that she directed. Under her kind and patient tutelage, we each had participated in plays and given little "pieces," as we called the short addresses required of good, Christian children. A small child of three or four, dressed in his or her Christmas best, might say:

> What are you looking at me for?
> I didn't come to stay.
> I just came to tell you
> Today is Christmas Day!

The audience would chuckle and applaud appreciatively, as though they hadn't heard this same little poem every Christmas since time began. Other children recited speeches about Jesus and the joy of His birth and assorted Christmas stories. Still others participated in a play about the Nativity. Several times at church and also at school where similar programs were produced—we didn't worry about the "separation of church and state" at Lovejoy Grade School in Villa Ridge, Illinois—I was chosen to be an angel who sang a Christmas song, usually "Silent Night." At the time, I imagined that the director or the teacher had chosen me for some angelic characteristics that she had detected. In retrospect I find my selection a bit puzzling because even then I was unable to carry a tune. "Silent night, holy night . . ." By the time I got to the high notes, my voice was straining, cracking. Maybe they just needed a bit of comic relief in a generally serious program.

On the way to the old homestead, we also talked about Grampa. Warm and touching stories, as well as humorous ones. We recalled that the previous evening Larry had asked our Aunt Gertie Nichols about rumors that Grampa had been quite the ladies' man. "Is it true that Grampa was going with that *young* woman?" he had asked, calling the woman in question by name.

"Yeah, it's true," Aunt Gertie had confirmed, with a little smile.

As Larry and Aunt Gertie had talked, I thought about the time I had visited Grampa in the veterans' hospital in Marion, Illinois, and he'd asked me to help him call this same young woman. She'd sounded so sweet on the telephone when I'd identified myself as Henry Motley's granddaughter and told her why I was calling. Discreetly referring to him as "Mr. Motley," she'd indicated that she had mail for him and needed to know his address. Then I had passed the telephone to Grampa, who had been unable to restrain a huge grin as he'd anticipated talking with her. Although at that time I had still been trying to determine whether the rumors about the two of them were true, I had stifled the urge to loll about close enough to "overhear" his end of the conversation. But that look on his face and the joy in her voice told me what I had wanted to know, and more. They loved each other.

During the drive to our old farm, we also talked about Grampa's funeral. The little country church had been packed. We'd seen childhood friends and neighbors with whom we had lost contact over the years. Sister Luke, now a widow, had been there, looking just as she had twenty years ago. No better; no worse. The oldest Riley boy—one of the Rileys who lived by Bethel, not the ones who had lived by us—was still singing in the choir, although his once impressive voice was now slightly flat. And so it went as we recalled each old acquaintance. "Boy, they all looked so old!" we agreed. In general our contemporaries looked at least ten years older than we did. Or so we thought.

"It's that hard life," we speculated. Most of the people who had remained in Mounds still lived in or near poverty, in one of the poorest regions in the entire country.

"Any one of them could have climbed up in that coffin and taken the place of the corpse!" Larry announced, as we all howled with laughter. Larry has a way of bluntly saying just what others are thinking but won't say.

We also discussed how touched we were by the response of people, most of them strangers to us, to the funeral procession. As we had driven to National Cemetery in Mound City, every motorist we passed going in either direction pulled the vehicle off the road and came to a full stop on the shoulder. Some held their hats over their hearts, while others bowed their heads, paying homage to the departed. Carl "Big Wind" Meeks, our one-time neighbor, pulled his motorcycle to the side of the road and held his baseball cap over his heart. "You don't see that in the city," someone said softly. We all murmured our agreement.

As we talked about our life in Mounds, we suddenly realized that we had passed our old house nearly a quarter of a mile back. So John turned the car around and retraced our tracks until we stopped in front of the little place where we had lived twenty years earlier.

"I thought it sat back farther from the road."

"I thought the little hill was taller."

"And that field over there was larger."

"I thought we had a huge front yard."

And so the discussion went as we realized that our former residence did not look like the pictures we had of it in our minds, even though some of us had seen it only a few years previously, when Grampa and Grandmommy had still lived there.

Our house in Mounds had been a small, boxy frame house. As a child I sometimes wondered why the rich people who lived in Massachusetts would have tacky houses with brown brick siding like ours, but I was sure they did because that's the kind Mudeah and Daddy said we had: Cape Cod. Our parents and paternal grandparents had built the house themselves. *Literally* built it themselves. For a number of years three generations of Motleys—Daddy, Mudeah, Larry, June, Grampa, Grandmommy, and later I—had lived there. They had chosen this style, they said, because we could expand it easily. We would add a porch, a garage, and additional rooms when times got better. During our ten years in Mounds, the family, numbering anywhere from six to eight members, lived in the original four rooms—a living room, kitchen, and two bedrooms. A utility room, originally intended as a bathroom, served as a storage area.

My Uncle Curtis and Uncle Billy, both carpenters who lived in Lansing, came to Mounds to make fancy built-in cabinets for the kitchen. One entire wall consisted of a long base cabinet with a sink in the middle. Behind the double doors beneath the sink, we kept a huge bucket to catch the water because we didn't have indoor plumbing. We always had to keep an eye on the bucket to keep it from overflowing—it made a real mess when it got too full, because kitchen scraps went into the bucket also. At the end of the day Larry or June would take the bucket and its contents to "slop" the pigs.

At one end of the kitchen counter, we kept a bucket or two of fresh water for cooking and drinking. Everyone drank from the dipper, carefully returning it to the bucket, unless it needed to be passed to the next person. Only the most pretentious of people— those whom Grampa called "hanckty"—insisted upon drinking from a glass or a jelly jar. Above the base cabinet, on either side of the window, Uncle Billy and Uncle Curtis had built wall cabinets. When the cabinets were done, the whole kitchen looked really nice. By then we had replaced the wood-burning stoves in the kitchen and the living room with gas heaters. Opposite the new cabinets was a huge open pantry where Mudeah stored the fruits and vegetables she had canned for winter. The attractive, neatly arranged jars of peaches, apples, blackberries, green beans, and other good things to eat gave the kitchen country charm. Ours was one of those authentic, homey kitchens, before the city folks started reading magazines and hiring decorators in an effort to make their new, modern kitchens look old-fashioned. Friends and neighbors came by to admire my uncles' handiwork and to allow as how they would like to have such nice cabinets and such a fine-looking kitchen.

At the time that we lived in it, I'd thought the house was fairly large, but when I looked at it years later, I realized that it was quite small. The living room was probably no more than ten feet square. A sofa on one long wall and a lamp table or corner table beside it took up the entire area between the adjoining wall and the door. We were very proud of the complete set of the *World Book Encyclopedia* that we kept neatly arranged on the corner table. "Wash your hands first!" we reminded anyone who touched the books. In the winter the heating stove stood in the center of the opposite wall. During warmer months Daddy and the boys set the stove in the smokehouse behind the main house. A couple of old chairs would then take up the vacated space.

After we had a telephone installed, it sat on a little gossip bench—a telephone table with an attached chair and storage space for the telephone directory—on another wall. A record cabinet with a record player on top completed the furnishing of the living room, until we got a floor-model television set, which had about a nine-inch screen. When the television didn't work, we had Irving, a funny-looking little white guy, fix it. Daddy would drive over to the junky, unpainted house Irving shared with his mother to get him. An emaciated little guy with a scrawny neck, Irving was one of those white people who were likely to be called "poor white trash," "peckerwoods," or "rednecks" openly by whites and secretly by blacks. I was never sure whether Irving really knew what he was doing. After fiddling around with the television for ages, he sometimes got it to work, as much it seemed to me, through luck as by any skill on his part, because he was as likely to announce that he couldn't fix it as that he could. He was a very pleasant, patient man, though. I had to give him that. He'd fool with the set for hours and not even charge us for it unless he could fix it. But then again, the idea of a "service fee" never occurred to any of us. If someone fixed something for you, you paid them. If they couldn't, you didn't. Everyone agreed that *that* was fair. Only a crook would attempt to charge someone who hadn't done anything!

During the family reunions, we often talk about our grandparents, recalling summers spent in Lansing with our maternal grandparents, Lee Gene Sr. and Bessie Jones—whom we called Papa and Grandma Bessie—and remembering experiences in Illinois with Henry and Anna Motley, our paternal grandparents. Tales of our two grandmothers are particularly intriguing because they were very colorful figures. Both Grandmommy and Grandma Bessie were women whose strength we had admired, but whose sharp tongues and harsh criticisms we had sought to avoid. Scrappy and argumentative, they were in many respects the antithesis of the ideal white woman of the late Victorian era into which they were born. Grandmommy freely corrected anyone's behavior and readily challenged any view with which she disagreed, including Grampa's. "Henry!" she would say sharply and then proceed to make her point. "I'll declare. Sometimes I don't think so-and-so has bat sense!" Muttering with disdain, she depreciated the one who had given her cause for concern. Even if no one had given her reason to comment, Grandmommy might well have had something to say.

Grandma Bessie was similarly straightforward in her observations. She was noted for putting her hands on her hips, tilting her head to one side, and then proceeding to "bless someone out," as she called it. "Durn it!" she would begin. Then she would go through a laundry list of complaints. She usually could be counted on to upbraid anyone in her presence for both real and imagined misdeeds.

"Shelley hasn't come to see me in a long time!" she once intoned. "She used to spend every summer with me. Do you remember that, Shelley?" she demanded.

"Yes, I do. We always had a good time at your house," I responded. My attempts at sucking up notwithstanding, she continued her verbal assault, mixing in large doses of guilt.

"I don't have much time left. I'm living on borrowed time," she continued, reducing me to the status of an ungrateful six-year-old who failed to pay proper attention to her dying grandmother. Eventually she turned her sharp tongue on someone else, but I knew that I could not rest too comfortably because she might return to me later. It seemed to make her uneasy to see anyone getting too relaxed in her presence.

As Grandma Bessie aged, she became even more caustic. She had warned her two sons, Curtis and Billy, after Papa's death that, "You'd better keep a wife or a girlfriend because I ain't sitting by nan 'nother sickbed!" Years later, after Uncle Curtis had died, a delegation of close relatives had gone to her hospital bed where she was recovering from surgery to tell her of his death. Seeking to reassure her that Curtis's soul had found repose, they told her that he had joined a church in Chicago, his home at the time of his death. They continued to talk about Curtis, although they were unsure whether Grandma Bessie comprehended that he had died.

"He'd even become a deacon," they noted.

"Well, he's a dead deacon now!" she had responded cryptically.

Our two grandfathers, on the other hand, were relatively quiet men. Both were particularly kind and indulgent toward children, especially their grandchildren. Papa often called us by unusual names, such as "doodle bug," which coming from elsewhere might have seemed less than complimentary. For years I had thought that he said "doo-doo bug," which was a little insect that rolled cow manure into little balls. Even so, when Papa said the words, they sounded affectionate, so I didn't mind. Grampa and Papa were both quick to offer us a nickel or a dime, usually suggesting that we buy candy, ice cream, or another treat. Unlike our parents, they never proposed that we save the money. When he gave me a larger sum, Grampa was apt to say that perhaps I might like to buy a pretty red outfit. This was at a time when many African Americans, especially those of the middle class, considered red too garish for clothing, even clothing worn by children. But Grampa and I thought little girls looked pretty in red. In fact, the *New Friends and Neighbors* reader at school had a picture of a red dress, complete with matching shoes and a purse, that I secretly coveted. I sometimes imagined that I might find that very frock on one of our infrequent shopping trips to Cairo. Although I never saw anything that remotely resembled it, even when we shopped in Chicago one summer, I really enjoyed thinking that if I did find it, maybe Grampa would buy it for me. That the one I had seen was worn by "the City Mouse" in a story about "The City Mouse and the Country Mouse" did not deter my interest. I did have reservations, however, about the likelihood that Mudeah and Daddy would allow me to wear the high-heeled shoes that perfectly matched the dress, but I hoped that I might be able to find a pair of T-strap flats instead. And, of course, bright red fingernail polish like the City Mouse wore was completely out of the question.

Lately the discussion of grandparents at the family reunion often includes our teasing Mildred about how much she is like Grandma Bessie, our maternal grandmother. After years of protesting that the two of them had nothing in common, Mildred has come to appreciate the similarities in their personalities. In fact, now Mil proudly speaks of herself as heir to Grandma Bessie's mantle.

The Three Musketeers

Larry, June, and Shirl. I secretly thought of us as "The Three Musketeers." My two older brothers and I spent a lot of time together while Daddy worked at the Illinois State Garage and Mudeah sewed and did housework for Mildred Campbell, a wealthy white woman whose husband was our family physician. We lived in Springfield, Illinois, at this time. We were there for about two years, from 1950 to 1952, while I was between the ages of four and six and June and Larry were three and one-half and four and one-half years older, respectively.

The boys and I were supposed to stay at home while our parents were gone, but we regularly left in search of more exciting ways to spend the day. Often we left as soon as Mudeah and Daddy were out of sight, returning only minutes before they did. They may have been aware of this, but they never acknowledged it. All in all, we were pretty responsible. At least, we didn't get into any serious trouble: no one ended up with permanent injuries, and we didn't destroy property or anything like that.

Sometimes we just went to play with our friends. Larry and June would leave me at a girlfriend's house, and I'd play with her until they returned. This way they could join the other boys without the embarrassment of having a younger sister in tow. We girls would play house, dressing and undressing our dolls. Or we played jacks, hop scotch, jump rope, and other "girl stuff." Now and again I could persuade the other girls to make mud pies, one of my favorite pastimes, but this was disdained by the prissier little girls who were afraid of getting dirty. Anyway, an expert mud-pie maker should be able to produce all kinds of things without getting dirty, except for her hands, I believed.

More often, I went with the boys. Crying and threatening to tell our parents were two fairly reliable ways of inducing them to take me with them, which I usually preferred to playing with the girls. Then we really had fun because we did "boy things." Sometimes they admonished me that certain activities were reserved for boys, but generally I did what they did. Except for going around without a shirt and a few other things.

We played marbles, shooting with a "steely" when we had one. Each of us had a sack of marbles, which we had acquired by winning some, buying others, and finding still others. We played at Isles Park on the swings, slides, and see saws. Sometimes we even bought candy or popcorn at the concession stand, but most of the time we couldn't afford such treats. We went sword fighting with our homemade swords, pretending to look for rival "gangs" but breathing a sigh of relief when we didn't find them. We played cops and robbers, or cowboys and Indians, expertly brandishing our guns. We hunted for buried treasure. One time Larry and June purchased a treasure map for ten cents, and we looked for hours for the designated spot. Eventually, I asked, "Why would those kids sell a treasure map for only ten cents? Why wouldn't they keep the map and find the treasure themselves?"

"Shut up, Shirl," my two brothers said in unison, as they tried to hide their embarrassment.

The *real* fun, though, was playing in the brickyard. We rearranged the huge concrete bricks to make houses with walls taller than we were. To get inside, we climbed on the side and then jumped into the house. It's a wonder that we weren't all crushed to death by the bricks. Yet we had little appreciation for the danger this presented. Daddy and Mudeah periodically warned us to stay away from the brickyard, both because of the danger and because it was private property. The workers at the yard hollered at us and chased us away when they saw us, but we always returned when "the coast was clear." Such admonitions probably made the brickyard even more intriguing to us.

The brickyard also had another source of interest to us: the water tower. We often talked about climbing the lattice-like steps to the top where the tank was located and then following the platform all around the tank. We imagined how far we would be able to see in each direction. Now that really looked like fun. Daddy and Mudeah warned us about the dangers of that as well. The only meaningful fear we had, however, was that if our parents caught us, we would likely get a "whuppin'." This was much more to be feared than being crushed by bricks or falling from the water tower.

One day June decided to climb all the way to the top of the tower. Larry and I agreed that it was the thing to do. June began his ascent, going higher and higher. Beyond the walls of our brick house, beyond the tops of buildings, beyond the tops of trees. Higher than any of us had gone previously. Larry and I could hardly wait until our own turns came. And, then . . . along came Daddy. Before we had noticed him, Daddy had parked his car on the street at some distance from us. When we first saw him, he was hurrying in our direction. "Daddy's coming!" Larry and I both called to June.

June quickly climbed down and the three of us ran home, a few blocks from the brickyard. We were terrified! We had to develop a plan. We reasoned that because Daddy hadn't been very close to us, he couldn't be certain that we were the kids he had seen. Because June was on the tower, he was the one most in evidence, so we focused on obscuring his identity. He changed his shirt as we prepared to deny that we were anywhere other than at home. When Daddy arrived a few moments later and started to talk about having seen us at the brickyard, we simply said,

"We weren't at the brickyard."

"Yeah, we've been at home all day."

"See, we're wearing different clothes than those kids."

Did Daddy have a "mad spot," the wrinkles that appeared in his forehead when he was really angry? Is that the reason he turned away from us? Or was he hiding a smile at the suggestion that he didn't recognize his own children? Anyway, we got the customary warning, but not the whuppin'. Luckily for us, Mudeah was not with him, because she was the one who administered whuppins. Daddy was usually content to yell at us, throwing in an obscenity or two for emphasis. He never had much of a stomach for physical punishment, especially of me, and later of my two younger sisters, his "girls." Thus, when we looked sufficiently pitiful and contrite, with me bursting into tears if necessary, we usually found that Daddy would not do anything more serious than threatening bodily harm. He might grit his teeth and declare menacingly, "I ought to wring your little necks!"

One time Larry and June talked me into splitting my March of Dimes money with them, replacing the six dimes with nickels. When I balked at first, they turned on the high-pressure technique, similar to the "good cop/bad cop" routine. "Aw, Shirl, that's crazy, giving them all that money. Do you think everyone else is going to turn in all their money?" Larry argued angrily. I turned to June for support.

"That's right, Shirl!" June answered kindly.

With a tremendous sense of guilt, moderated by the prospect of buying candy, gum, soda, ice cream, or other treats, I finally gave in to their pleas. Later, when I got to school, I found that every single child in my kindergarten class had a card full of dimes. When it was my turn to announce the amount that I had collected, the other kids eyed me suspiciously when I said that I had only thirty cents. One even said, "I bet you spent the rest!" I was mortified.

"I did not!" I protested loudly.

The teacher stood up for me. She smiled kindly and said something nice like, "Everyone brought in as much as they could." Then I felt even worse, because I really liked Miss Potoff and I didn't want her to know that I was a little thief.

Several months later, I stole several balloons at the local dime store in order to impress Larry and June and because I wanted a whole bouquet of balloons—like the clown had in a book I had seen. I'd simply stuffed them into my jacket pocket and forgotten about them until the next time that I wore it. When I found the balloons there later, I really felt ashamed as I recalled how I'd sneaked up to the counter at the five-and-dime and grabbed a handful of the colorful balloons. I'd also envisioned myself in the reform school to which Mudeah and Daddy had said they sent children who got into trouble. I pictured the jails on televisions and in the western movies, except with a bunch of dirty, snotty-nosed children, some of them with long pigtails like my own. After these two forays into criminality, I decided that I wasn't cut out for a life of crime.

Our house in Springfield was a modest one, but at the time I thought it was rather large and nice. It had three bedrooms, in addition to the usual living room and kitchen. I had my own bedroom, which had at one time been a porch but that a previous owner had enclosed and made into a small bedroom. I enjoyed having my own room, and I played in it a lot. Until nighttime. And then I was afraid to sleep in it because it was on one side of the kitchen and the other two bedrooms were on the other side. I was sure that a host of ghosts and other supernatural beings lurked in the corners, under the bed, outside the door, or some place. In any event, I didn't want to take any chances, so I preferred to sleep in the room with my two brothers. They both said they'd like to have it as their own room since I didn't want to sleep in it, but it remained mine. After we moved from that house when I was six, I didn't have my own room again until I was in my thirties and divorced from my first husband.

The Kindest Man in the Whole World

During the summers Larry, June, and I often visited our maternal grandparents, Papa and Grandma Bessie. They lived in rural Lansing with two of their children, Lee Gene Jr., whom everyone called "Billy," and Leora, whom we called "Toots." Toots was about seven years older than I and Billy was about ten years older. My grandparents' three grown children—my mother, Cora; Aunt Theresa; and Uncle Curtis—were much older than the two children still at home and had their own families.

Daddy and Mudeah usually drove us to Arkansas; occasionally our Uncle Curtis, who lived down the road a piece from Grandma Bessie and Papa, came to Illinois and got us. The two-hundred-mile trip could take anywhere from a few hours to the better part of a day, depending on how many times we had to stop and fix a flat or take care of some other problem with the car. Especially when we were in Uncle Curtis's car, which was usually even more unreliable than our own, it was a long, long trip. Before we left home Mudeah always cautioned us to "Be sure to go to the bathroom." For many years I thought there were no restrooms between Mounds and Lansing. Later I discovered that there were restrooms at many service stations, but they were all reserved for white people. Blacks had to go into the cotton fields to relieve themselves, a humiliation adults tried to spare the children, as well as themselves.

Papa was born in Sardis, Mississippi, on December 27, 1890. His mother was Sarah Archibald Jones from South Carolina and his father was Powell Jones. Papa had six brothers, including Will, Thomas, Richard, and Louis. Neither my mother nor my grandmother could remember the names of the others, suggesting that they'd had little, if any, contact with them. My Aunt Toots recalls Papa telling her about his mother, a Native American, who sometimes rode a horse bareback with her beautiful, long hair blowing in the wind. Even her name is shrouded in mystery. According to some sources, her name was Sarah Archibald Jones; according to others it was Elizzer Jones. Perhaps it was Sarah Elizzer Archibald Jones, or Elizzer Sarah Archibald Jones. When asked for additional information about his mother, including the name of her tribe, Papa became uncharacteristically reticent, according to Toots. Apparently the family was rather secretive about her Native American ancestry, possibly trying to obscure it because they had lived in Mississippi and thus should have been evacuated during the Trail of Tears or earlier forced Indian migrations to the area west of the Mississippi River.

Papa was the kindest person I have ever known. Called "Mr. Genie" by many friends and neighbors, he was well-known and much admired. Even when he had something negative to communicate, he said it with great kindness. For example, he could temper Grandma Bessie's often vitriolic outbursts by merely saying "Now, Bess." Whereupon she would calm down and, even more amazingly, she would stop fussing. Of his grandchildren, as with all chil-

32

dren he encountered, he always said "That's a fine girl," or "That's a fine boy," to any comment, whether negative or positive, from another adult. Or sometimes, he would say "That's Granddad's boy," or "That's Granddad's girl." In any event, the point was, as far as he was concerned, children could do no wrong and he did not appreciate opinions to the contrary.

One time my Uncle Curtis was angry with me over some misdeed, and he told Grandma Bessie about it and she got angry, too. Both were really giving me a bad time as I hung my head in resignation. At least with Grandma Bessie, I knew she would confine herself to "preaching"; she didn't whup us as Mudeah did. Suddenly Papa said, in his usual calm manner, "Now, now, she's a good girl." I ran over to him and buried my head in his lap, as he gently patted me. Uncle Curtis and Grandma Bessie stopped chastising me, and that was the last I ever heard about the matter.

Papa chewed tobacco and spat the juice into a coffee can or a spittoon filled with ashes. In an attempt to emulate him, Larry, June, and I made "snuff" from cocoa and sugar and put it in our cheeks or between our front teeth and our lips. Then we practiced long-distance spitting, hoping to match Papa's prowess. We wanted to be able to say "spit-too-y" and then accurately direct our spittle into a can, making a little "ping" against the side, just like Papa.

An avid baseball fan, Papa could simultaneously watch one game on television and listen to another on the radio. When the action got really exciting, he would lean forward in his huge old leather-and-wood chair and put his ear close to the radio. Papa was hard of hearing, and occasionally he had problems following a play.

He also liked to listen to boxing matches—which everyone called "the fights"—on the radio or watch them on television. They came on late on Saturday nights, and we children were permitted to stay up to listen or watch them, too. Sometimes we'd fall asleep in the middle of the floor, and the adults would awaken us when the fight began. Papa would get really excited over the boxing matches, almost as though he were coaching one of the contenders. It was a lot of fun just watching Papa enjoy himself so much.

In looking at Papa's life, I began to see, while still a child, some of the problems faced by blacks in the South. I also saw that Papa was a very admirable person who was neither bent nor broken by the economic hardships and the racial oppression of his time. He handled every situation with dignity, kindness, and fairness. Papa became one of my heroes.

A very intelligent man, Papa was a former schoolteacher, as were most of his brothers. He'd taught at the colored grade school in Lansing from about 1915 to 1919, where he'd earned approximately sixty dollars monthly. His brother Richard, whom his nieces and nephews called Uncle Bud, was a schoolteacher in Charleston, Missouri.

I was shocked by my mother's response when I asked her whether Papa was a Democrat or a Republican. She said he was a Republican. I had presumed from my parents' staunch commitment to the Democratic Party that all intelligent people were Democrats. And certainly anyone in our family would be a Democrat. But she said that he was a Republican because in Arkansas, the Democrats were against Negroes having rights. She went on to indicate that he did not vote because Negroes in Arkansas were not allowed to do so. And, further, white Democrats in that state were in favor of denying Negroes the right to vote. That was the first time I had ever heard anyone in our house say anything negative about Democrats.

Papa was also a carpenter, and he built a lot of structures in the Lansing area. He had even built the Bethel African Methodist Episcopal (AME) Church, of which he and Grandma Bessie were members. Papa had been a founding member of the church in 1916. His name, along with six others, is listed as a trustee in the cornerstone. When we drove through neighboring communities, Billy and Toots would point with pride to many structures that their father had built or remodeled. Like the stereotype of the master carpenter, Papa's own home was often in need of repair. The steps sagged, the screen door did not close properly, and there was no sidewalk. A few people made nice brick or flagstone walkways, but not Papa. After a rain we stepped gingerly between mud holes or we placed boards from the steps to the driveway so that we could walk without getting mud on our feet.

Papa was also a cotton farmer. A sharecropper actually. For years I had thought that he was very rich because he produced so many bales of cotton each season. He also employed many other black people to chop cotton and to pick it. And he drove a huge tractor. The simple unpainted house in which he and his family lived was a clue to his modest economic stature, but I did not realize this at the time. In fact, it seemed quite a nice house to me. It had six rooms and a small back porch. There was a store across the street where we could buy sodas, candy, and other treats, as well as groceries and other staples. Later, Papa and his family moved to a larger house, one with a veranda that ran the entire width of the house and a portico at the back of it.

I learned of Papa's sharecropper status when I asked my mother about his presumed great wealth. He did not own the land, or the cotton, or the house, or the tractor. All these things belonged to some white guy who lived, rather appropriately, in a white house. Papa was only entitled to a "share" of the crop he grew. When he died, although he had cropped for the same man for years, Grandma Bessie had to move off the land shortly after the funeral.

One summer when my brothers and I were visiting Papa and Grandma Bessie, we heard about the lynching of a black man who was an acquaintance of my grandparents. This was one of the most traumatic experiences of my life—and probably of my brothers' lives as well. The man was a member of a socially prominent, relatively well-to-do black family, which lived fairly close to Papa and Grandma Bessie. One day the man's family reported him missing. Shortly afterward, the local newspaper reported that his partially burned car had been found. Close by were indications of another fire, one in which a few charred bones and the soles of a pair of shoes suggested that someone had been burned at the stake. Ultimately, the identity of the victim became evident. The gossip in the black community indicated that he had been "going with" a white woman. But the adults were very circumspect around children, so we learned few details about either the illicit relationship or the man's eventual murder because of it. This lynching intimidated me to the point that I wanted to leave Arkansas immediately. Grandma

35

Bessie had regularly commented that my outspokenness around white folks would "get us all lynched." Heretofore I had thought that she was joking. Now, I feared for my life. I wondered exactly how they lynched a child. Did they burn children at the stake, also? Would they really lynch a child for "looking white folks in the eye," as Grandma Bessie claimed? Indeed, under what set of circumstances might a child be lynched?

The following summer we found out the answers to these questions. Fourteen-year-old Emmett Till of Chicago was visiting in Money, Mississippi, when he was lynched in August 1955. Till was thrown into the Tallahatchie River after having been mercilessly beaten, reportedly for whistling at a white woman. We saw pictures of his body in *Jet* magazine. His grotesque, bloated face is indelibly etched in my memory. Even now, over forty years later, I can recall the horror of that picture and the sick feeling in the pit of my very being as I saw it for the first time.

These two lynchings—of my grandparents' neighbor and a child—made me wonder about white folks. How could they be so cruel? How could they be so hypocritical? Everyone in the Lansing area knew that a pretty black girl of about sixteen was "keeping company" with the white man who owned the grocery store in Lansing. Every day she walked past our grandparents' house to the store, where she sat for hours. She could eat any of the candy, cold cuts, or anything else he sold and drink soft drinks—plus put peanuts in them if she wanted to—for free. Sometimes the store owner would close the store in the middle of the day, and everyone knew that they were in the back room. But no one ever proposed to lynch either of them. So why . . . ? But I could not discuss these things with the adults, because such topics were not fit subjects for conversation with children.

The lynching of my grandparents' neighbor let me know I needed to be very careful around these southern white folks, even more so than around the ones in our own area. I had never heard of anyone in Mounds being lynched, at least. It seemed to me that white people could not be counted on to be fair and to do the right thing. Daddy and Mudeah did point out that there were some "good white folks," like Senators Hubert Humphrey of Minnesota and Adlai Stevenson II of Illinois. The ones they mentioned were usually those that we had seen on television at the Democratic National Convention or read about in the newspaper. I don't recall them doing a lot of bragging about the white folks in Mounds, however.

Many years later, after Papa's death on December 3, 1968, we returned to Arkansas for the funeral. It seemed as though everyone wanted to pay last respects to "Mr. Genie." Many people spoke to us of his kindness. They stopped by to visit my grandparents' home, to bring food, and to "set a spell." His funeral was held at Macedonia Baptist Church, the larger of the two black churches in Lansing. Macedonia always let the AME folks use their church when they needed it. At Papa's funeral, there was standing room only. Even two red-faced white men, the landowner and his son, were there, serving as honorary pallbearers. Although I resented their presence, it was a tradition that the landowner serve as honorary pallbearer for a respected "cropper."

The procession to the cemetery stretched for what seemed like miles. At the grave site, we all gathered about to hear the minister's last words. And, finally, the Masons conducted a secret ceremony in honor of their brother, who was a Mason to the thirty-second degree. They walked around his grave, chanting words unintelligible to the uninitiated. Even though I didn't understand anything they said or did, I recognized that there was beauty in this final homage to Papa. Papa, who chewed tobacco, loved baseball, and was kind to everyone.

What Comes Up Comes Out

Grandma Bessie, my maternal grandmother, was the quintessential matriarch. She reigned over an extended family, which included her two remaining children (four having preceded her in death), grandchildren, great-grandchildren, and great-great-grandchildren. She lived with her son Billy and his family in Lansing until her death on November 3, 1994—the day after her birthday. Although she was in good health until a few years before her death, for at least forty or fifty years she had predicted her own imminent demise. She warned that if anyone crossed or neglected her, she would come back as a "haint" and avenge herself. If it is possible to do so, Grandma Bessie will find a way.

Grandma Bessie was born Bessie Melvina Smith in Evadale, Arkansas, on November 2. Although she claimed to have been born in 1901, other evidence—including an entry written by my grandfather in the family Bible, her marriage license, and her youngest child's birth certificate—suggests that she was born as early as 1898. Her parents were Horace Smith and Ida Rankin Smith from Lake Cormorant, Mississippi. Grandma Bessie said that her mother was a half-blood Indian, although she did not know her mother's tribal affiliation nor anything more about her Native American background. Grandma Bessie, the eldest of three children, had a sister, Beulah, and a brother, Jack.

Grandma Bessie's father, Horace Smith, was a hearty man who reportedly walked the fifteen to twenty miles between his home in Memphis and Lansing in order to visit his daughter. Grandma Bessie recalled that even when her father was seventy years old, he would make the trip, following alongside the railroad track. Horace Smith worked at a brickyard in Memphis. Grandma Bessie's maternal grandfather was Giles Rankin, who was from Clax, Mississippi. Giles Rankin, a member of the Knights of Pythias, also claimed to have served in the Spanish-American War in Cuba, further indicating that he had lost a thumb there. This latter information presents some problems of credibility, however. Rankin would have been in his mid-seventies at the time of the war. Also, he lived in Mississippi at the time. It is virtually unimaginable that a seventy-four-year-old black man from Mississippi would have served in the war. Perhaps when he'd returned home after an otherwise unexplained and lengthy absence, and with an injury, Rankin had thought it prudent to offer an explanation that would be socially acceptable to his family.

Grandma Bessie was a very pretty woman in her old age. She must have been a stunning beauty as a girl and as a young woman, such as when she got married on Christmas Day, 1915. Papa was just two days short of twenty-five. My grandparents had six children, but the eldest, Geneva, was killed in a house fire in early childhood. The others were Theresa, born in 1918; my mother, Cora, born in 1920; Curtis, born in 1923; Lee Gene Jr., born in 1935; and Leora, born in 1939.

My first recollections of Grandma Bessie are of when she was about fifty years old and I was five or six. At that time she was approximately five feet three inches tall, very light complected, with long, wavy, silver-white hair, which was worn in two braids crossed atop her head. She claimed that her hair, formerly very dark brown or black, had turned white from being "worried to death" by her children and grandchildren.

Grandma Bessie often worked in the fields chopping and picking cotton, as well as in the vegetable garden planting, weeding, and harvesting. She, like everyone else in the area, wore a big straw hat with a wide brim to protect herself from the extreme heat, which was often in excess of ninety degrees. She insisted that her children and grandchildren wear hats too, which she bought for us at the store in Earle, a few miles from her home. I really liked my summer straw hat and I wanted to wear it back in Illinois, but Mudeah said it made me look too country.

An old-fashioned woman in many respects, Grandma Bessie cooked over an old woodstove, washed laundry using a scrub board and tubs, and heated her flatirons on the cook stove. She hung the laundry outside on a clothesline to dry. She continued to use many of these old-fashioned devices long after she had access to modern conveniences. Whatever she was doing, however, she usually stopped in order to watch her favorite daytime television programs, "Truth or Consequences" and "Queen for a Day."

Grandma Bessie could make delicious molasses cakes—similar to gingerbread—and banana pies with vanilla wafers on top. I don't remember her other cooking when I was a child, though. In her later life, however, her cooking wasn't particularly good. In fact, sometimes it was darned near inedible. I recall, for example, that a friend of hers once brought her fresh okra, which he'd grown himself. Grandma Bessie managed to overcook and underseason it until it had virtually no taste at all. And she used to fry thick pieces of country bacon, leaving them swimming in their own grease until they were totally soaked.

Grandma Bessie insisted that her children and grandchildren take cod liver oil or castor oil every day to preserve good health. She also used assorted home remedies when a person was ill. For certain ailments she rubbed our chests with a foul-smelling ointment. For others, one might wear an equally foul-smelling poultice around the neck. Still others necessitated taking elixirs. Coal oil and sugar was, I believe, for a cold. But one might also be given sassafras tea, which we really liked. All in all, if one "felt poorly," it was a good idea not to tell Grandma Bessie, because the "cure" could be worse than the ailment.

We attended church nearly every Sunday when we were in Arkansas. We usually walked to Lansing, a one-half-mile to one-mile distance—depending upon which house Grandma Bessie and Papa lived in at the time. We wore our Sunday-go-to-meeting clothes and carried our good shoes in our hands so they wouldn't get dirty in the inch-deep dust along the roadside. When we got to the church, we washed our feet with a damp cloth and changed into our Sunday shoes. Grandma Bessie, Toots, and I carried parasols to shield us from the sun. I liked the way that Grandma Bessie always called them "parasols" in the southern fashion, rather than "umbrellas" like we did in Illinois. Parasol was such a pretty, lady-like term. I thought it would be really nice to have a fancy ruffled umbrella like Little Bo Beep or the ladies in the musicals at the movies.

Most Sundays we went to the Bethel AME church, but occasionally we attended Macedonia Baptist, just around the corner from the AME church. Compared to the Baptist church, the AME Church was very staid, so we children often preferred the Baptist church. One or two of the Baptist women could be counted on to "shout," which just about tickled us children to death. First the minister would begin to preach, starting off relatively calmly but becoming louder. After a while he was shouting, prancing, and dramatically modulating his voice. He would wipe his brow with a handkerchief and prance about the pulpit, often while repeating the same phrase over and over until he evoked a response. If none was forthcoming, he might yell, "Can I get a witness!"

"Yes, Lord!" the congregation would respond.

"Lord, Lord, Lord!"

"Ha' mercy, Jesus!"

At this point one or several people, sometimes the entire choir, would begin to hum, possibly bursting into song. By now the congregation would have reached a fever pitch, and at least one woman would begin to moan and cry and to rock back and forth in her pew. This woman, or another one, might suddenly leap to her feet, toss herself backward, and nearly fall. The ushers would rush forward and begin to fan her furiously, talking softly to her. Then another woman would spring to her feet, swinging her purse dangerously as everyone ducked to avoid being knocked out cold. She might heist her dress above her knees and dance down the aisle while we children struggled to keep from laughing. We were told that the women had "felt the Holy Spirit," but we weren't always convinced that their experiences were genuinely holy ones. We thought the women were just trying to get attention, especially if they were particularly well-dressed at the time. Grandma Bessie would quietly come to where we were seated and usher us out of the church. She was about as skeptical as we were, however. She sometimes said that certain women "just liked to show out." Always very outspoken, Grandma Bessie might well have told them that herself.

After church we would remain in Lansing, spending time with our friends, going for a "sody water" at the little store across the road from Macedonia Baptist, or perhaps going to the homes of other children. We went back home for Sunday dinner most of the time; occasionally we went to a friend's or a neighbor's for dinner. Grandma Bessie never expected us to eat after the adults had eaten, like many did, especially if the minister was present. She claimed that ministers were crooks anyway. In her later years—when she had been widowed—she said she'd rather be married to a gambler than a minister because with a gambler you *knew* he was just trying to beat you out of your money while a minister pretended that he wasn't. One never knew when Grandma Bessie made this kind of dramatic statement whether she did it from conviction or for its shock value. At her funeral, the minister spoke of Grandma Bessie's financial contributions to the church and the minister, perhaps suggesting that we might all take that as a model for our own behavior. I didn't dare steal a peek at my siblings because I knew that they were thinking the very same thing that I was. I smiled through my tears as I recalled Grandma Bessie's admonition that ministers were worse than gamblers.

Grandma Bessie praised the role that her AME denomination had played in the family's education. Her daughter Theresa and Theresa's friend Mildred had both gotten scholarships to the AME church-affiliated Shorter College in Little Rock, Arkansas, in the late 1930s, while her son Billy had gotten one to the same institution in the 1950s.

Miss Bessie, as friends and acquaintances generally called her— her children sometimes playfully called her that as well—was very active in the Eastern Star, an organization composed of women whose husbands or sons were members of the Masons. She sometimes attended Eastern Star conventions in Hot Springs, Arkansas, and other places. Her white uniforms and colorful sashes always looked so impressive to me as she packed them along with her other belongings into a little suitcase, which she called a valise. Sometimes she rode along with a friend to the convention. At other times, Papa or one of my uncles would drive her to her destination. Then we children might get to go along, although we wouldn't spend the night there. I was always struck by the authority Grandma Bessie commanded from the other women. I could tell when she was in charge because she would put her hands on her ample hips, tilt her head to one side, and talk nonstop while the other person nodded her head in agreement or in resignation.

Grandma Bessie and her daughter Cora, my mother, constantly warred with each other. The two of them could parlay almost any disagreement into a major battle. They argued over which of them was fatter. Which was taller. They once argued over the relative merits of regular aspirin and buffered aspirin. They argued over whether a given day was a "nice day" or not. As I witnessed their conflicts over many years, I concluded that the two of them simply did not like each other. Nor was either inclined to mask her antipathy toward the other in order to spare hurt feelings. In fact, they seemingly went out of their way to make sure that no possible opportunity for conflict was overlooked. Why they had such a strong animosity toward each other was never altogether clear to me. Mudeah said her own negative feelings toward her mother were because Grandma Bessie had always favored the other children, especially Theresa, the oldest. This was indeed the case by the time I was old enough to remember their relationship. Grandma Bessie was very quick to compliment her other children, especially her second born, yet equally quick to criticize Mudeah. Ironically, however, Mudeah herself had a favorite child, June, and made no effort to hide this from her other children or from other people. Interestingly, June was also Grandma Bessie's acknowledged favorite grandchild. An additional factor that might account for the problems between my mother and grandmother was that both were very uncompromising and mean as hell.

Grandma Bessie has always loved to be the center of attention, often sacrificing sensitivity to other people's feelings in her quest for the limelight. At my mother's funeral, Grandma Bessie would not have surprised me had she climbed into the coffin and attempted to trade places with Mudeah. Not so much due to grief, but because she hated to see Cora getting all the attention! Instead, she contented herself with upbraiding her grandchildren after the funeral. We had assembled at my sister Carol's house in St. Louis during a visit of several hours. Grandma Bessie chided my two sisters and me for not having invited our mother to live with us when she was ill, leaving that to be done by our brother Calvin. Then, in a parting salvo, she made a very mean-spirited comment to Larry, who had said that the next time she saw him he would be good-looking and skinny. "You may be skinny, but you'll never be good-looking," she had snapped nastily. Having thus commanded everyone's attention, if not their affection, she was ready to return to Arkansas. Turning to the door, she indicated to Billy, his wife, Bessie, and Aint Puddin' that she was ready for the journey home.

Aint Puddin'? Oh, yes. She is a relative of Billy's wife. She was sitting alone in the living room of Carol's home because she was too "shamefaced" to join others in the kitchen. She sat alone, pulling a coat over her head if anyone walked into the room. She dipped snuff, though, so periodically she had to spit. Then she was obliged to walk into the first-floor powder room, located in full view of the kitchen assemblage. After the Arkansas contingent had left, we found that she had poor aim and inadvertently had spat on the floor beside the toilet several times. When Carol first saw the tobacco juice, unaware that Aint Puddin' took snuff, she attributed the stains to other things. She yelled, "Oh, damn! You should see what this bitch did!" We told her that it was the juice from tobacco, which was sufficiently disgusting, but far less so than what Carol had presumed.

Then Calvin said, "Carol, she spat in the living room fireplace, too!"

Carol was livid. "Oh, yeah," she said sarcastically, "She's too shamefaced to talk to people, but she can spit all over the house!" She ran into the living room to survey the damage. She did find several pieces of facial tissue, no doubt used to wipe tobacco juice from Aint Puddin's lips, behind the sofa. But Carol found no other surprises.

Grandmommy and the Mysterious Chifforobe

Anna Barnes Motley, my paternal grandmother, whom my siblings and I called Grandmommy, was about five feet three or four inches tall and of medium-brown complexion. Neatly dressed and carefully coiffed, she maintained a trim figure all her life. Her family was from Wynne, Arkansas, where her father owned a grocery store.

I have few personal recollections of Grandmommy because I spent little time with her. She was in a state hospital in Anna, Illinois, during much of my early childhood. Although her doctors did not pronounce her "cured" of her mental illness, she was able to leave the hospital in the mid-1950s. At that time she went to Chicago to live with my Aunt Gertie, her oldest child, where a large, supportive family was able to provide the continuing care that she needed. Meanwhile, Grampa continued to live and work in Peoria. In 1959 both Grandmommy and Grampa moved to Mounds after his retirement from the Caterpillar Tractor Company. By that time we had moved to Springfield.

Grandmommy was always very nice to me, but she didn't talk very much. When she was first being taken to the state hospital, I was the only one she would allow to sit beside her in the truck. "This baby is the only one of you who's got any sense!" she'd said. Although I was so young—about three or four—that I don't recall this incident, I was told about it later. It convinced me that she herself was quite smart, and I saw no problems "with her mind," as people called psychological problems at that time. Many times when Daddy and Mudeah drove to Anna to visit Grandmommy, we children went along, but we had to wait in the car while they went inside because children were not allowed in the facility. Daddy parked the car in the parking lot, beside the beautiful, tree-lined driveway of the hospital. Daddy and Mudeah generally took Grandmommy little, green, seedless grapes and other fruits and several small brown jars of snuff. As we waited for our parents to return, I would think about Grandmommy, trying to recall her from earlier years, but I couldn't form a clear picture in my mind. I'd also wonder about what went on inside that mysterious building. Because on the outside it was so pretty and well-maintained, I envisaged it as very nice inside as well. I imagined that the doctors and nurses were all very kind and helpful, and that the patients played assorted board games all day long. Patients with lap robes over their spindly legs were pushed about in wheelchairs. Later, when I'd seen a few movies about psychiatry, I thought that the psychiatrists, hoping to determine what had caused their mental problems, would talk to patients as they reclined on chaise lounges. Because the process took only a couple of hours in the movies, I couldn't understand why it was taking years to figure out the causes of Grandmommy's illness. Maybe her doctors weren't as smart as those in the movies, I speculated.

Daddy now speaks fondly of his mother. When we were children, however, I rarely recall his having mentioned her. As he talks, I often wish I had known this strong-willed, independent woman as he had. I mean, really known her beyond my own cursory acquaintance with her. "No one was going to push her around!" he proudly observes. Even when she was in the state hospital, she managed to have some control over her surroundings. When Daddy and Mudeah went to visit Grandmommy, other patients might linger nearby, hoping to be included in the conversation.

"Come on over here," she would command. "I want you to meet my son and his wife." After a brief introduction, she caustically instructed the other patients to leave her alone with her guests. "Go on now! They didn't come to see you!" As the others scurried to comply, Grandmommy might add, "I can't stand anyone hanging around me, looking like a fool!"

Grandmommy emerges in Daddy's stories as a rather argumentative person who was more bark than bite. When he and his siblings wanted to go somewhere, such as to the movie theater, his mother generally instructed the children to ask their father's permission. But before he could respond, especially if he appeared on the verge of saying "no," she would intercede.

"Oh, it won't hurt them none to go!" Then, turning to the children, she would say, "Go on now! He doesn't care if you go to the show." Because Henry Motley rarely challenged his wife, they knew that they were free to go at that point.

Daddy relates an incident in which an insurance salesman, who regularly had come to the house to collect the premium, offended him over his mother. "What's your first name?" the man had asked her. Before she could reply, John, who was about twelve or thirteen at the time, responded protectively,

"Why? Why do you want to know her first name?"

"Because I want to be able to call her by her first name," the man responded. "I like to call my clients by their first names."

"You've been calling her Mrs. Motley all this time, haven't you? You can just keep right on calling her Mrs. Motley," the boy said firmly. "She can't call you by your first name, can she? So why should you call her by hers?"

"When you get grown, you'll have to leave the South. These folks down here will kill you," Anna Motley firmly but gently warned her son after the astonished salesman had left. She no doubt was both proud of her son and frightened for his safety. His bold manner and imprudent words were not what southern white men expected from black people, particularly not from a black child.

Daddy further recalls that when he and his siblings were children, his mother constantly admonished them about many things, often working herself up into quite a rage. She might, for example, warn him and his brothers, Harry and Vernon, against marrying a stupid, ugly woman. "We weren't even old enough to date yet," Daddy recalls.

"The problem is, if you marry some stupid, ugly woman, you'll have a bunch of stupid, ugly children," she insisted. Afraid to respond, they said nothing. "Then you'll bring them to me and expect me to take care of them," she continued. "And there ain't nothing I hate worse than a bunch of silly lookin' younguns!" By now she had become quite enraged, as she imagined herself beset by a bunch of silly looking, stupid, ugly children, the product of a union between one of her sons and an ugly woman. Her sons had learned that they were well advised to remain silent because anything they said could be misunderstood at that point.

Years later Daddy married Cora Lee Jones, my mother, who was both intelligent and pretty. Nevertheless, Grandmommy didn't like her, and the feeling was mutual. Sharing a household for several years only deepened their antipathy toward each other. My brother Larry claims that one of the things that made it clear that Grandmommy was mentally unstable and a threat to others was her determination to harm Mudeah. Larry recalls that Grandmommy once physically pursued Mudeah, brandishing a knife. "I'm not taking anything else off this bitch!" Grandmommy had shouted as Mudeah ran into the fields, seeking protection from Daddy and Grampa, who were working there. Larry and June, about five and four respectively, ran after their mother and grandmother.

"We wanted to see what Grandmommy would do. She was mad as hell," Larry recalls now.

"Why was Grandmommy so angry?" we ask.

"I don't know. She said something about how Mudeah thought she knew everything. But Mudeah wasn't saying anything that day. She was just running. She could run, too! Grandmommy was right behind her, though. And June and I were right behind them both."

My first recollection of Grandmommy was when she came for a visit to the farm in Mounds after she'd been released from the hospital and had moved to Chicago. I was very apprehensive about her. I hadn't seen her in a number of years, and the near-total silence of adults about her and the whispered tales of my two older brothers combined to heighten both my fear and my curiosity. How would she look? Would it be safe to be alone with her? I wondered. I recalled also that Larry had said that she believed in "hoo-doo," which he explained was similar to voodoo. I knew nothing of either, but based upon the black folklore I'd heard and a few movies I'd seen, I thought voodoo had something to do with sticking pins into dolls that represented the enemies one wanted to harm. I'd seen movies about people being turned into zombies, presumably by those who practiced voodoo. And Larry told us about strange ceremonial dances associated with voodoo, which our grandmother had done.

"She used to do little chants and dances," he claimed. As his siblings watched in awe, Larry demonstrated. "Step it off!" he shouted, and then he proceeded to do an intricate little march.

As Aunt Gertie's large, late-model car pulled into the driveway, we all went out to meet her and Grandmommy. Minnie Lee and Annie Lee, Gertie's pretty twin daughters, probably were with them. Her two older children—Leroy, whom everyone called Lee Boy, and Bert—probably were at home. Occasionally Lee Boy made the trip, but I don't recall ever having met Bert.

A well-dressed, brown-skinned woman emerged from the car, smiling pleasantly as she greeted everyone. It took me a moment to realize that this was my grandmother. During the visit, which lasted several days, she talked little, but she smiled a lot. She wore a different pretty dress each day. And they weren't old-lady-looking dresses either. They were stylish frocks that any woman would have been proud to wear. In fact, I had never seen anyone who had as many beautiful outfits as she had in my entire life. I noticed, too, that she didn't appear to have a single gray hair on her head.

Grandmommy looked through her chifforobe, which had sat for years unopened in the bedroom that my brothers and I shared. The three of us, accustomed to being very inquisitive, hadn't messed with Grandmommy's stuff. We hadn't even looked inside her wardrobe. We'd been afraid that we might see some of her hoo-doo things—even though we had no idea what hoo-doo stuff looked like—or that she might somehow know we'd been bothering her belongings and cast a spell on us or something, perhaps turning us into bats or spiders. The three of us had always maintained good relationships with our paternal grandmother, especially because she was inclined to think that kids had better sense than adults, but we didn't want to press our luck. We vividly recalled that before she had gone into the state hospital in Anna, we had been wary of her, even though she had neither done nor threatened to do any harm to us. We had found both her mental illness and her interest in hoo-doo rather mystifying and frightening. And her chasing Mudeah while brandishing a knife had made her image even more fearsome. So, it struck us as prudent to keep our hands off her belongings.

I watched as Grandmommy began to pull things out of the wardrobe. Will there be knives, swords, magic potions, mysterious dolls? Will bats fly out of the chifforobe? I wondered. Should I pretend not to notice what she is doing? But my grandmother made no effort to hide her treasures. She had looked at me and smiled several times, showing me various items, although making few comments about them. Just clothes. Old clothes. They were a bit out of style, but otherwise they were quite unremarkable. I recall little else about this visit with my grandmother. Although I was not yet prepared to abandon the fears about her that I'd harbored for so long, I did recognize that my concerns had been exaggerated. During subsequent visits she remained pleasant, but distant. And I was respectful but similarly aloof. I don't think that I ever completely got over my fear of her. That was my loss, I realize now as I listen to my father speak so kindly and lovingly about my grandmother.

Grandmommy died in 1978 in a nursing home in Mounds. Larry, June, Carol, and I went to the funeral, which was held in Cairo. The only time I saw my father cry was at his mother's funeral. After struggling to maintain his composure, he slumped forward, dropping his head into his hands, and his shoulders shook so slightly that one scarcely could tell. My stepmother tenderly put her arms around him. Sitting directly behind Daddy and dry-eyed until that point, I too broke into tears, as did Carol.

"That really got me. Seeing Daddy cry," one of my brothers quietly commented as we drove back to the St. Louis area the next day.

"Yeah. I've never seen Daddy cry," someone else murmured.

"Yes," we all agreed, no doubt on the verge of tears just thinking about it.

We Had It Just About Right

Grampa Henry Motley worked at the Caterpillar Tractor Company in Peoria for thirteen years, from 1946 to 1959. Many times he made the long drive from Peoria to Mounds to see us. Larry, June, Carol, and I, and later Calvin and Alvin, looked forward to his visits. When we saw his car coming over the "little hill," we would all run out to the road and wait for him. Sometimes we would run down the road to meet him and he would pick us up and drive us home.

"Hi, Grampa."

"Hi, Larry"

"Hi, Grampa."

"Hi, June."

"Hi, Grampa."

"Hi, Shull." He always called me "Shull." I thought he couldn't pronounce "Shirl" or "Shirley" or he actually thought my name was "Shull," so I always responded to "Shull."

"Hi, Grampa."

"Hi, Cal." He always called Carol "Cal," to which she always responded also.

"Hi, Grampa."

"Hi, Calvin."

And so it went. We each greeted Grampa in turn, and he always responded with a separate greeting for each of us. The baby, Alvin, was too young to speak.

Carol, Calvin, and I spent most of the summer of 1959 with Grampa in Peoria. Our family had moved to Springfield from Mounds that summer. June remained in Mounds to finish his senior year at Douglass High School, and Larry was in Carbondale, where he had just begun his freshman year at Southern Illinois University. Alvin, the baby, had died of pneumonia in January 1959, when he was just under one year old. The remaining five family members—Daddy, Mudeah, Carol, Calvin, and I—had made the move to Springfield.

That summer Carol, Calvin, and I took a bus from Springfield, and Grampa was to meet us at the Peoria bus station. While we waited for him, we decided to go to the restroom. We had to carry our suitcases up a long flight of steps to the restroom. As we began our trek, a woman stopped us. "Could you help me with my luggage?" she asked politely, pointing to a huge trunk. "I'll pay you," she added generously.

"Yes, ma'am. I'll be happy to help you," I responded, thinking I could at once do a good deed and earn perhaps a quarter. Holding our own suitcase with one hand, I grabbed a strap on the side of the trunk with my free hand. The woman took hold of the other strap.

Substantially overweight, the woman struggled under the burden of the trunk. After considerable tugging, we got to the top of the stairs, with me having done most of the work. Carefully depositing her trunk inside the restroom, the woman opened her purse to give me the aforementioned remuneration.

"Oh, no, thank you," I protested in the fashion obligatory for good-mannered children of the 1950s. But she insisted. She reached into her coin purse and fished around for a long time. I started hoping for more than twenty-five cents. Finally she located a coin and ceremoniously presented me with five cents. I was disheartened (and still out of breath), but I graciously accepted the nickel and even thanked her for it.

When we found that the facilities included a pay toilet, I deposited the required money in the coin box on the door and ushered Calvin and Carol into a stall. Because Calvin was only three, I didn't dare send him to the men's room alone. As we emerged from the toilet, standing there was the woman whom I had assisted. Smiling with familiarity, she commented that it was a pay toilet. We, of course, agreed. "Would you hold the door for me?" she asked, perhaps a bit sheepishly.

Hold the door, I thought. She means to use the toilet for free, which offended my sense of propriety. But I was unaccustomed to refusing an adult's request, so I agreed. Once inside she began to make suspicious and unpleasant sounds. This continued for some time. An offensive odor drifted from the stall as she continued her disgusting noises. Suddenly it occurred to me: not only is she using our money to go to the toilet and expecting me to hold the door, but she also will expect me to carry her trunk back down that long flight of steps!

Without further hesitation, I let go of the door, allowing it to close and lock. I turned to Calvin and Carol, hurrying them out of the restroom door. With only our own small bags to encumber us, we moved down the stairs quickly and into the lobby where we caught sight of Grampa.

"Hi, Grampa."

"Hi, Shull."

"Hi, Grampa."

"Hi, Cal."

"Hi, Grampa."

"Hi, Calvin."

As we left the station, I glanced over my shoulder toward the steps, wondering if our friend had found anyone to release her from the restroom as yet. But I saw no sign of her. My concern was for our safe getaway, rather than for her freedom from the toilet stall.

We had a good summer with Grampa. He lived in a small, nicely furnished apartment on the second floor of a large house. The landlord and his family lived downstairs, and his grown daughter and her family lived in a two-room apartment across the hall. I took care of Calvin and Carol while Grampa went to work at his job at Caterpillar. While he was away, we played on the swing set in the large, tree-shaded back yard. We also played games with the landlord's grandchild and younger daughter. Hopscotch, jump rope, hide-and-seek, jacks. Accustomed to spending the summer working on the farm, this was a relatively carefree existence. The fact that I was the primary caretaker for two younger children was easy by comparison.

Sometimes on the weekends, when he didn't have to work, Grampa would insist that I go to the movies or do something with my friends while he babysat Carol and Calvin. My friends and I were routinely cautioned to be back before dark. We were very responsible, so we always returned early. But one time we lost track of time and got home almost an hour after dark. I was sure that Grampa would be angry. That really frightened me because I had never seen him angry, and I didn't know what he would do. When we got home, the landlord and Grampa were out looking for us. I knew we were in big trouble. A little while later, I heard Grampa's footsteps on the stairs. I braced myself for him to yell at me, and possibly for a whuppin'. But when Grandpa came in, all I saw in his eyes was relief.

"Hi, Shull."

"Hi, Grampa."

"I was scared something had happened to you. Maybe somebody had gotten after you or something," he said. That was all. He wasn't even angry. Boy, did I ever love Grampa. I decided two things at that time. One, I would never frighten him like that again. And, two, when I had children I would never physically punish them. This was one of numerous occasions on which I vowed that I would not spank my own children. Most of the times when I made such a commitment were when I was being whupped. I would want my children to feel about me the way that I felt about Grampa and his not spanking me, rather than the way I felt about Mudeah who would definitely have spanked me mercilessly, preaching all the while. With Mudeah I would have been remorseful because of the whuppin', rather than because of my misdeed.

Grampa was very generous, providing us with enough money to buy treats every day. I think he gave us ten cents apiece nearly every day. Five cents was enough for most items we wanted. We had more spending money than we'd ever had. We could choose between buying something when the "Street Treat" ice cream wagon came or we could go to the confectionery a block or two from the apartment. The confectionery sold ice cream, penny candy, and other edible delights, as well as small games and toys. Ice cream cones were five cents for one dip and ten cents for three dips. There were assorted flavors, including my favorite, blackberry.

Grampa was doing quite well financially at that time. He earned over three hundred dollars monthly, and he worked regularly except when they had a strike. He was a janitor and oiler of heavy equipment. I don't know his exact income in 1959, but in 1958 he had earned $3,700 for eleven months, having lost one month while on strike. He retired from Caterpillar later that year, on September 30, 1959, due to his age and physical health.

After retirement Grampa moved to Mounds. Grandmommy joined him there from Chicago, where she had been living with her eldest daughter, Gertie. Grampa and Grandmommy were able to live quite comfortably on Grampa's three pensions. He received a monthly check from Social Security for $112, a monthly check from Caterpillar for $34, and a veteran's pension of $78.75 when he first retired. By May 1978 he received a Social Security pension of $1,600 annually, an annual pension of $900 from Caterpillar, and a veteran's pension of $1,620.

During their twenty years of retirement in Mounds, Grampa and Grandmommy made many improvements to the house. They added a large bathroom complete with plumbing, a carport, and an enclosed front porch. Their grandson (and my brother) John recalls that Grampa was very proud of his and Grandmommy's efforts in improving the home. John had seen the house and thought, as I did, that it looked rather tacky because Grampa had insisted on doing most of the work himself and he did not have a great eye for detail or a mastery of carpentry. But as John listened to Grampa describe the house, he came to appreciate that the two of them saw two different houses. Grampa saw a small house with few amenities that he had expanded to a larger one with many modern conveniences. He said to John, as he had to me,

"We got it just about right. Me and huh." Grampa had said proudly. Grampa always referred to Grandmommy as "huh," rather than by her name, Anna. As we discussed Grampa's sentiments about his home and comfortable lifestyle, John and I began to realize that they did, indeed, have it "just about right."

Grampa's Bell-Bottom Trousers

As I got off the elevator, I stood for a moment to get my bearings. Assorted medical personnel bustled around the nurses' station. A little old man, slightly stooped, walked slowly down the hallway, his hands clasped behind his back, his head lowered as though in contemplation.

"Grampa!" I exclaimed.

"Shull!"

Grampa hurried over to me, threw his arms around me, and kissed me on the cheek. I was touched—and very happy I had come to visit. Grampa had always been very kind and attentive but never affectionate. "Shull, is it really you? I was just thinking about you, trying to remember your last name so I could call. How'd you know I was here?" he asked.

"Carol called. She said that Daddy told her that you were here."

He grabbed my hand and led me down the hallway, proudly introducing me to everyone he saw. "This is my granddaughter Shull." Everyone greeted me happily. There were few visitors at Cochrane Veterans' Hospital in St. Louis, and everyone was genuinely pleased when someone—anyone—had company. Thereafter, when I made my almost daily visits, by the time I arrived at Grampa's room he already knew I was on my way. Sometimes I saw a pajama-clad patient hobbling or even running to inform him that his granddaughter was coming.

As I passed the other men, they grinned broadly and called after me, "How are you doing today?"

"He knows you're coming."

Grampa would emerge from his room, also grinning, as I approached. "Hi, Shull."

"Hi, Grampa." We'd hug and kiss each other and then he'd take my hand.

"I want you to meet this old guy. He's been worrying me to death to meet you," he would say. And then we'd make our rounds. Having a frequent visitor increased his own bragging rights substantially.

"Hi, Henry. Is that your granddaughter?" The standard rhetorical question.

"Hi, Henry. How're you doing?"

"Hi, Shirley." I never could figure out how they knew that my name was Shirley, rather than Shull.

Grampa talked about his past a lot when he found out that I was interested in family history. He was an excellent storyteller. I particularly enjoyed his mimicry of certain people, especially of pretentious ones, whom he described as "hankty." He could mimic both males and females so well that I felt as though I could hear them myself. He told me about the way the older folks used to disapprove of the younger ones' attire when he was a young man. He talked about his first pair of bell-bottom trousers and about his first spats and what a sensation they had caused. Grampa wasn't particularly concerned with other people's assessments of him; thus, I thought that there was a message in the latter stories about not worrying about what other people might think, because the older ones have always been inclined to disapprove of the younger ones.

He also told me about a black woman who had sat and stared at him in a bus station where they were both waiting. Finally, she had spoken to him. "I declare. You're the blackest man I ever seed." She added gratuitously, "You're fair [good-looking], but you're so black!"

"Grampa! You're making that up!" I had responded.

"That's what she said. 'You're the blackest man I ever seed,' " he had repeated, grinning broadly. I was never sure why he had told me this story, or even whether or not it was true. But I gathered from it that he was reinforcing his point that one ought not be concerned unduly with the things others thought and said.

Grampa talked about his move to Illinois from Arkansas during the Great Migration of the post–World War I era. His work on the Illinois Central Railroad took him through Cairo, where he noticed that entire families worked together in the fields of their small farms. This convinced him that Cairo would be a good place to raise children and to own a farm. So in 1921, shortly after the birth of their first son—my father, John—Grampa and Grandmommy moved their family to Future City, just north of Cairo. Future City was right on the Mississippi River and was subject to periodic flooding, so many homes there were built on stilts eight to twelve feet off the ground. Grampa and Grandmommy had planned to save money and purchase a farm in the area at a later date.

Grampa worked at Bruce's Mill as a laborer and on the Illinois Central Railroad during the family's seven or eight years in Future City. Daddy recalls the years there as ones when the family primarily interacted with other blacks and had limited contacts with whites. Thus, they purchased their groceries from black-owned stores, attended all-black schools taught by black teachers, and had other social communication with blacks. In 1928 the family moved to a farm in Charleston, Missouri, where Grampa's mother, his four younger siblings, and several nieces and nephews lived. His father had died the previous year, and his mother, Emma Holloman Motley, requested his help in sharecropping the farm on which they lived. Within a year, Great-Grandmother Emma had returned to Arkansas. Meanwhile, Grampa, Grandmommy, and their family remained in Charleston, eventually moving into town when Grampa got a job with the Works Projects Administration (WPA) of the New Deal.

Grampa, Grandmommy, Daddy, and Mudeah returned to Illinois years later, moving to rural Mounds in Pulaski County, a few miles north of Cairo and Future City, where they purchased a farm. Larry and June were born in Chicago, when my parents lived there for two years and Daddy worked in a meatpacking house. Long before I had read *The Jungle,* Upton Sinclair's exposé about the meatpacking industry's abuses, I'd heard Daddy's stories about them.

After its residency in Chicago, my family returned to the farm in Mounds where my paternal grandparents still lived. This is where my parents, my grandparents, and Larry and June lived when I was born on January 29, 1946. Grampa and Daddy, with help from various neighbors, had built the small four-room house that became the residence of assorted Motleys over the next thirty years or so.

While he was at Cochrane, Grampa called me one day to ask me to come to the hospital as early as possible because he needed to talk to me about something important. Once I was there, he explained that the doctors thought that he might have cancer and they wanted to operate on him. He said that he didn't understand the whole deal, but he knew I would since I was well educated, so he wanted me to be with him when he spoke with the doctors. "Ask them whatever you need to know. Then you can let me know if I should have the operation or not," he'd said. I was horrified, first because of the possibility that Grampa had cancer and second because he wanted me to decide what he should do. My protestations notwithstanding, he insisted that I was more knowledgeable on the subject than he was.

He and I met with the doctors, with Grampa looking to me to ask intelligent questions. After they'd left, he turned to me and said,

"Well, Shull, it's up to you." I couldn't induce him to say another word about the matter, so ultimately I advised him to have the operation. On the appointed day, I was beside myself with worry. I went to the hospital before he was prepared for surgery, then I went to Southern Illinois University at Edwardsville (SIUE), where I had a couple of classes, and then I returned to the hospital while he was still in the recovery room. The biopsy revealed that his abdominal tumor was benign. I was so relieved that I cried until I was too weak to produce a decent tear.

Gracious and considerate, Grampa said one day, "Shull, you don't have to visit me every day."

I replied, "But I like to visit you, Grampa. Besides no one else is as happy to see me as you are." And we both grinned and held hands. Shortly thereafter, Grampa was released from the hospital, and my husband Allan Carlson, our daughter Fae, and I drove him home to Mounds.

Grampa increasingly suffered from health problems as he aged, however. In 1976 he was hospitalized once again, this time at the veterans' hospital in Marion, Illinois. When we learned he was in the hospital, my sister Carol, Allan, and I went to visit him. When we walked into his room, we found that he was doing reasonably well, no longer in the life-threatening situation he'd been in earlier.

"Hi, Grampa."

"Hi, Shull."

"Hi, Grampa."

"Hi, Cal."

"Hi, Grampa."

"Hi, Allan."

We visited with him for a while and then decided to go out for something to eat before returning later. "Grampa, we're going to get some lunch. We'll be back later. Would you like us to bring you anything?"

"No, but give Cal something to eat. She's might near as po' and skinny as me," he replied.

On another visit, the nurses were surprised to find that he recognized me, because they had thought that he was very disoriented. One said to him, "Mr. Motley, who is this?"

"Well, her name was Shirley, when I knowed her." Shirley! He had called me Shirley. I had never heard him call me by my real name.

Because he was still hospitalized at Christmas time 1976, Allan and I invited him to spend the holidays with us. Mudeah visited, also, as did Allan's mother, Marion Hadley Carlson, who lived in Osco, Illinois, near the quad-city area of Rock Island-Moline-East Moline-Davenport.

For health reasons, Grampa and Grandmommy were forced to abandon their farm and home in Mounds, and both moved into nursing homes in 1978. Grandmommy moved to a nursing home in Mounds. Grampa lived first at a nursing home in Creal Springs, near Marion, for several months, and later moved to Halstead Terrace Nursing Home in Chicago. I had worked with the social worker at the hospital in Marion to get him moved to a nursing home in my neighborhood in Edwardsville, but without any luck. I presume that, meanwhile, Aunt Gertie had requested that he be moved closer to her.

A notation regarding Grampa's condition on May 30, 1978, when he was in the Halstead Terrace Nursing Home in Chicago, indicated that he was "senile, somewhat demanding and on occasion very stubborn." I had seen him shortly before that time and did not find him to be senile. In fact he was mentally very alert, although physically infirm. He was, however, "somewhat demanding" and "very stubborn." He told me that he liked to "fool with" the nurses by refusing to do what they said. "Sometimes I go too far with it, though," he'd confessed with his characteristic broad grin. When they wanted him to take medication that he did not care to take, he accused them of "being in cahoots with someone," perhaps the doctors or the drug companies. He would tell them, "How much are they paying you to make me take that? I'll double it, if you'll leave me alone." The nurses and aides would become angry over this, he indicated, but he thought it was funny. So did I. Besides, I really liked his sense of humor and his fighting spirit.

Grampa's refusal to take the medication struck me as a way he exercised control over his life at a time when his physical strength was waning. Two strokes had left his legs weakened, and he was unable to walk. Thus, he spent the last few years of his life in a wheelchair. This was a very difficult adjustment for a man who had been very active all his life. Refusing medication, if only temporarily, restored some decision-making power to him. When I had visited him at the veterans' hospital in Marion earlier in 1978 and in 1977, the nurses sometimes had asked me to induce him to take his medication. When I asked him to take it, he would say "Just sit it there and I'll think about whether I'm going to take it or not." After a brief wait he would say, "I'm going to take it for you." That is, I'll take it for your benefit.

Mildred's Awakening

"Shirl," my sister Mildred says when I answer the telephone. "Have you written about my awakening in the family history?" She laughingly continues, "Do you know what I mean?"

"Yes, when you felt Grandma Bessie's spirit infuse your body," I respond. "No, I haven't, but it would make a good story." I had thought of writing about that situation, but I had been reluctant to do so because I wasn't sure whether Mil would find it objectionable. And I didn't want to hear for the rest of my life about my indiscretion in telling a story that she didn't want told. Thus, it seemed prudent to mind my own business.

"Yeah, that would be a good story," she continues, adding gratuitously, "I knew you'd know what I was talking about." We are both laughing as we recall the entire scenario.

"You know, I'd have to tell the whole story," I warn.

"Yeah, I know. You could parlay that motherfucker into a whole chapter!" Mildred notes, sounding like Larry now. My petite, youngest sibling, who is the very picture of propriety, sometimes says things that others recognize as true but shrink from saying because they are impolitic.

After we've talked a while longer about what should go into the chapter about the awakening, we hang up the telephone. It is now my job to figure out how to tell this story about my sister and our grandmother in a tasteful, sensitive manner. After all, this is a story about Grandma Bessie's funeral.

For many years Mildred's five older siblings have teased her about how much she is like Grandma Bessie. Grandma Bessie had a well-deserved reputation as being sharp-tongued, as does Mildred. But Mildred felt absolutely no affinity for our grandmother. "She doesn't even remember my name," Mildred would complain. "She just calls me 'the other one.'" Mildred would mimic our grandmother, "'Well, here's Callyn, and . . . the other one. Have you gotten yourself a husband yet?' She acts as though my only reason for living is to get a husband!"

"Yeah," we all agree. But then we remind Mildred of her own equally direct manner. To illustrate the point, I might tell once again about the way Lloyd Jordan, her boss at that time, literally had backed out of her office as she reprimanded him for something that he'd forgotten to do.

"I'll get to it right away, Mil," he had reassured her as he'd reached the door and hurriedly made his exit, hoping to avoid any further comment by her. Isn't he her boss? I'd thought as Lloyd had disappeared into the corridor.

Or someone might remind her of what she'd told Daddy after his second divorce, "You don't need to even think about getting married again. You can see that you're no good at this marrying thing. Just stick to dating." Then she had told her brothers and sisters that if Daddy dated another evil woman, we would all have to get them both straight because we weren't going to put up with another disagreeable woman. When we'd all laughed as though we presumed that she was joking, she had said,"And I'm not joking either!" To Carol and me she had added, "I know I can't count on the Motley men because they're so wimpy, so it'll be up to us."

As the discussion about Grandma Bessie resumes, someone notes that she had refused to remarry after our grandfather had died. She'd said repeatedly and emphatically, "I'll never marry again. I was married to Gene for fifty-four years and he didn't try to boss me around, and I'm not going to let nan 'nother one try to boss me around either!" Sometimes I liked to imagine a man attempting to tell Grandma Bessie what to do. Now that was a very entertaining picture. Nonetheless, she had many potential suitors who had tried to change her mind about remarrying. One man, a minister, had even solicited the assistance of her grandchildren and great-grandchildren in the hopes of winning Grandma Bessie's hand, but to no avail. She had only smiled and said once again that preachers were crooks—actually she had said that they were even worse than crooks—and then she had gone on to make numerous other disparaging remarks about clergymen. But being a widow who does not wish to remarry was one thing; never getting married in the first place was quite another, according to our grandmother's social expectations. Thus, she constantly beseeched her grand-daughters to marry.

"Surely you can find someone to marry you!" she had urged, as though at a certain age we should have married virtually any willing candidate.

Our Uncle Curtis and Uncle Billy, our mother's two brothers, hadn't helped matters with their own constant admonitions to their nieces. "You know, with all that schooling you're getting, you won't be able to find anyone to marry you," Uncle Billy had warned. Mildred was pursuing a law degree at that time, and Carol a master's of business administration. Carol would later make the husband hunting even worse, in their estimation, by getting a doctorate in marketing. Because I had married—albeit I had divorced after thirteen years—they weren't as concerned about me. They periodically did hint, however, that it was about time that I began my quest for another husband, although clearly this was less a priority than my sisters' stalled searches. When I introduced Harry to my grandmother and uncles, first as my fiancé and later as my husband, they had been particularly pleased. Not only had I found another husband, but also I had chosen one whom they really liked. The latter was a bonus.

As I considered how to write the story about Mildred, I thought about the trip we'd taken to Lansing to attend Grandma Bessie's funeral, where the awakening had occurred. My siblings Calvin, Carol, and Mildred, my husband Harry, and I had driven down from the St. Louis area, where we all lived, to Memphis, where we had met our brother John, who had flown in earlier. Our brother Larry, who lived in California, had been unable to attend. "I can't do anything for her now. Right?" he had said, adding, "So I might as well go later when I can stay longer."

The six of us had spent the night at a Marriott Hotel in Memphis, and then we had driven to Lansing the next day. En route we had told stories about our many visits to our grandparents, focusing on the "good ole days" when we had been children. We also had speculated about the various family members and friends whom we might see in Lansing and Earle. We would assemble at Uncle Billy and Aunt Bessie's house in Lansing. Our Aunt Toots had taken the train from Portland, Oregon, and had already arrived in Lansing. Some of our cousins would be there. Derik and Jerome Jones, Uncle Billy's two children by his first wife, Katherine, would be present, as would Katherine, who lived a few miles from Lansing in Earle. Phyllis Benton, Aunt Theresa's daughter, whom most of us had met only once over twenty years ago, planned to attend, but her three brothers—William Jr., Rellie, and Gregory Benton—did not. I was really looking forward to talking to Phyllis about our mutual interest in family history. She'd sent me some of her research on genealogy and some wonderful old family photographs, as well as other primary data, and we had talked on the telephone about family history.

We would also see Uncle Curtis's five children, Jean Alex, Curtis, Tommy, Ray, and Carl Jones. Mattie May, who was the mother of the latter four and Uncle Curtis's second wife, from whom he was divorced, might be there as well. May had been one of my favorite adults when I was a child. I recalled her as a kind, easy-to-talk-to woman who seemed to have an instinctive understanding of human psychology.

I could scarcely wait to see Jean—called Emma Jean when we

were children—because I hadn't seen her in over thirty-five years, since she and I were about twelve and eleven respectively. We had become close friends as children, when we had visited our grandparents during the summers. She had lived in Seattle, Washington, with her mother after her parents' divorce. Now she lived in Anchorage, Alaska. Outgoing and fun, Jean was very popular with both family and friends. Even Grandma Bessie had bragged about her. My brother John recalled, however, that Jean had overstepped herself with our grandmother when she'd tried to get Grandma Bessie to agree that she was her favorite grandchild. "Am I your favorite grandchild, Grandma?" she'd asked solicitously. We all gasped at Jean's audacity in raising the issue.

"No!" Grandma Bessie had replied sharply, waving away any suggestion that anyone other than John, whom Grandma Bessie continued to call June, held this status.

The stories continued as we drove through Crawfordsville, Arkansas, only a few miles east of our destination. We remembered the many Saturday nights that we had spent there, just hanging around on the streets. At that time, Crawfordsville had been a rather attractive small town; now the ravages of economic decline had hit it, as they had many other towns in the area. We noted also that Papa and our Uncles Curtis and Billy had built many houses and renovated still others in Crawfordsville and the vicinity. Uncle Curtis had made large built-in kitchen cabinets for many. We'd never actually seen the interiors of these houses, but we were confident that they were particularly beautiful after Papa and our uncles had finished with them. We further recalled that Earle had been the setting for some of our Saturday night forays. Whether it was Crawfordsville, Earle, or elsewhere, the scenes were likely to be almost identical. We went into one of the small, family-owned shops and bought soft drinks, ice cream, candy, or other treats, and then ate them outside as we talked to the other black people who had come into town for the evening. Teenagers and adults courted, children played, and we all had an opportunity to see those who lived too far away and were too busy for visiting during the week.

"Miss May Ella will be there," we had speculated, our excitement mounting as we came closer to Lansing. Miss Mary Ella Miller is a long-time family friend and a retired schoolteacher whose school we had attended when we were in Lansing. Along with the other black children who lived in the district, we had walked to the little, segregated, one-room school in the middle of nowhere. There we had studied reading, writing, and 'rithemetic, and played games during recess and at lunchtime before returning home in the late afternoon. Patient and dignified, Miss May Ella was the prototype of a black schoolteacher. She, like many black schoolteachers throughout the country, including those in our own southern Illinois community, loved teaching school. And she loved the children whom she taught. She never said this in so many words, but her attitude and the pleasant expression on her kind, round face told us how important we all were to her.

Miss May Ella had no children of her own. She and her husband, Murray, lived in Lansing, only a few doors from Macedonia Baptist Church to the east and about one block from the Bethel AME church to the north. She was a member of the latter, which was also Grandma Bessie's church. In fact, Miss May Ella had been a family friend of the Joneses for many years. She had taught Billy and Toots in school, and she and the Joneses had belonged to the same church for many years. Whenever she saw the Motley children, she would ask, "How is B.B.?" using our mother's childhood nickname, which her old friends still called her. "How is your daddy?" she always added, since she'd known him for many years as well. She was one of the few people in Lansing who continued to ask about Daddy after my parents' divorce in the 1970s after over thirty years of marriage and seven children.

We finally arrived at Uncle Billy and Aunt Bessie's house in Lansing about a half hour before Grandma Bessie's funeral, which was to be held at Macedonia Baptist Church, the site of most large African American community gatherings in that small town. The cousins whom we had expected to see were present, except for Phyllis, who had remained home due to illness, and Jerome, who would arrive later, after we'd left.

Following the funeral and the burial, we had returned to the community center, across the street from the church, to talk and to eat. There had been many delicious foods: turkey and cornbread dressing, ham, cornbread, rolls, greens, mashed potatoes, candied yams, and sweet potato pie. Aint Puddin', Aunt Bessie's aunt, had made an absolutely outstanding white coconut cake that reminded me of the ones Daddy used to make for Christmas when we lived in Mounds. Later, we had all returned to Uncle Billy and Aunt Bessie's house. It was here that it became clear to some of us that our grandmother's mantle now rested comfortably upon Mildred's shoulders.

During the post-funeral visit at Bessie and Billy's house, some people played cards, others talked, and still others played dominoes. Mildred had sat quietly, seemingly deep in thought, for a long time. Then she turned to our brother John and said, "Well, John, your mother's dead. Your grandmother's dead. You're nobody's favorite any more!" As he sat in stunned silence, she added, "And don't try to suck up to Daddy. We know you're good for that, but I'm his favorite!"

Everyone was taken aback at first. No one spoke. Then we began to laugh self-consciously, a bit embarrassed. We stole sidelong glances at John, trying to assess his reaction to Mildred's comment. After his initial surprise, John, too, laughed. But he didn't make any of the glib comebacks that are his stock-in-trade.

"That's when I knew that she was the one," John said later at the family reunion, when we were telling our brother Larry about the incident.

Mildred says it was during Grandma Bessie's funeral that she had realized for the first time that she was, indeed, like our grandmother. As speaker after speaker rose to eulogize "Sister Bessie Jones," a theme developed: Grandma Bessie was very outspoken and undiplomatic. Or as one person had characterized her, "What comes up, comes out."

"What comes up, comes out?" Mildred recollects. "That does sound like me!" As she listened to the various eulogies, she had thought, "Okay, this means they know she was a bitch. They just don't want to come straight out and say it, so they resort to euphemisms." One speaker had said that Miss Bessie Jones always was very involved in what was going on in the community. Another observed that she kept the younger women in the Eastern Star and other organizations to which she belonged "in line." Someone else noted that she always had advice to offer, although she didn't say that those to whom she had given advice had sought it. All of these things might well be said about Mildred, who now proudly embraces her role as heir to Grandma Bessie.

2

Stories about Mudeah

Family Reunion: Remembering Mudeah

"**M**udeah could cook. She could make anything without a lot of fancy ingredients. Without herbs and spices. All she used was salt and black pepper. And onions."

"Yeah, she might put some chili powder in her chili, if she had it."

"She'd cook everything in those big cast-iron skillets, too."

"Remember, she fried everything in lard. And it would be delicious. Not greasy either."

"She'd have the heat turned up so high, you'd think it was going to burn, but it didn't. I don't think she ever burned anything."

"I've never been able to make sweet rolls like hers," John says. He's tried for years to bake like Mudeah. "Once I had it just about right," he adds.

And so the discussion about our mother goes at the family reunion. Many of our recipes are attempts to reproduce hers, although Mudeah almost never cooked from a written recipe. Like many country cooks, she added a bit of this and a pinch of that, often pouring the ingredients into her open palm rather than using measuring spoons or cups to determine the appropriate quantities.

Mudeah was a pretty woman, with a medium-brown complexion and thick black hair that grayed prematurely. Petite in stature, she was chronically overweight by twenty or thirty pounds. "Pleasingly plump," she called it. Self-confident and gregarious, Mudeah clearly held herself in high regard.

When we'd lived in Mounds, Mudeah frequently had milked the cows, worked in the fields, and driven the tractor, but not as often as Daddy had—except for the milking, which she did twice daily until Larry and June were old enough to help Daddy with it or to entirely take over the duty. Daddy cooked, canned, ironed, cleaned, changed diapers, and the like regularly—although not as frequently as Mudeah did these things. My family, like that of many African Americans, was more equalitarian than that of many white Americans. Either parent would have been offended at the mere suggestion of incompetence to perform all chores—whether traditionally female or male—with equal skill. I recall my own amazement and confusion when the feminists of the 1960s spoke of the historically separate spheres of women and men. Women took care of home and children; men worked outside the household, earning a living. This was so different than my own family experiences that I was unable to see that these charges had validity for the larger society, especially for middle-class whites.

Women in the Motley-Jones family in general and Mudeah in particular are not noted for being demure, deferential to men, or lacking in either intellect or self-confidence. While my parents probably expected that all of us would eventually marry and have children, they urged us all to wait until we were at least in our late twenties to do so. More than marriage or children, they emphasized that we should go to college and prepare for a profession. I recall Mudeah saying many times that I should not become interested in the opposite sex until after I'd graduated from college and had worked a few years. I was quite sure when she said this that she was totally out of touch with reality. "I got married at twenty-one," she said repeatedly, "and that was still too young."

My mother was always very outspoken, sometimes to the point of extreme insensitivity to other people's feelings. When we lived in Mounds, the whole family occasionally visited neighboring families. Sometimes during these visits, the men and women would get into verbal sparring matches, usually with Mudeah as one of the most vocal and most effective of the female contingent. Mudeah's logic and knowledge were striking as she often bested the men. Preacher Brooks, a lay minister, liked to get on the subject of biblical admonitions to women. Mudeah was more than his match because she knew the Bible better than he did. She often pointed out the context in which a given point was made, indicating that it was different from the one in which he had placed it. She would go on to strengthen her argument by pointing out other biblical passages in support of her own belief in the equality of the sexes. When the men began to resort to blustering illogic, I knew that she'd outdone them, and so did they. I was really proud of Mudeah when she argued the men down like that. I always got the impression that Daddy was proud of her too, although I never heard him say so. There was something about the way he'd laugh and shake his head, though, that revealed his pride and approbation.

Mudeah also told us about the sexism she had personally encountered, although she did not actually use the term "sexism." One example that had really angered her occurred when she was a senior in high school. She and Daddy had attended the same school, where both were honor students. He was chosen as class valedictorian. Mudeah said that she should have been valedictorian because she had received better grades than he had, but because she was a female and he a male, they gave the honor to him. The most striking thing to me was not whether this was an objective account of the situation. I had a hard time believing that anyone was smarter than Daddy, although I did not totally discount the possibility that Mudeah was. What interested me was the implication that decisions were based on gender rather than the objective criteria on which they were purported to be based.

Mudeah talked a little about "the olden days," but she was always more reticent than Daddy when it came to storytelling. I liked to hear her tell about when she and Daddy had met. They had met through my mother's Uncle Richard, her father's brother, whom she called Uncle Bud, and his wife, whom Mudeah called Miss Snow or Mother Lemmie. Mudeah lived with them while attending high school in Charleston because there was no high school available for black students in the Arkansas town where she lived. This was an experience shared by countless other blacks, especially in the South. Years later, in 1956, my Aunt Toots, Mudeah's sister, came to live with us in Mounds in order to attend high school. There were secondary schools for blacks in Arkansas by this time, but hers did not offer all of the courses she needed to qualify for nursing school. Even though Douglass High, the black school in Mounds, did not offer all of the same courses as Thistlewood High, the white high school, Douglass had more than the black school in Earle, Arkansas.

Daddy recalls Uncle Richard Jones as a sharp contrast to his brother Lee Gene, my grandfather, whom I called Papa. Richard Jones, according to Daddy, was a strict disciplinarian who was intense, even intimidating, in his demeanor. His brother, however, was gentle and kind. Daddy says Papa was one of the nicest people he has ever known. Uncle Richard had been a principal and a teacher at a segregated black grade school in Charleston. Daddy had been one of his students. After Uncle Richard took over as principal of the school, he precipitated dramatic improvements. He was critical of many practices of the school system, such as the dog-eared textbooks and other cast-offs that blacks received when whites got new ones. Daddy saw Uncle Richard as a person who was quite willing to challenge the whites who controlled the school board and the superintendent's office. As a result, they were sometimes obliged to yield to his demands for better books, equipment, and other things for the black school. Interestingly, my mother saw her Uncle Bud in quite a different light than my father did. She described him as a very "tough on the outside, mush on the inside" person. She did not find him at all intimidating, and she was amused that others often were "fooled" by his veneer of harshness.

Mudeah talked about my birth on January 29, 1946, in Charleston, at Mother Lemmie's boarding house. Mother Lemmie was a widow now that Uncle Richard had died. Later I got to know her as a very kind and attentive person. Larry, June, and I enjoyed our infrequent visits to her place. At my birth, Larry and June were disappointed that I was a girl and protested to Daddy, "We don't want her. Do we, Daddy?" Luckily for me, Daddy did want me. Perhaps even luckier for me, the boys eventually reconciled themselves to having a little sister, because a few months later the two of them were responsible for saving my life. They were about three and four years old at the time. I had been asleep on a bed next to an open window and had somehow managed to get trapped in the window. When my brothers discovered my predicament, one went outside and stood under the window, prepared to catch me while the other pushed me through it.

The family returned to Mounds shortly after my birth. The home we lived in had few modern conveniences. There was no indoor plumbing and no electricity, and the house was heated by wood-burning stoves and illuminated by kerosene lamps. Nor was there a telephone. Often we had no car or any other reliable motorized vehicle. Some years later, in about 1951, we did get electricity, and four or five years later we got a telephone.

We shared a party line with several other neighbors. Every home had a special ring, such as two longs, or one long and one short, which was how the telephone company supposedly insured privacy. But it was obvious that people listened in on other people's conversations. Several times one of my siblings or I walked into the house only to witness Mudeah in this eavesdropping mode. With a sharp "Shush!" she attempted to silence the intruder, but no doubt this was heard also by the legitimate user of the phone. Usually she hung up at this point, possibly muttering weakly, "I didn't know anyone was on the line." We children sometimes eavesdropped as well, hoping to hear some juicy morsel of gossip.

Mudeah was never one to mince words. I recall that one time I came home from school excited to tell her about what I'd learned about President Abraham Lincoln. Rather than the profuse praise of Lincoln that I'd anticipated, she said simply, "Hmpf! Lincoln was a racist!"

Shocked, I asked, "Why do you say that?"

"Because he was, Shirley," she responded. And that was that. She would say no more about the matter, either then or later. It took me many years to realize why she had spoken of the Great Emancipator with such derision.

"Mudeah and Grandma Bessie couldn't stand each other," some-one observes. For years we've tried to understand why these two—mother and daughter—who were so much alike conflicted so much.

"It's because they were both so damned evil," Larry says in his usual matter-of-fact way.

"Yeah, they were both two evil women." Everyone agrees. Some-times we talk about which one was more evil, perhaps adding Grandmommy, our paternal grandmother, to the competition.

Daddy and I once had a discussion in which we agreed that it wouldn't be fair to simply declare an over-all winner. It would be better to divide things up like assorted Olympic events and to em-ploy Olympic-style judging, where the lowest and highest scores would be eliminated and then you'd average the remaining votes. For example, there might be a category for "Saying Something Evil Without Provocation," and another for "Saying Something Evil With Provocation," and so on. Thus, one person might win in one event, and another person in a second.

At the family reunion and other family gatherings, I am some-times called upon to tell a favorite story about Mudeah's insensi-tivity, which could take a nasty turn.

"Shirl, tell them what she said to that guy in her office. You know, the one . . ." And I do, indeed, know the one.

Mudeah and I were standing in line at a check-out counter, chat-ting and laughing while we waited our turn with the cashier at the Zayre store in Springfield. I looked around to find a young man waving in our direction. Because he was unfamiliar to me, I glanced at Mudeah to see whether she knew him, but she had turned her back to him.

"Mudeah, do you know that man over there who's waving at us?" I asked.

"I told that damn fool Daryl not to act like he knows me in pub-lic!" she said angrily.

"But why would you say that?" I asked.

"He's handicapped!" she snapped, as though that explained everything.

Daryl, with whom she worked, had cerebral palsy, and she was embarrassed to acknowledge publicly that she knew him. She'd also been very outspoken—cruel even—in making him aware of the disdain in which she'd held him. When he'd proudly announced to her that he was getting married, rather than give him her best wishes, Mudeah had told him that he should make a premarital agreement. After he'd asked why, she'd said that obviously the young woman was marrying him for his money because she could not possibly love him since he was handicapped. She'd also told Daryl that his fiancée, whom he had happily insisted did not have a disability, was "cross-eyed." Mudeah had added, "You just can't keep your head still long enough to see."

As we share such stories, making light of them now, we are all keenly aware of the injustices in them. Our mother's insensitivity and that of our grandmothers serve as a reminder to us of the biases we find so abhorrent. We can all recall as well instances when we were the object of their derisive comments. The recounting of these experiences suggests to us a need to examine periodically our own views toward our families, friends, and other people. These stories also are an indication that we make an attempt to see our family in a realistic light, rather than merely recounting those tales that make us proud and happy. For us family history is about the bad times as well as the good ones.

Mudeah was without a doubt the best money manager I have ever known. A frugal shopper, she taught her children by example how to get the best value. Thus, she clipped coupons for groceries and incidentals, raised a vegetable garden, and made almost all of her own and her three daughters' clothing. She also managed to have a small savings account even during times when our income was very low.

Mudeah's frugality went to extremes, however. She generally allowed us to have only a few inches of water in the bathtub even after we had moved to Springfield and had indoor plumbing and a bathroom. For many years, until I had my own home and paid the bills myself, I thought that water was very expensive. The heat was always turned down very low in the winter. The temperature rarely got above the sixties when she and we children were home alone. Before Daddy came home, however, she would turn up the heat so that it would be warm enough for him. Indeed, Mudeah did many things to ensure Daddy's comfort that I am not sure he was aware of at the time, or even now.

"Remember that time she made you wear her shoes, Shirl," Larry reminds me.

"Yeah, I remember," I respond, my cheeks beginning to burn with embarrassment as I recall that humiliation.

My siblings sometimes contend that I run a close second to Mudeah when it comes to frugality. The fact that I once drove a vehicle for twelve years and 160,000 miles suggests that they have a point. By the time I sold my 1977 Oldsmobile Cutlass Supreme, even Daddy had begun to make jokes about how I "didn't really have a car." He'd speculated once, half jokingly, that I never had to yield the right-of-way because other drivers recognized that I "didn't have anything to lose." Startled at first, the next time I went for a drive, I noticed that it really was true. I could sit at a stop sign for ten minutes without another car pulling out in front of me.

My husband, Harry, says the hallmark of my own penny-pinching is the pot that I once used for making popcorn. He likes to tell about the first time I offered to make popcorn for him and how stunned he was when I dragged out a thirty-year-old aluminum pot that was blackened with soot and missing its handle. He was even more surprised when I produced the most delicious popcorn he'd ever had—large, white, fully popped kernels to which I added lots of melted butter. "Wow! It's delicious!" he'd noted, as though surprised that it was edible.

The conversation turns back to Mudeah as someone recalls her admonitions to my sisters and me regarding the appropriate behavior for "a lady." A lady does not: Sit with her legs gaped open; laugh or talk loudly; chase boys or call them on the telephone; or wear cheap jewelry, clothing, or perfume. A lady does not swear, chew with her mouth open, or smoke cigarettes. Nor does a lady permit men to "hang all over her, flocking around her like flies to honey."

Mudeah loved little children. She would play with them, cuddling and kissing them and calling them by assorted pet names. "Little devil" was Mudeah's highest accolade, as in "Oh, he's a cute little devil" or "She's a sweet little devil." As one grew older, Mudeah became less tolerant and admiring. By age eleven or twelve, one was apt to have real difficulty in relating to her and was less likely to be called by these love names.

"Tell me about the kids," she used to say. When she was very ill with the bladder cancer that ultimately claimed her life, she didn't feel like talking much herself, but she wanted to hear stories about the children in the family—her own children, grandchildren, and great-grandchildren. She once told me that she thought Krystle and Kraig, my daughter Fae's children, were so cute that they should have little dolls made in their likeness. For their part, they really loved their great-grandmother who always smiled at them so approvingly. "I think everything they do is just fine," she'd once said.

One day I took Kraig and Krystle to Springfield to visit Mudeah. Mudeah smiled broadly and happily, nodding her approval as the two children inspected her apartment, including various knick-knacks in the living room. She gave each of them one or two articles that they had admired, and they settled down to play. They were so engrossed in play that they did not notice when Mudeah left the room and went into the kitchen. Suddenly Krystle looked up and realized that her great-grandmother was no longer in the room. "Where's Great-Grandma?" she asked, her voice quavering.

"She's in the kitchen. You can go in, if you want to," I said.

Krystle went into the kitchen and returned almost immediately, holding her great-grandmother by one hand and a box of crackers in the other. Great-Grandma smiled even more broadly than she had earlier. She immediately conferred the highest love name upon Krystle.

"She's a little devil," Mudeah cried emphatically. Always the loving child, Kraig ran to grab Great-Grandma's other hand, as well as some crackers. He, too, won the top praise. "They're both little devils!" Mudeah proclaimed happily. I nodded my assent, proud to be the grandmother of two "little devils." But I was a bit jealous, also. I didn't recall ever having reached "little devil" status. Yet in less than fifteen minutes, both Krystle and Kraig had acquired that stature.

Mudeah had struggled with mental illness for many years, but her physical health had been very good except for problems with her back. Her recurring schizophrenia had been controlled with medication for years—since an earlier bout with the illness in the late 1960s. We'd learned only two months before her death that Mudeah had cancer. The oncologist who first discovered the cancer had said that she'd probably live another six months to a year. Hoping for a better prognosis, we took her to a bladder cancer specialist at Barnes Hospital in St. Louis. Although the specialist had contended that, "No one can say how long anyone has to live," it was clear from the pained look on his kind face that Mudeah was gravely ill. We'd been shocked and eventually devastated. Mudeah had been only sixty-eight, and it had never occurred to any of us that she would die so young. Her father had lived to be almost eighty; her mother at eighty-seven still enjoyed good health. Mudeah's funeral was held in Springfield on January 30, 1989. She'd died on January 27 at Barnes Hospital in St. Louis.

Mudeah's Quilts and the Family Jigsaw Puzzle

Mudeah almost always had a patchwork quilt in some stage of preparation. After dinner, on winter afternoons, or at any time that she had what might have been leisure time otherwise, she worked on handmade quilts or sewed on her sewing machine. She began a quilt by choosing a pattern from a book or from ones neighbors had shared with her. Every now and then, she made one based on a pattern included with the cotton batting that she bought at the big general store in Mounds. She then cut the pattern for the individual squares or sections from newspaper, preserving the original one for future use. Then she was ready to cut the pieces of fabric and sew them together by hand. Usually the patterns were of the "scrap" design, where she used leftover pieces of fabrics from garments she had made. A gingham check from my pinafore, a print with little valentines from Carol's "turnaround" dress, a bright solid from Toots's skirt, and a plaid from Larry's and June's shirts all might be included. Occasionally she made a quilt using two or three pieces of fabric purchased especially for the purpose, but usually this was too expensive.

Some quilt makers sewed pieces randomly with little concern for the aesthetics of the finished product, but Mudeah was far more discerning. Thus, her quilts were both functional and attractive. She "set together" the completed squares using a single fabric, providing symmetry that was very beautiful. To the completed quilt top, she added a cotton batting and a bottom layer made of muslin or another inexpensive but durable fabric. The three layers would then be placed on a huge quilting frame, which took up much of our small living room.

Mudeah then quilted the coverlet with periodic assistance from friends and neighbors who came to visit. Often when we came home from school, Mudeah and Mrs. King or someone else would be sitting at the frame, quilting and talking. Mrs. King was the most accomplished quilter. She made beautiful piecework quilts, some of which she sold. She often made elaborate designs as she quilted. Her stitches were always tiny, neat, and even. Mudeah never removed Mrs. King's work when she left, as she did with others' work that did not suit her high standards. After some helpers had left, she would remove stitches that were too long, or uneven, or both, while railing about the importance of producing an attractive finished product, "Nobody wants these old, long, sloppy-looking stitches. Look at that! Her work looks worse than the baby's!" This was, of course, a supreme insult. In fact, Mudeah did allow the baby—Carol or me, as the case might be—to assist her. She left the children's work in place, however.

"Shirley did this. See how nicely she sews," she would boast to

Daddy or to a friend, although usually not directly to me or to any other of her children. I secretly listened as she proudly displayed my other efforts at sewing, perhaps comparing two or three quilts and demonstrating the progress of "the baby's" stitches. Overhearing such praise, I was both proud and puzzled. To me she had said, "This looks okay, honey. But you know you can do better than this. Don't you? Look at this stitch. It's too long. Look here, this one is crooked. And this one. . . . You could do better if you would go on and use a thimble, like I've been telling you." Having totally deflated my ego, she would then instruct me to do some chore, thus ending the little lecture.

Years later one could look at the completed quilts, recalling their history and that of the family and the community in the process. "Old Lady King quilted this part right here, girl," Mudeah would say to a friend. "She stayed a long time that day, so I knew she wanted something. She finally said to me, 'How's Mr. Motley?'" Mudeah chuckled, recalling that Miss King had a crush on Grampa and was trying to think of a way to get him to marry her.

"She said, 'Lordy, Lordy. That's such a hardworking man. Nice looking, too. Do you think he'll ever marry again?'" Mudeah continued. Miss King always spoke as though Grandmommy did not exist, because she was either in the state hospital in Anna or living with Aunt Gertie in Chicago. Mudeah no doubt went on to tell about how, eventually despairing of getting Grampa to the altar, Mrs. King took a different approach to marriage. She decided to go down South and find herself a husband.

"I'll buy him a new truck," she'd announced to all her neighbors. Mrs. King left for a week or two and returned married to Mr. Luke, whom she had not previously known. And she bought him a truck. She had left home a single woman, walking into Mounds to catch a train, and returned riding in a truck beside her new husband. Mr. Luke was a nice man, affable and hardworking. The two of them worked side by side on her farm until his death some years later.

One evening Mrs. King—this was before her husband-hunting trip—quilted with Mudeah until it was nearly dark. This was very unusual because she generally preferred to get home before sun-down. Eventually she said that she really hated to "stay in that big, old house alone," even though her house wasn't all that big. "I was wondering, Cora, if I could get one of your chi'ren to stay with me," she asked. I was chosen for this duty. So she and I walked the mile between her house and ours.

When we got to her house, I found her to be the most gracious hostess I had known until that point, and one of the most gracious of my entire life. She was very kind and attentive, as well as solici-tous for my comfort. She showed me many beautiful quilts she'd made. Some she'd made for sale to various people who had asked her to do so. Others she'd made for her two sons, her granddaugh-ter, and other relatives.

"Would you like me to cap some corn for you?" she asked. That was her terminology for making popcorn. I immediately accepted. I loved popcorn. Mrs. King had a reputation for making delicious popcorn that she had grown herself. It was, indeed, particularly de-licious and she kept making big pans full until I said that I'd had enough. I think it was the first time in my life that I'd had enough popcorn. She also left our bedtime to my discretion, even though I was at most ten or eleven years old. I liked this because we got to stay up later than my usual bedtime and because I got to make the decision. The next morning she insisted on making me a hearty breakfast. When I got ready to leave, she said very nicely, "I sho' hate to see you go. But I really appreciate you staying with me." In a community that was very reticent to openly pay a compliment, this was major praise. Whenever I saw her after that incident, I re-membered what a lovely hostess she had been. And what good popcorn she had made.

Wilson Green, a one-time neighbor, would visit on some days when Mudeah was quilting. He'd appear unannounced, like most of our guests, and Mudeah would cordially invite him to stay awhile. "Have you had your dinner yet?" she'd ask, knowing that Wilson was always hungry. Besides, it was the neighborly thing to do. She would fix him a nice meal. Perhaps ham and eggs with biscuits. Or maybe the beans or whatever she was making for our supper would be done, so she'd give him some of those with a big hunk of cornbread. And she'd make a fresh pot of coffee and have a cup with him. Wilson probably had visited all the other neighbors fairly recently, so talking with him offered Mudeah a chance to catch up on the local gossip.

Wilson invariably became drowsy after eating, and he'd fall asleep. When we got home from school, he'd be sitting straight up in a chair, snoring with his eyes wide open! Now that was spooky. I never did understand how a person could sleep with his eyes open as he did. He looked kind of like a chicken, I always thought, because chickens sleep with their eyes open sometimes. When we walked in, he'd continue to sleep, and Mudeah would admonish us to be quiet so as not to disturb him. Such precautions were unnecessary, however. Once Wilson fell asleep, you couldn't awaken him even if you tried. Eventually he would wake up and continue talking just like nothing out of the ordinary had occurred. While Wilson slept, Mudeah would continue to work on her quilt.

Quilts were used on all of our beds. I used to think how wonderful it would be to have a nice, store-bought blanket. My favorite quilt was a red-and-blue one that someone—I don't think it was Mudeah—had made years earlier. It remained on my little twin bed during the entire time we lived in Mounds, which was about seven years. When we moved to Springfield in 1959, the quilt was left behind, much to my disappointment. As we unpacked in our Springfield apartment, I asked Mudeah, "Where is my quilt?"

"That old thing? I left it in Mounds. It was just a rag," she'd replied. Left behind? Just a rag? I was incredulous. I loved that quilt. I recalled all the years I had covered myself with it. Nights when I had drawn comfort from its weight on my body, both for the physical warmth and for some psychological pleasure I drew from it. I thought of the nights I had made little accordion-style pleats between my fingers with it and fallen asleep with the little pleats still tucked between my fingers. I thought about the nights I had awakened, screaming and pursued by ghosts. Daddy would come running into the room each time as though he really thought that there was a genuine crisis. Each time, he reassured me that I'd just been having a nightmare and that there was not a ghost lurking in the corner of the room where I was sure I had seen one this time. Then he'd cover me with my quilt and tell me to go back to sleep. I don't recall his ever having been angry or impatient with me about interrupting his sleep so often. A rag? Left behind? I dared not complain, so I didn't say anything—but I sure missed my quilt.

Walking in Mudeah's Shoes

We were generally well dressed even though our economic status was somewhere between poor and lower middle class—usually a lot closer to the former than to the latter—because Mudeah was an excellent seamstress. I sometimes complained because she made very simple clothing, refusing to decorate it with the appliqués, lace, and fancy topstitching that I liked. Occasionally, she would put a little rickrack on a dress, but even this was rare. Mudeah would buy a pattern, usually *Simplicity* or *McCall's*, which might be very pretty. But when she made the garment, it lacked the finishing touches that had made it so pretty in the pattern book. She would comment derisively, "Doing that mess just takes a lot of time." Then she would point proudly to the quality of her work—the straight seams, the well-turned collars, the perfect buttonholes—and show me what "real quality is." What I wanted was a really pretty dress; I didn't care that much about its quality. I liked the dresses, pinafores, and wide skirts that Fay, the little white girl down the road, wore. Her mother sewed also, and she included the fancy touches I admired so much. Virgie Wilkerson, Fay's mother, could not make a decent buttonhole, though, so she often had Fay bring pieces to Mudeah, whom she paid to make them for her. Sometimes she asked Mudeah to do other things too, such as inserting a lining in a garment. This reinforced Mudeah's conviction that her own sewing was much better than anyone else's. She would examine the garments made by Mrs. Wilkerson, pointing out their many flaws.

"Look at this. She couldn't make a straight seam if you paid her to do it. She doesn't know how to make a buttonhole, even though she has a special attachment to do it. It makes perfect buttonholes, but she doesn't even know how to put it on her machine right," Mudeah gloated. Even so, it seemed to me that Virgie Wilkerson made Fay very pretty outfits. Sometimes when I saw Fay in downtown Villa Ridge, close to where we went to our separate, segregated schools, she'd be wearing something that I recognized as having been made by her mother. It always looked really nice. In fact, she was one of the best dressed of the white girls. But I dared not say this to Mudeah because she did not generally appreciate candor. More correctly, she didn't appreciate anyone who disagreed with her, especially her own children.

Virgie Wilkerson had, in fact, been paid at one time to sew. There was a sewing factory in Mounds on Front Street, where she had worked. I asked Mudeah one time why she did not get a job there, rather than going all the way to Chicago to work. Also, I figured that if "ole no-sewing Virgie Wilkerson" could get a job there when she couldn't even make a decent buttonhole, surely Mudeah would be hired. But Mudeah informed me that the factory hired only white women. That struck me not only as unfair, but also as stupid. Why hire less competent people to do the work when they could get someone with Mudeah's talents? I wondered. As much as I liked Mrs. Wilkerson's sewing, I did see Mudeah's point. Mrs. Wilkerson did come to Mudeah a lot to do those things that she couldn't do herself. Mudeah went on to explain once again, as she, Daddy, my teachers, and countless other blacks had done before and after this incident, that "Negroes have to be twice as good to get half as much as whites."

Negroes have to be twice as good to get half as much as whites. It didn't make a lot of sense to me at the time, but I took it to heart and vowed to be at least "twice as good as whites." And I wouldn't be sewing in any ole factory, either! I'd go to college and then I'd become a schoolteacher, or a doctor, or a lawyer. Daddy and Mudeah spoke of the possibility of becoming an engineer, but I didn't see why I'd need to go to college to drive a train, which didn't seem all that much fun anyway except for the part where you got to blow the whistle and wave at everyone at railroad crossings. I didn't tell them that, though; I didn't want to hurt their feelings when they were just trying to be helpful.

When Mudeah's sixteen-year-old sister, Toots, came to live with us, I believe that one of the reasons for their constant conflict was their competition in sewing. Toots's sewing incorporated both the high quality of Mudeah's work with the aesthetics of Virgie Wilkerson's. Thus Toots's own attire, as well as clothes she made for others, was very pretty, stylish, and well made. When Mudeah turned her sister's work over in her hands, seeking to find fault, she rarely found anything wrong. Now that really infuriated her: she had lost ground in the arena where for years she had had no real competition. Mudeah did not like that at all. So she picked at Toots for other reasons: Toots changed outfits too often. She spent too much on fabrics and accessories. She selfishly kept most of the money that her father sent her, rather than dividing it equally among herself and her nieces and nephews. She was lazy. She paid too much attention to Eugene Hughes, who was from the poorest part of Mounds, and she "thought he was cute." Actually, I thought Eugene was cute myself.

Because neither Mudeah nor Aunt Toots could make all of our clothing, we had to purchase some of our attire, such as undergarments, socks, and shoes. This often presented a problem, especially the shoes, because our income was always very modest. We children often used our money from farmwork to buy these things, but we were not always able to earn enough for all the clothes that we needed. Also, we bought the fabrics for the items Mudeah made, and this took a lot of our earnings.

One year my shoes wore so thin on the bottoms that I needed another pair soon. When I told Mudeah and Daddy about this and showed them the holes wearing through the soles, they didn't say anything. I had expected them to say that we would have to make a trip into Cairo soon to select my new shoes. Obviously, they didn't have the money at that point. Then Mudeah came up with a solution: I could wear her shoes. Oh no, I thought. I didn't want to wear Mudeah's shoes. Her shoes were a pair of white nurse's shoes, which were totally out of style. Indeed, they had never been in style. At that time kids usually wore black-and-white or brown-and-white saddle oxfords, penny loafers (without the pennies), and a few other styles. They did not wear white shoes of any sort, except for the occasional white bucks popularized by the singer Pat Boone. Further, Mudeah had very wide feet, which stretched her shoes far beyond the size of my own very narrow feet. Worst of all, Mudeah had huge bunions on the side of each big toe. Any pair of shoes that she wore more than a few times took the shape of her feet, including the bunions. On the side of her wide white shoes, the imprints of her bunions were very clearly defined. I was mortified, but they were the only shoes available, so I wore them. I polished them well and tried to push in the bunion imprints, but to no avail. It was clear to everyone that I was wearing my mother's shoes. I expected the kids at school to tease me, but no one did. I was very popular at Lovejoy Grade School, but this popularity was more likely to insure that one was teased. Maybe they empathized with me.

Facing Mudeah

Mudeah went to Chicago for the summer of 1958 in order to work in a sewing factory. She took with her the youngest child, Alvin, who was three or four months old. He was born on February 20, 1958. They lived with her aunt and uncle in a comfortably furnished second-floor apartment on Roosevelt Road.

Toots, Mudeah's younger sister, baby-sat Alvin until she decided to get a sewing job also. Meanwhile, Daddy, Carol, Calvin, and I went to visit Mudeah for a few days. After Mudeah and Daddy had talked about the baby-sitter problem, they asked me how I'd like to remain in Chicago to baby-sit. It was a rhetorical question in as much as they had already decided that was the best thing to do. I was not anxious to stay there, because I enjoyed earning money picking fruits and vegetables during the summer. Further, I was not anxious to be with Mudeah because by now she and I had problems relating to each other.

Impatient and authoritarian, Mudeah was not inclined to give the kind of guidance and positive attention sought by a preteen daughter. For my own part, I had absolutely no understanding of her strictness. Nor could I appreciate her insistence that I share my resources, financial and otherwise, with my younger sister. I also objected to her demanding that I take Carol with me to my friends' houses when I went to visit. My own attitude, then, was far from supportive of my mother's authority. Rarely did I overtly challenge her, but I did resist in covert ways. I sometimes muttered under my breath, taking care that I was not within easy "swinging distance" of her. I also waited until Daddy came home or in from the fields and pouted or cried in order to gain his attention. Daddy was a fairly easy touch when it came to his girls. The sight of one of us either crying or preparing to do so was generally sufficient to get his support. Mudeah became very angry with us when he intervened or offered any comfort to us or if he disagreed with her on matters of child rearing. Sometimes she warned us that she would "get us when your Daddy leaves." And sometimes she did just that. Sometimes it was worth it, however. I was quite sure at this point in my life that one of Mudeah's main purposes on earth was to make sure that I never had a good time. If I were to remain in Chicago, I would have two months without Daddy's protection and moderating influence. I wasn't sure how much support I could count on from Aunty and Uncle. Mudeah and Aunty were quite close, so I hoped that this might be to my advantage in that I was sure that Aunty would see that Mudeah was too strict with me.

Baby-sitting Alvin, whom we called Bud, was relatively easy. He was a sweet baby who didn't cry much. He and I stayed at Aunty's apartment each day and played, napped, and went for walks. Sometimes I took him to one of the nearby stores or confectioneries. One day as I carried him, we passed two young men. One said, "Mama and baby. Baby is as big as Mama." I was shocked and tempted to reply, but I restrained myself because I had been told about the ruthless men one might encounter on the streets of Chicago and I couldn't tell whether these two qualified for that label. So I just kept walking. It struck me as really stupid that they thought that I, a twelve-year-old who looked even younger, was the mother of a child.

In the evenings I sometimes visited Toots, who lived across the street from us. She had a baby, Eugene Jr., who was just two days younger than Bud. I liked her husband—Eugene "Gene" Hughes Sr., her high school sweetheart—a lot, but he was rarely at home when I was there. Indeed, I had a crush on him because he was so cute and because he was a former high school basketball star as well.

Mudeah always warned me that I must be home from Toots's house before dark, and I was very careful to do this. Defying her on something like that would undoubtedly have meant that she would whup me. After a problem I experienced with Uncle, however, it became worth the risk to remain at Toots's apartment rather than to be alone with him.

Uncle had always been someone whom I had liked a lot. Sometimes when he went for one of his "runs," he would take me along with him. I don't know what he did, but he would go into his friends' homes, sometimes for quite a while, and I waited in the car as he instructed. Because he was so nice, I didn't object. Uncle worked evenings, and often he, Bud, and I would be the only ones at home during the day. When he was awake, he might sit and talk to me, but usually he slept or "went on runs." One day Uncle was talking to me about his premonition that he was going to "win big hitting the numbers." He said he'd had a tip on a "bumbershoot" or perhaps it was "bumper shoot." He used a term with which I was not familiar. I looked at him quizzically. He said, "Do you know what that is?"

"No," I responded.

He leaned forward, coming closer to me, and said, "This is what it is," as he poked his index finger into my breast. I was stunned and very frightened. I quickly put one hand up and moved his finger away from me, no doubt with a look of horror on my face. After that incident, I was afraid to be alone with Uncle. I tried to avoid him after that terrifying experience. Sometimes I would take the baby onto the huge, rather tacky back porch. Other times I took Bud for long, long walks. Except for the one incident where the man thought that Bud was my son, I did not feel particularly uncomfortable walking down Roosevelt Road. The only problem, as I saw it, was that the baby was very heavy, and because he didn't have a stroller or anything, I had to carry him the entire time.

Occasionally Toots came home before Mudeah, and then we might go to visit her. One day Bud and I were visiting Toots, while I kept watch to see when the lights at Aunty's came on, indicating that either Mudeah or Aunty was there. Because Toots did not have a telephone, I couldn't call them. Because Uncle was there, I made a point of staying away from our temporary home. It began to get dark and I saw no indication that either woman had returned, so I was faced with a difficult decision: should I go home and risk Uncle's touching me again, or should I stay at Toots's and face a whuppin'? I decided to stay at Toots's. Eventually it appeared that Mudeah was back from work, so I took Bud and went home to "face the music." My only hope was that Aunty was also there and would stop Mudeah from spanking me. But Mudeah was alone. And she was both worried and angry.

"Where have you been? I've been worried to death!" she yelled. What could I say? I did not dare tell her that I was afraid of Uncle and why because I feared that she wouldn't believe me. Besides I knew that even if she did believe me, we could not afford to go back home because we needed the money that Mudeah's job at the sewing factory provided. By staying with Aunty, walking to and from work most days, and taking her lunch from home, Mudeah had been able to save most of her pay.

So I said simply, "We were at Toots's. I didn't see the light come on, so I didn't know that you were back yet." I knew that this would not save me, but it was the truth, although not the whole truth. She did, indeed, give me a whuppin'. Quite a severe one at that. She raised welts on my body; my back and buttocks burned long after she had stopped. But at least Uncle had not had an opportunity to touch my breast, so I felt it was worth it.

It took years before I mentioned the incident of Uncle's sexual abuse to anyone. I believe that the first person I ever told was my daughter, Fae. This experience had sensitized me to the fact that trusted adults sometimes took unfair advantage of children. I wanted her to be aware of this and to know that, if anything like that ever happened to her, she was to tell me immediately and I would believe her and also support her, regardless of the consequences.

Several years after telling Fae, three girlfriends and I were sitting around my kitchen table. The conversation turned to sexual abuse. One friend noted a statistic that indicated that a very high number of children—especially girls—were sexually abused. I told my girlfriends about my own experience. Two of my three girlfriends had been sexually abused by adult men when they were children. Still later, I told my sister Carol about Uncle. Her response reminded me of something that I had forgotten. "Oh! That's the reason you always kept me away from him."

"I kept you away from him?" I said proudly, even though I didn't recall that I had been so protective of her.

"Yes," she said, "I always liked him a lot, but you would not let me go near him."

Trying to Bargain with God

"Oh, baby, Mama thought you were getting better," Mudeah said. The telephone had rung early in the morning, before even she had awakened. She'd answered it quickly, afraid that it was a call from the hospital in Cairo where Bud had been a patient for nearly a week. She'd talked quietly, saying only a few words, and then had hung up the telephone. Then she'd said, "Oh, baby, Mama thought you were getting better."

She talked to Daddy, but too low for me to hear what she was saying. I knew then that our little brother, less than one year old, had died of pneumonia. He'd been sick for a few days before being taken to the hospital in Cairo, where Mudeah worked as a nurse's aide. Mudeah had sat by his bedside every day and nearly every night since then. Last night she had come home because she'd needed to get a little sleep before returning to her vigil today.

I had awakened as soon as the telephone had begun to ring. Early-morning calls, like late-night ones, were always bad news. We'd all dreaded just such a moment. I began to cry softly, almost secretively. I didn't mind people seeing my crocodile tears, but I didn't like anyone to see the real ones. Mudeah entered the room, saw me crying, and said brusquely, "Shirley, what's wrong with you?" The question startled me and gave me hope. Maybe I didn't have a reason to cry. If I did, if the baby was dead, Mudeah wouldn't have had to ask me why I was crying. So maybe I'd misunderstood the early-morning phone call and the whispered conversations.

"I thought Bud was dead," I said, hoping she'd tell me how silly I was being. Meanwhile Larry and June, whose bed was across the room, had awakened. Or maybe they had awakened earlier.

"Yes, Bud is dead," she said simply. Larry and June cried too. I don't remember what happened next. Whether we children got up and got dressed at that point or later, at the usual time. Mudeah and Daddy probably got dressed and went to Cairo to the hospital to sign the requisite forms and to make arrangements for the funeral.

I was distraught. My little eleven-month-old baby brother had died! After all my prayers to God. My promises. And he'd still died. That was the first time I'd ever asked God to do anything for me— to let my brother live because he was just a baby. I'd promised God that I wouldn't ask for anything else from Him ever again if He'd just let my little brother live. I promised I'd do anything He wanted, if He'd just let me know what He wanted from me.

When Bud's illness had gotten worse and his condition was listed as critical, I'd tried a new approach. I'd asked God to take me instead. Although I was terrified of dying, I'd decided I'd rather die myself than have Bud die. I'd gotten in thirteen whole years at least. "Besides," I'd whispered to God, "Mudeah loves him." I thought she'd miss me less, or maybe not at all. My mother and I had so much conflict that I thought she didn't love me anymore. Maybe she never had, but I was pretty sure that if she had once, she no longer did. Daddy probably loved me, I'd thought, although he never actually said it. He was nice to me most of the time, and he stuck up for me when Mudeah was mean to me. But it might be kind of a relief to him not to have so many conflicts with Mudeah over me. Larry, June, Carol, and Calvin would miss me, but they would miss the baby, too, so it was just a trade-off for them.

"Do you want to go to school? You can stay home if you'd like," Mudeah or Daddy had said before the two of them had left. But Carol and I decided to go on to school. I didn't want to stay home all day where everyone was bound to be crying and looking sad. Mrs. Buckley, my schoolteacher, and her husband, stopped by as usual to pick us up and drive us to school in Villa Ridge, although we now lived in Mounds, where we had moved recently. We'd decided to finish the school year at Lovejoy, where I was in the eighth grade and Carol was in the first. Larry and June attended Douglass High School, a few blocks from our house.

Carol and I didn't even tell the Buckleys about Bud's death because I didn't want their sympathy. Nor did I want them asking for details of his death. Or asking if I was okay or if they could "do" anything. Later that day, though, the word got afloat at school. Apparently someone had asked Carol why she and I looked so sad and she'd told them. Even then, I refused to say anything more than to confirm, "Yes, my baby brother died this morning." But I didn't want to hang out with the girls in the cloakroom or anything like that. My schoolmates looked at me curiously, with sympathy, wondering how to comfort me, but I simply wanted to be left alone.

We had a graveside funeral at a little cemetery in Mounds. Mainly family and very close friends attended, I think. It was one of the first times I'd ever seen my mother cry. Daddy appeared to be on the verge of tears. All my siblings and I sobbed bitterly. I really wished then that God had just taken me instead, like I'd asked him to do. At night I lay in bed thinking about Bud, wondering what I might have done differently so that he wouldn't have died. Maybe if I'd held him more often and not let him crawl around on the cold floor. Or perhaps if I'd paid more attention when he'd first gotten sick and realized that it wasn't just a cold that he'd had. Although Mudeah and Daddy had taken him to the doctor, who'd given him an assortment of medicines and sent him home at first, it still seemed to me that I should have noticed something that no one else had. Eventually the doctor had recommended hospitalization, but perhaps that had come too late, I thought. I'd picture Bud's tiny chest rising up and down through his labored breathing, and I'd think I should have known something—although I wasn't sure what.

Anxious to see my brother again, I came up with yet another proposal to God: if He would just let me see Bud again, I'd not even tell anyone else. I'd just meet Bud at the appointed spot, under the prescribed circumstances. Maybe over by the pond on our farm out in the country, because that was deserted. I wouldn't mind walking the several miles between our house in town and the farm, but I'd have to come up with an explanation for my lengthy absence.

Five years later, when my mother-in-law discovered that I'd had an infant brother who had died, she wanted full details: How old was he? How old was I? How did he die? Was he terribly ill first? Where did we live? "I don't want to talk about it," was my only response.

"I don't want to talk about it," remained my stock reply for many years as I continued to grieve over Bud's death. Openly crying, other than at the funeral, was not something that Motleys did. We thought it was "brave" or "proper" to hold all that grief and pain inside, I suppose. Rarely did anyone even make reference to Bud after his death, as though that would make it easier to bear his death. I guess we didn't want to "pick at old wounds." So we just kept it all inside where it became even more painful. Or at least that was how it was for me.

My sister Carol and I talked about Bud's death after we were both adults. Comparing notes, we found that we had gone through much of the same inner turmoil—private mourning and crying, extreme guilt, attempts to make deals with God. "I thought it was my fault," my sister had said. Only six at the time, she too had thought that she should have held him more, or played with him more, or done something to prevent his illness.

When Mudeah became mentally ill years later, she'd said once that maybe Bud's death was her fault. "Your fault? How?" I'd asked, shocked that she'd blamed herself.

"I should have done something," she had said.

"But what more could you have done? You took him to the doctor. You sat by his bedside day and night when he was in the hospital. You hardly slept for a week. What more could you have done?" I'd responded.

"Maybe I should have prayed more," she had replied, her voice still pained as she recalled her son's death. "Your Daddy thinks it was my fault. He said so once."

"Daddy knows it wasn't anyone's fault, Mudeah. He knows you and everyone else did all you could."

"Do you really think so?" she'd asked hopefully, sounding almost like a young child. Do you really believe it wasn't my fault? was her unspoken question.

"Yes, I really believe that. It wasn't anyone's fault," I had said firmly. And at that moment I knew that was the truth. Over thirty years after my brother's death, I had finally accepted that it wasn't my fault either. But I sure wished we'd talked about it at the time and that I had cried a lot right out in front of everyone. I wished we'd talked about Bud, recalling his sweet disposition and sunny smile, and his handsome little face. We should have shared assorted memories from his short life. And we should have talked about his illness and his death. All of that would have been very painful, but I don't think it would have left us with the almost unbearable emotional wounds that festered like open sores for so many years.

3

Stories about Daddy

Family Reunion: A Father's Story

Daddy always attends the family reunion now. He missed the first few because he was married to his second wife and Motley family gatherings weren't all that comfortable for her. She didn't seem to like to be reminded that Daddy had been married and had a whole family before he'd met her. Okay. There's no sense in evading the issue. She was a bitch. She could have gone toe to toe any day with Mudeah and Grandma Bessie for the Olympic Evil Competition. Further, Motley men are not noted for their willingness to meet family conflict head on, although in the public arena they are as fierce as tigers when it comes to defending their families and their principles.

Daddy has really come into his own since getting a divorce several years ago. He used to say that he didn't like to be away from home for more than a day or two. He didn't want to leave the house, or the garden, or some woodworking project he was doing. Now he loves to travel; he'll take off for a week or more at a time. He has gone to Hawaii, Puerto Rico, Canada, and England, in addition to numerous places within the continental United States.

Daddy, who earned bachelor's and master's degrees after becoming a grandfather, is retired from his position as a counselor with the Illinois State Department of Vocational Rehabilitation. Now in his seventies, he is still a handsome man who likes to be "dudey," as Grampa, his father, used to call a fashionably dressed man. His shoes are always shined. His pants are always creased.

Lately he has taken to wearing silks—jackets, shirts, even robes and pajamas.

Even when we were growing up in Mounds and had very little money, Daddy was a real dudey dresser. I can picture him now: shirt starched and carefully ironed, often with a threadbare collar that Mudeah had "turned" to the underside; knife-creased slacks, usually inexpensive; and shoes spit-shined to such a high gloss that you could virtually see yourself in them. The soles of his shoes sometimes had holes the size of a dime, so he carefully cut pieces of cardboard to put inside them. "Daddy, don't cross your legs," we cautioned.

"Oh, yeah," he'd laugh, planting his feet firmly on the floor. He joked that if he held his feet up too high, the bottoms of his shoes would fall all the way to his ankles and flap around them. The finishing touch to Daddy's sartorial splendor was his hat—only worn outside, of course, Daddy being a gentleman and all. It had a wide brim that he turned down over one eye, kind of like Humphrey Bogart in *Casablanca*. We learned something looking at Daddy getting all dressed up, though: how to make the best of what you have. And how to look good. Even now my sisters Carol and Mildred immediately discount as a possible suitor any man who doesn't dress well and whose shoes aren't properly shined.

Daddy is quite the gentleman now, but I can recall when he was not so staid. It used to be when he got angry he could raise holy hell, yelling and swearing, or he would get what we children called his "mad spot," deep furrows in his brow. We kids would quietly go about our chores, doing our homework, or whatever we were supposed to do at these times. Eventually he would relax, and his mad spot would disappear. He might even start joking or tell us about the incident that had made him so angry.

Daddy sometimes talks about his pride in his six children, declaring their successes to be "unheard of" in their excellence. That's his highest compliment: to say that something is so outstanding as to be "unheard of." Thus, several years ago when Carol earned a Ph.D. in Marketing from the University of Georgia at Athens and was appointed to the faculty of the School of Commerce at the University of Illinois at Urbana-Champaign, he lauded her accomplishments as "unheard of." "That Carol 'Ree is something!" he declared, referring to her by the pet name he has used since she was a small child, when she had told someone, "My name is Carol, but they call me Carol 'Ree." He proudly says of Mildred, an attorney who is a recent past president of the Mound City Bar Association, the St. Louis Chapter of the National Bar Association, "That Millie-gal is something! Did you see how she snatched the gavel from the past president? The fellow acted like he didn't want to give it up!" Then he goes on to boast about what a fine attorney she is. Daddy is the only one who dares to call Mildred "Millie-gal"! About Larry, an auto mechanic and part owner of an auto repair shop, Daddy declares, "That boy was always good with his hands. I remember when he was a little boy he would tell me I wasn't fixing something right and then he'd fix it!"

Daddy refers to all of his sons, now in their forties and fifties, as "boy." Similarly he refers to his daughters, who range in age from their thirties to their fifties, as "gal" or "girlie." He's the only one who can get away with this, too. Of John, who is a senior vice president with The Travelers Property Casualty, Daddy observes, "That boy is really respected by a lot of people! He knows his stuff." Calvin, who has his own auto mechanic business, elicits high praise also. "I swundle, that boy is something! Why you remember what all of his professors down at Rolla said about him? He even introduced me to the president, who spoke very highly of him." He likes to introduce himself at Southern Illinois University Edwardsville, where I am a history professor, and at conferences where I have a significant role, as "Dr. Portwood's father." He says of each of our accomplishments, as well as of those of the group: "It's just unheard of, I tell you. It's simply unheard of!" And we all beam as though no one has, in fact, heard of such things.

Mudeah and Daddy often talked about issues of politics and race when we were very young. During the Democratic National Convention, we were permitted to stay up at night as late as we wanted.

Those were the only times when we'd fall asleep in the middle of the living room floor at our own home, although at Grandma Bessie and Papa's, we'd sit up late every weekend, watching the fights on television or listening to them on the radio. Daddy and Mudeah were fervent Democrats. They were both strong supporters of Adlai Stevenson II and Hubert Humphrey. We were never permitted to watch the Republican National Convention, nor did Daddy or Mudeah watch it.

Daddy still maintains an antipathy toward the Grand Old Party (GOP). Several years ago, Daddy, Mildred, Harry, and I went to the Illinois State Fair in Springfield. It began to rain, so Mildred, Harry, and I ducked into a tent. We suddenly realized that Daddy had remained in the rain, but finally he stepped inside when the rain got heavier. We looked at him quizzically. "I've never in my life been inside a Republican tent," he explained. We were in the exhibit of the Illinois Secretary of State, a Republican. We tried to assuage his concerns by pointing out that this was a display—at public expense—by a state official, even though he was a Republican. To this day, I doubt that Daddy has ever voted for a Republican.

Both our parents were very active in local Pulaski County politics. I can recall going to political meetings with them. They each had held political patronage positions, also. Daddy had such a job when we'd lived in Springfield the first time, when I was between the ages of four and six. He later became a deputy sheriff in Pulaski County. And, finally, when we'd returned to Springfield when I was thirteen, he'd worked for the Illinois Superintendent of Public Instruction. Mudeah had worked in several positions with the Illinois State Auditor during the 1960s.

When we were young children, our parents made us aware of racial issues. We could also see the racial tensions and signs of inequality in our own geographic area and elsewhere. In Pulaski County we had economic and sometimes political relationships with whites, but socially there was limited contact between the races. Our schools, churches, families, friends, doctors, schoolteachers, and other professionals were black. Occasionally a black person had a white doctor or dentist, but that was not the usual situation. Most African Americans went to the two black physicians in our area, the older Dr. Robinson or the younger Doctor Chambliss, until his death at an early age.

When the Civil Rights movement began in the 1950s, Daddy and Mudeah, like other blacks in Mounds, were very aware and supportive of it. We gathered around the television set in our own or others' homes—many people didn't get their own televisions until much later. We got together in the girls' cloakroom at school and in the classrooms. We loitered before and after church and other places to talk about Dr. Martin Luther King Jr., Rosa Parks, Daisy Bates, and the "Little Rock Nine," and many others. The teachers at our all-black school spoke of the movement, sometimes speculating on the impact that it ultimately might have on Mounds, Villa Ridge, Cairo, and elsewhere in our own area. We envisioned going to the white school across town because it had many amenities that our all-black school lacked—new books and desks, a cafeteria, indoor plumbing and toilets, and a different teacher for each of the eight grades. We wanted our own teachers to be there, too. We were so proud of the many black people who were willing to risk their lives for their own rights and our rights.

Daddy and Mudeah taught us that skin color alone was not the determinant of whether one was a good person. Somewhere along the way, I did develop the idea that generally whites had biased views toward blacks, however subtle these attitudes might have been. Even so, I never regarded all whites as racists. We noticed that some whites, even some in the South, supported the Civil Rights movement.

Sometimes we had very positive experiences with whites that reinforced the point our parents and teachers had made that fairness and equalitarian values are not race-linked characteristics. I recall Daddy's telling stories about whites who had been supportive of him or other blacks. He also told many more tales about the racism that he had experienced.

Daddy is largely responsible for my own, as well as some of my siblings', interest in history. Daddy often shared stories about his own life, especially his childhood. We really liked to hear about when he lived in the Charleston, Missouri area, during the Great Depression. He and his brothers would go rabbit hunting in order to provide food for the family, or they'd pick blackberries or gather pecans to sell to the white folks in town. Mudeah was more reticent, rarely talking about her own life experiences. Appeals to her to tell us a story only evoked an occasional response, but Daddy was more forthcoming. I'm not sure that he realized until much later what a significant impact his stories had upon his children.

My brother John credits Daddy with prompting his own interest in history, as we all discovered a few years ago. John was guest curator of a museum exhibit, "We Also Served: African-Americans in the U.S. Military—Selections from the John H. Motley Collection," which included pieces from the colonial era through Desert Storm and was based largely on his own extensive collection. It opened at the Wadsworth Atheneum in Hartford, Connecticut, in February 1995 and ran through June 18, 1995. On the night of the grand opening, John gave an introductory presentation about the exhibit. Most of his siblings and Daddy were present because John had told us we'd better be there (and because we really did want to see the show). When John introduced us to the audience, he commented that he traced his own interest in African American history to Daddy's influence. I thought Daddy was going to cry at first, because he looked so touched by his son's accolades. He smiled proudly and probably thought, "Well, I'll swundle. I didn't know that boy had gotten his interest in African American history from me."

Taking a Mile

Daddy periodically went from our farm in Mounds to a livestock auction in Charleston. One time he'd gone there hoping to buy additional cattle or pigs. After making his purchases, he had stood in line for a long time waiting to pay for them. He was, as usual, the only black person present. White men kept cutting in front of him. At length their rudeness and presumptuousness made him angry, and so when yet another man nonchalantly stepped in front of him, Daddy objected, "Wait a minute. I've been here all day waiting to pay my bill. I've had enough of this!"

"Well, I'll be damned! You give them an inch, they'll take a mile!" replied the man who'd stepped in front of Daddy.

"You can just go straight to hell!" Daddy responded. The man was stunned. He had probably scarcely looked at Daddy until this point. All he'd seen was some nigger and thus established that it was appropriate to get ahead of him. The man looked around angrily at Daddy and then at the crowd of white men. Meanwhile Daddy reflected upon the words that had escaped his lips, wondering if they might be the last ones he'd ever utter. Here he stood facing a bunch of southern white farmers, who were accustomed to stepping in front of and on top of blacks if it served their purposes. The last thing they'd expected was a "mouthy nigger" who would challenge the propriety of their behavior. The whole idea was a surprise and an affront to the system of Jim Crow to which they had grown accustomed and from which they had benefited. The crowd grew restive, staring angrily at Daddy.

Another white man, the one behind the cage who was collecting the money and who was probably the owner, interrupted. "Why this man is right! He's been here all day trying to pay his bill. He's waited patiently all this time, but you guys have been breaking in front of him! I've sat here and watched you!" With that, the other man moved out of the way and Daddy regained his place in line, all the while wondering what would happen when he left the premises. Would they wait for him outside? Would they exact a toll from this nigger who didn't know his place? When he stepped up to pay his bill, the man who'd spoken up for him apologized on behalf of the others. "I'm sorry for the way these boys have treated you." At least the last words he would hear in his life had been kind ones, Daddy thought. When he went outside, he walked to his truck, loaded his livestock, and drove home without further ado.

Forty years later, Daddy still recalls this incident, shaking his head in disbelief that one person was willing to speak up for him and also struck by the impact that this single voice had made upon the group. The crowd might have turned on him, too. Being a nigger lover was even worse than being a nigger. One couldn't help the latter, but there was no excuse for the former. They might have refused to patronize his business in the future, bringing him economic ruin. Or . . . the possibilities were numerous. Daddy is amazed also at his own audacity in vocally rejecting traditional black/white relations.

As I listen to the story for the umpteenth time, I enjoy it as much as I did the first. And I recall, also for the umpteenth time, that I am not surprised by Daddy's boldness. That is the way I have always seen my father: willing to go against the crowd to stand up for the principles in which he believes. I am not sure that as a child, however, I fully appreciated how incredibly dangerous Daddy's behavior was. I did not realize that his actions were life-threatening at times. All I knew was that he always made me feel proud and safe.

My father's example is probably what rendered me an outspoken person who is willing to take risks in support of my own principles, even when they are not the most popular ones. When I speak up in my classes, in meetings, and elsewhere for the rights of African Americans, Native Americans, and other ethnic groups; women; the poor; and others, I always picture in the back of my mind Daddy standing before a potential lynch mob. Or Daddy running the white man off our farm. I always think that if he could stand up for his principles then, considering the enormous risks he took at the time, I can face the more limited ones now, such as the disapproval and the questions about whether or not I am a "team player." In fact, at times I don't want to be a team player because I would be ashamed of myself if I were. At these times I think about Daddy and what Alexis de Tocqueville said about "the tyranny of the majority," and I think about other people whom I admire for their high principles.

When Daddy reads this vignette, he will no doubt think, "Well, I'll swundle. I didn't know that's how you felt. So the ole boy's right up there with that French fellow de Tocqueville, huh?" Then he'll grin real big, like Grampa, and maybe blow his nose or clear his throat.

The Family Gunslinger

We gazed in awe, curious about why Robert "Bob" Aldrich, sheriff of Pulaski County, had come by our farm to talk to Daddy. The sheriff drove his police cruiser, which made an impressive sight with the red light on top and the two-way radio inside the car. We could actually hear periodic radio transmissions. As he got out of the car, the sheriff said "Car 9-5-1 to Cairo 10-8," or something like that. Cairo's response was rather scratchy, but audible: "Cairo to 9-5-1, 10-4." This was exciting.

Sheriff Aldrich looked like the stereotype of a southern sheriff. He was a very tall, heavyset man, well over six feet and close to three hundred pounds. He also swore constantly. He and Daddy had had a cordial relationship for many years because they were both staunch Democrats and had worked together in assorted political campaigns.

The sheriff and Daddy shook hands and talked amiably. They were too far away and spoke too quietly for us to hear what they were saying. They shook hands again, and the sheriff got back into his car. After calling Cairo again, Sheriff Aldrich took off in a cloud of dust down the one-and-one-half-lane macadam road. In seconds he topped the "little hill," and in less than a minute he was over the "big hill" and totally out of sight.

Daddy came into the house to tell Mudeah about his conversation with Sheriff Aldrich. We listened in, as we frequently did. We were all very skilled at eavesdropping on our parents' discussions. Rarely did we giggle aloud or make other telltale noises. The sheriff had asked Daddy once again to be his deputy. Daddy had turned him down previously, but this time he demurred. The farm was not as profitable as we had anticipated. The regular income would make a big difference in our economic status. We were a family of six—Daddy, Mudeah, Larry, June, Carol, and me. After consider-

able discussion, Daddy and Mudeah agreed that Daddy would accept the sheriff's offer. Daddy indicated that he had told Sheriff
Aldrich that if he were to agree to become a deputy, he would insist
upon having authority over both whites and blacks. Typically in
Pulaski County, a black deputy would have authority only over
other blacks. Aldrich had readily agreed to that condition, no doubt
having anticipated that to be Daddy's stance.

Daddy's 1956 appointment as deputy sheriff of Pulaski County
was in part a recognition of the importance of the black vote to the
Democratic Party. Sheriff Robert Aldrich, a Democrat, no doubt recognized that his own and his party's political future would be more
secure with the additional black support that this appointment was
likely to garner. The party had gained a stronghold among Pulaski
County blacks in the late 1940s and early 1950s, over a decade after
this development had occurred in many other northern areas. My
parents had been instrumental in securing this support. Further,
many blacks who were active in politics were Republicans, such as
George Cross and Dr. Alphonsa Robinson. Both Cross and Robinson sat on the local school board. Robinson, who had a large private
practice, also served as a public health physician who inoculated
children at area schools. Thus, the appointment of a well-known
African American Democrat to a high-profile political patronage
position seemed a prudent move.

Other blacks had served as deputy sheriffs in the area, but the
limitation on their power whereby they had authority only over
other blacks placed them in a nebulous position when they confronted white lawbreakers. At the least this was humiliating; at the
most it could cost the deputy or other persons their lives.

We were all in favor of Daddy's becoming deputy sheriff. We
were fans of the cowboy heroes. We had seen all the cowboy movies
that we could afford to see at the small, racially segregated theater
in Mounds. Occasionally we saw cowboy programs on television
when we visited friends and relatives who had televisions. We
knew about Matt Dillon, the Lone Ranger, Roy Rogers, Gene Autry,
and the others.

I pictured Daddy as a combination of the cowboys I liked best. He would wear an outfit, including a hat, similar to the Lone Ranger's. He would have a large badge in the shape of a star with "SHERIFF" in huge letters. He would carry at least one six-shooter—maybe two—in a special, fancy black holster, slung low over his hips. As he walked, his fingertips would nonchalantly brush the top of his gun, as though in warning to potential evildoers. At any moment, he would be prepared to "slap leather," drawing his gun in less than the blink of an eye. Rarely would he need to fire, but if forced to do so, he would be an expert marksman. He would let most people off by merely shooting something from their hands. He would wound them in the leg, if absolutely necessary. More serious injury would be unnecessary, Daddy's reputation having preceded him. There would be no gratuitous violence because Daddy was a very good man, like Roy Rogers. Before returning his gun to its holster, he would twirl it expertly, perhaps blowing the smoke from the barrel if he had had occasion to shoot. As he walked down the street, people would clear the way for him out of respect and admiration, perhaps mixed with a tiny bit of fear. All talk would cease, as every eye turned in his direction.

Anticipating that the word of Daddy's appointment as deputy sheriff would have gotten afloat by then, Larry, June, and I could hardly wait to go to school the following Monday. Clearly everyone did know. As we entered the school bus, Mr. Robinson, the driver, said, "I hear your Daddy is the high sheriff." My brothers indicated that he was the deputy. The kids were all grinning. At school the teachers also commented on Daddy's new status. All the kids there knew, also. Later, some teased me, claiming that they saw Daddy walking down the street, trying to walk like Wyatt Earp. I pretended to be angry, knowing that this was meant as an insult. Secretly, I was pleased because I thought that Wyatt Earp on television was very handsome and that he had the sort of swagger that befitted a lawman. He meandered just perfectly. After that, I was inclined to liken Daddy to Wyatt Earp in my fantasies.

After school we were anxious to get home to see the new uniform. But it was a disappointment. Daddy wore a khaki outfit—matching shirt and trousers. It wasn't at all like the Lone Ranger's. Daddy's badge was a small shield, rather than a huge star. And the major disappointment: he wore a shoulder holster with a small snub-nose .38. The hat, at least, was fine, and he wore it tilted appropriately over one eye. And Daddy did swagger very nicely. He explained that, rather than a gun and a holster like the cowboys', his were like those of Sergeant Joe Friday on *Dragnet*. Friday also carried a badge in the form of a shield. On the whole, it was a more sophisticated look, he explained. We were not altogether convinced, but . . . well, maybe that was okay. After all, Joe Friday was on television.

Occasionally Daddy gave us a ride in the sheriff's cruiser. Larry, June, and Toots got to experience this thrill more often than the younger kids and I did, however, because they were in school in Mounds and Daddy sometimes dropped them off there before proceeding to work. Villa Ridge, where Carol and I went to school, was in the opposite direction from where he was headed most days. Every now and then, Daddy would drive Carol and me to school. Now that was fun! We'd beg him to turn on the siren and the flashing light and to go really fast. But all we could persuade him to do was to sound the siren very briefly. We could hardly wait until we drove up to the school and everyone looked out of the window when they heard the crunch of a car on the rocks.

The Man Who Looked Like Papa
and the Great Bank Robbery

The car drove past National Cemetery just outside Mound City. Daddy, driving the sheriff's cruiser, turned on the red light and gave pursuit. Almost immediately the driver saw the official vehicle and pulled onto the shoulder. "What's the problem, officer?" a very pleasant and courteous man asked.

"You just ran a stop sign, sir," Daddy responded, stunned by the man behind the wheel. This man looked and sounded just like

John Motley Sr., Shirley's father, ca. 1949.

Graduation exercises for a summer extension course, Lincoln University, Jefferson City, Missouri, ca. 1939. *Back row, third from left*: Cora Jones, Shirley's mother. John Motley Sr., Shirley's father, is beside her to the right. *Second row, sixth from right*: Theresa Jones, Shirley's aunt. Courtesy Phyllis Benton.

Emma Jean Jones, Shirley's cousin, with her father, Curtis Jones, ca. 1957.

Lawrence "Larry" Motley, Shirley's oldest brother, approximately twelve years old, ca. 1953.

John "June" Motley, Shirley's brother, approximately eleven years old, ca. 1953. Courtesy Leora Jones Hughes.

Leora "Toots" Jones, Shirley's aunt, in her graduation photograph, Douglass High School, Mounds, Illinois, 1957. Courtesy Leora Jones Hughes.

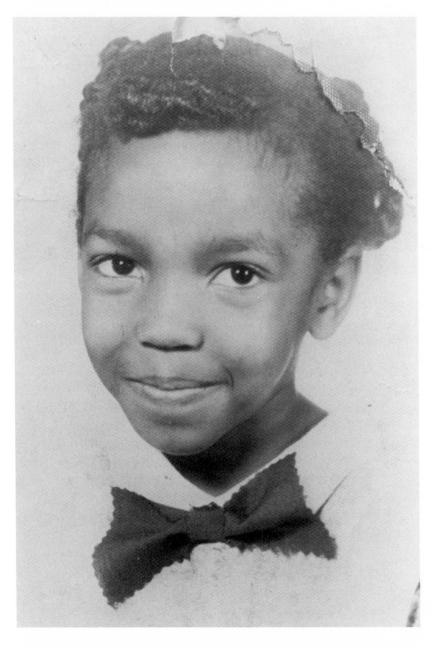

Carol Motley, Shirley's sister, in her first grade picture, Lovejoy Grade School, Villa Ridge, Illinois, 1959. Courtesy Carol Motley.

Pinning ceremony for the Springfield (Illinois) Urban League teen club, Tomorrow's Scientists and Technicians (TST). *Front row, far left*: Shirley. *Standing far left:* Executive Secretary of the Urban League, handing pin to Vivian Bird, the club's adviser. *Back row, far right*: Kay Culver, Shirley's junior high school girls' counselor, 1960.

Award ceremony and banquet sponsored by the Springfield NAACP in honor of the students' induction into the National Honor Society. *Left to right:* William Wheatley, Carolyn Carey, Shirley, Allan Woodson, Janet Armstead, and Dr. Edwin Lee, who is presenting them with gold filigreed fountain pens, 1963.

Lee Gene Jones Sr., Shirley's grandfather, with his grandchildren.
Left to right: Eugene Jr., Beverly, and Christopher Hughes, ca. 1963.
Courtesy Leora Jones Hughes.

Back row, sixth from right: Shirley at Steagall Hall, Thompson Point,
her dormitory at Southern Illinois University, Carbondale, 1963.

Cora Motley, Shirley's mother, with Shirley's siblings, Calvin and
Carol Motley, opening Christmas presents, 1964.

Faelynn Carlson, Shirley's daughter, with her grandfather,
John Motley Sr., on their birthday, August 17, 1966.

Shirley teaching a class at Forest Park Community College, 1976.
She began her teaching career there in 1972.

Left to right: Fae Carlson, Shirley, and Shirley's siblings, Mildred, Carol, and Calvin Motley, after Mildred's graduation from the University of Illinois at Urbana-Champaign, May 1982.

Wedding photograph of Fae Carlson Monroe and
Kraig Monroe Sr., August 9, 1986.

Four generations of Motley women. *Left to right:* Cora Motley,
Fae Monroe, Krystle Monroe, and Shirley.

Shirley's grandchildren: Krystle Monroe, holding the Velveteen
Rabbit, and Kraig Monroe, with Bear, two years after their move to
California and at about the time that Shirley began telling
them stories about family history, December 1989.

Shirley and Harry's wedding. *Left to right:* John, Carol, Larry, and
Mildred Motley; bride, Shirley, and groom, Harry Portwood;
Fae Monroe; and Calvin Motley, March 14, 1992.

Family members at Shirley and Harry's wedding. *Front row, left to right:*
Krystle Monroe; Vanessa Motley, Shirley's niece; Fae Monroe; and Kraig
Monroe. *Back row, left to right:* Michael Johnson and Ramirez Roberts,
Shirley's nephews. Krystle was the flower girl and Kraig the ring bearer.

Family reunion, August 1994, Godfrey, Illinois. *Front row, left to right:*
Michael Portwood, Ruby Rosas, John Motley Sr., Kraig Monroe, Mary
Portwood, Krystle Monroe, and Fae Monroe. *Back row, left to right:* Shirley;
Ramirez Roberts; and Mildred, Carol, Calvin, and John Motley. Michael
and Mary Portwood and Ruby Rosas are the children of Deborah
Portwood, Harry's daughter, and Antonio Rosas.

Shirley and John Motley with Mary Ella Miller,
their favorite schoolteacher, 1994.

Shirley with her grandchildren, Krystle and Kraig Monroe, July 1999.

Papa, my maternal grandfather. He even had Papa's kindly demeanor. He was just like Papa, except he was white! The man smiled pleasantly, obviously unaware that he had passed through the sign without so much as slowing his vehicle.

He profusely apologized, admitting, "I didn't even see the stop sign." He promised he'd obey it next time, though, because Daddy had been kind enough to point it out to him. The two talked briefly. Then the man headed back toward Cairo, on his way to his home in Kentucky.

Several months later the sheriff's office received a call from Virgie Wilkerson's sister that two suspicious-looking men were hanging around Villa Ridge, east of Lovejoy Grade School. Deputy Motley answered the call. Driving along Highway 51, Daddy spotted a black 1949 Chevrolet with two white men inside parked just off the highway. He proceeded to the house of the woman who had called, where he questioned her about what she'd witnessed. When she indicated that there were two white guys in a black car, Daddy pictured the vehicle he'd just seen and rushed back to see whether it was still there.

The car and the men were gone, but on a hunch that something was amiss, Daddy decided to pursue them anyway. He turned north on Highway 51 and drove three or four miles without any sign of the vehicle. Meanwhile, a report came over the car radio that the First State Bank of Mounds had been robbed by two white men, one described as thirty-five years old and heavyset. Again, a picture of the black Chevrolet and the two white men he'd seen earlier came to mind.

Daddy drove south along Highway 51 into Mounds and on to the bank. He described the two men he had seen outside Villa Ridge. "Yes, that's them," a witness to the robbery responded. Meanwhile the suspects had doubled back to Mound City, where their car was later recovered, parked about a mile south of National Cemetery, close to Cairo and near the Ohio River. Apparently the two had stationed a paddleboat there, which they had rowed across the river into Wickliffe, Kentucky. Pulaski County authorities notified their Kentucky counterparts, who picked up the men and arrested them.

Daddy, accompanied by Ralph Griggsby and Brother Rabbit, two black law enforcement officials from Pulaski County, went to get the bank robbers and return them to Pulaski County. Because Sheriff Aldrich was out of town, Daddy was the chief law enforcement officer for Pulaski County. The three black officials walked into the court house in Wickliffe, where the county jail was located. A crowd of men, numbering into the hundreds—all of them white—had collected in the lobby, no doubt hoping to get a look at the notorious criminals who'd robbed the bank. The sight was an intimidating one—a roomful of white guys, most wearing bib overalls, probably none accustomed to seeing black men in positions of authority. But Daddy drew himself up to his full height and swaggered in real coolly, wearing his sheriff's uniform, his hat tilted to the proper angle, his gun in his shoulder holster. He no doubt looked a lot calmer than he felt as he sauntered over to an officer on duty. Daddy told him that he was a deputy from Pulaski County, Illinois, and that he had come to pick up the prisoners.

"Wall, there's a lot of folks in the room. I don't know why you'd want to go in there. You better wait," the officer drawled slowly, barely looking at Daddy. Daddy repeated that he was on official business, because it appeared that the man had misunderstood him the first time. Once again the officer told him, rather rudely, that he'd better wait because there were too many people in the room already.

"Have you been in there?" Daddy asked politely, although rather brusquely.

"Wall, yeah."

"Well, then. I'm going in there, too, man. I'm the representative of the county sheriff of Pulaski County, Illinois. I've come to retrieve the prisoners." Meanwhile the talking in the room had stopped as all eyes focused on Daddy and the Kentucky officer. Questioning looks turned to hostility. "This was the kind of situation that could well have turned into a necktie party, with you-know-who wearing the necktie," Daddy noted later.

Suddenly out of the crowd stepped a familiar figure—the man with the face and the voice like Papa's. The man stuck out his right hand and clasped Daddy's in a warm greeting. The two exchanged pleasantries, genuinely pleased to see each other. "I was never so happy to see anyone in my life!" Daddy observed when he subsequently told the story.

Throwing an arm around Daddy's shoulder and turning to face the crowd, the man addressed them. "I want all of you to meet the nicest fellow I've ever met in my life," he began. "This is the finest gentleman in the whole world." He then proceeded to tell the assemblage about their previous meeting. He spoke of how polite and cordial Daddy had been when he'd stopped him for running the stop sign. Their pleasant discussion. Daddy's letting him go with a friendly warning to be sure to obey the sign next time. Within minutes the tension had dissipated as the mob turned into a friendly gathering. Smiles replaced the scowls and hostility. Murmurs of approval graced lips previously set in hardened disdain. "I've never seen a crowd change like that before," Daddy now says.

The two chatted briefly as Daddy told the man why he was there. Parting with a handshake and a good-bye, the two went their separate ways. Daddy turned back to the Kentucky officer, who then quietly ushered him into the jail to retrieve the prisoners, the crowd making way for them as they passed. "Nice meeting ya, sheriff," some called to the finest gentleman in the whole world.

After Daddy had gained access to the jail, he confronted the prisoners. One looked at him and said, "There's the man that jumped us up." To Daddy he said, "We saw you."

As the story unfolded, Daddy found that he had been in an extremely precarious situation when he had spotted the car earlier. The suspects were two parolees whose possession of illegal weapons, including a sawed-off shotgun and a machine gun, violated their parole. "If I'd gotten closer, they'd likely have killed me because they were on parole and were in possession of illegal weapons," he calmly says now with traces of his old Wyatt Earp demeanor showing.

The bank had posted a reward for the capture of the robbers, which Daddy, Virgie Wilkerson's sister, two Illinois State Police officers, and one other person shared. At the ceremony in which the cash reward was bestowed upon them, the Illinois State Police officers refused to stand beside Daddy for the official photograph. But Virgie's sister quickly moved over beside him, proud to share the honor with him. The state police officers looked on with disdain.

4

School Days

Family Reunion: "When You Go to College"

"**N**ow, when you go to college . . ." was a common theme that our parents emphasized when we were children. As far back as I can recall, Mudeah and Daddy regularly reminded my siblings and me that they expected—assumed, in fact—that all of us would go to college and pursue a profession. "When one of you graduates, then you can help the next one," they said, emphasizing our familial responsibilities to our younger siblings. They said little about the schools we should attend. That was a decision left to each of us. They did point out that Southern Illinois University (SIU) was conveniently located about thirty miles north of our farm in Mounds. We knew about traditionally black Lincoln University in Jefferson City, Missouri, because Daddy had attended it "back in the olden days." Daddy, Mudeah, and Aunt Theresa had taken a summer extension course in Charleston, which was sponsored by Lincoln University. Daddy also had attended Springfield Junior College, a small Catholic school, when we lived in Springfield, Illinois, during the early 1950s.

We had heard of Shorter College in Little Rock, Arkansas; Fisk University in Nashville, Tennessee; Tuskegee Institute in Tuskegee, Alabama; Wilberforce University in Wilberforce, Ohio; and other predominantly black colleges because they were frequently noted by our parents, teachers, and others. We were personally acquainted with black physicians and dentists, and we had heard about some of the schools that they had attended—Meharry Medical College in Nashville and Howard University in Washington, D.C., for example. Dr. Alphonsa Robinson, a black man, was the physician for most blacks in our area who could afford medical care. But almost all blacks knew him professionally because the county employed him to go to the black grade schools to inoculate the children each year. Most blacks also had social contact with the doctor because he regularly attended black community activities, even though he was apt to appear rather arrogant and aloof. He and his son, Alphonsa Jr., were always tastefully and expensively dressed when they attended basketball games at Douglass High School in Mounds. The doctor's mansion near the high school sat on a large, heavily wooded lot along Highway 51, the road that led to Villa Ridge and other points north. It was the nicest house in Mounds and one of the finest in the entire area. Dr. Robinson's financial success and his high social status spoke well for the value of a college and professional education.

As the Motley siblings and our families sit around the kitchen table at the family reunion, we recall the many, many family discussions about college during our childhood. We remember our early career aspirations as children. When June had said he wanted to be a physician, I had announced, "I want to be June's nurse."

"Why don't you be a doctor, too? Then you can be his partner," both Mudeah and Daddy had said.

"Okay," I responded. Although I had never seen a woman doctor, I thought that if Mudeah and Daddy said I could be one, and if June could be one, I could be a doctor.

At other times I had wanted to be a lawyer, mainly because it was the profession that Daddy had wanted to pursue. "Yes, you'd make a good lawyer," Mudeah and Daddy had said encouragingly. "You'll have to study hard in school. And you'll have to save your money. College is expensive."

When I'd entered high school, both parents continued to emphasize a professional career. Mudeah said that we should each be able to support ourself and to "make something of yourself."

More important than my mother's views in encouraging me to go to college were my father's actions. He had earned a number of college credits, including at Lincoln University right after he had graduated from high school, when he was nineteen. Dropping out of Lincoln after only one year, he'd continued to pursue his education in adulthood, including at Springfield Junior College, which had a reputation as a rigorous and excellent institution. He had taken a prelaw curriculum and had planned to attend a local law school, but it had closed the semester before he was to have enrolled. I recall many nights Daddy would go to class after dinner, returning around bedtime. Often he would study at home on the nights that he didn't have class or on weekends. When I was a junior in high school in 1961, Daddy enrolled full-time at SIU in Carbondale, which both Larry and John—as we now called June, when we could remember it—attended at the time. I was proud to announce to friends, acquaintances, teachers, and anyone else who would listen that my father was in college. A number of years later, Daddy received his bachelor's degree in education from SIU. Still later he returned to the same institution for a master's in rehabilitation administration.

Larry had been the first of the Motley children to go to college when, in September 1959, he'd entered SIU. "I cried when my baby went to college. But I didn't let him see me," Mudeah said years later. I was shocked to hear her say this because she had never seemed particularly nurturing or emotive when it came to her older children. Besides, her relationship with Larry was the worst of the lot, even worse than her relationship with me. The two of them had so much conflict that I'd assumed that she had been happy when he'd finally gone to college. "He was so little. He was smaller than the other kids," she had continued, sounding as though she was picturing the scene at that very moment.

We were all so proud of Larry. This was the beginning of putting into action "the plan" whereby each of us would go to school, graduate, and help our younger siblings. That way we'd all graduate from college and get good jobs. Larry, June, and I talked about how we would buy Daddy and Mudeah each their own new car. I thought we should buy Mudeah a Mercury because it was a big, luxurious vehicle, and Daddy a Chevrolet or an Oldsmobile because he said they were the best ones. We'd also talked about building them a big, new house. I liked to imagine the expressions on their faces when they saw the cars and the house. For myself I wanted a nice house and a car, pretty clothes, and a gold tooth with a star on it. I'd envied the shiny, gold teeth of friends and acquaintances who had moved to the city when they returned for visits. I'd thought that they really looked attractive, as well as prosperous. My gold tooth would be right in front where it would be noticed every time I opened my mouth.

Meanwhile, Larry had found that his education at Douglass High had not provided enough courses in mathematics to permit him to enter an engineering curriculum as he had planned. Taking remedial courses would have been an option, but since he had to work long hours in order to put himself through school, he did not have the time for all of that and regular classes as well. He decided to take another major, eventually deciding on business.

John entered SIU the following year. And three years later, in September 1963, after graduating from Feitshans High School in Springfield, I went to the same university. At this point, we had four family members in the same college. I was quite sure that *Ebony* would do a big cover story on us, which I further imagined would bring both fame and fortune to the family. On the drive to Carbondale, Daddy began talking about my college education. He said that after I had gotten a baccalaureate degree, I could go on for a master's, and finally a doctorate. I was astounded! I had trouble enough fathoming getting one degree, much less three. In fact, I had considerable fear that I would flunk out of college in the first quarter. I soon discovered that it took a minimum of two quarters to flunk out of SIU. So then I figured I had a six-month reprieve on possible humiliation.

For the first time, I was actually afraid that I might not be able to do what my entire family and I had planned for so long. But I constantly reminded myself of earlier successes. I buoyed my spirits by remembering the encouragement I had received from family members, friends, and acquaintances. At Feitshans High School, all of the black students had been so proud of the fact that there had been 5 of us in National Honor Society—Carolyn Carey, Janet Armstead, Allan Woodson, William "Billy" Wheatley, and me. Five was a disproportionately large number because there were only 34 blacks in a class of 172 students. Further, there had been only 19 students in National Honor Society. Even those black classmates who were themselves poor students and who previously had offered no encouragement to those of us who were good students were now very proud.

The Springfield branch of the National Association for the Advancement of Colored People (NAACP) gave a banquet and award ceremony at the Holiday Inn for the five black National Honor Society students. We sat at a long head table where everyone in attendance could see us. Throughout the program our parents and the other guests kept beaming at us proudly as we tried to look worthy of the honor. The NAACP gave each of us a beautiful, gold-filigreed fountain pen. I thought that mine, which I still own, was a particularly elegant one because it was black. They insisted that we each "say a few words," although we had decided initially that Allan Woodson, our senior class president, would speak for us all. "No, no. We want to hear from all of you," they'd insisted.

We took turns giving brief speeches, telling them of our plans for college and thanking them profusely for the fountain pens. I don't recall what I said, other than that I used the word "reiterate" and everyone was really impressed by that, as a number of people commented to me later. My high school English teacher, Gladys Black, had insisted that we learn a list of new words each week, and that had been one of them. Friends, family, and others offered encouragement in diverse ways. Mrs. Antonacci, our Italian American next-door neighbor, who had always been very friendly and kind, gave me a silver dollar, which I still have over thirty years later. Aunty, who had a huge gold tooth that I'd long admired except for the fact that it stuck out of her mouth too far, gave me a portable typewriter, which was a very lavish and later a very much utilized present. Dorothy Jacobs, a friend of my mother's, gave me an almost-new blanket. "I know this isn't much, but I know you're getting ready to go to college and I wanted to give you something," she'd said. Often when I covered up with it I thought of her saying "I wanted to give you something."

Another of Mudeah's friends—I think it was Mrs. Campbell, the white woman for whom Mudeah had done housework and sewing before she had gotten her job as a clerk with the Illinois Secretary of State—gave me a huge steamer trunk, which was in very good condition. I was able to fit all of my clothes and other items that I'd planned to take to school into this trunk and the two-piece set of Samsonite luggage that my parents had given me. When Daddy and I arrived at Thompson Point, the residence area where I was to live, I noticed that some kids had numerous suitcases, trunks, and boxes full of things. My own meager belongings seemed very limited by comparison.

Nearly twenty years later, in 1982, my own daughter, Fae, went to school at SIU. We were driving down the street and noticed two young black students, each of whom had a large Pullman suitcase. They had even less than I'd had when I'd first arrived in Carbondale. Fae turned to me and asked, "Where are their other things?"

"Their other things?" I had responded. "They may not have any other things."

"Oh, sure they do! They have to have more than that!" she had said, incredulous that anyone should have only one bag. She herself had a carload of belongings, leaving scarcely enough room for the two of us in my large 1977 Oldsmobile Cutlass. The trunk and back seat as well as under her feet contained all kinds of things: a stereo record and cassette player, clothing, and many personal items. She had left her television set and electric typewriter at home, as well as many clothes and other things. Her roommate had agreed to share her television in return for using Fae's stereo. They would rent a small refrigerator the first semester; Fae's father and I bought her one for Christmas that year, so she had her own refrigerator to take the second semester.

"Oh, of course," I replied with biting sarcasm, unbecoming to someone's mother. "They're probably having their other belongings brought down by the family chauffeur."

"You mean, you really don't think they have other things?" She had finally gotten the message that many people had only modest possessions when they went to college.

Among the six Motley siblings, we now have twelve college degrees. Larry has a bachelor's in business from SIU; John, a bachelor's in accounting from SIU and a law degree from DePaul University in Chicago; Carol, a bachelor's in communications from Sangamon State University in Springfield, Illinois (currently the University of Illinois at Springfield), a master of business administration from Washington University in St. Louis, and a Ph.D. in marketing from the University of Georgia in Athens; Mildred, a bachelor's in English and psychology from the University of Illinois at Urbana-Champaign and a law degree from Washington University; and I have four history degrees—a bachelor's from Southern Illinois University at Edwardsville (SIUE), a master's from SIUE and one from Washington University, and a Ph.D. from Washington University. Calvin, who has pursued majors in both business and engineering, plans to complete his degree in the latter field. The assorted degrees we have attained are due in no small measure to our parents' steadfast insistence that we must go to college.

We Motleys also tend to continue our schooling into our adulthood. My nephew Ramirez once commented to me, "It seems kind of funny having an aunt who's going to college." What he meant was "an aunt of your age . . . ." Except for Mildred, who enrolled in law school immediately after completing undergraduate school, we have received graduate degrees after working for a number of years first, and in some cases after having children.

Whenever we discuss college experiences, Carol begins to fidget and look uncomfortable after a certain point. She knows that before all is said and done, we will start saying things like, "So whatever happened to Askia Ammar?" or something along those lines, in reference to the name that Carol had taken when she went to Howard

University. If there is anyone present who has not heard about Askia Ammar, we will feel obliged to tell this person about her. Or if everyone has heard about her, we'll talk about her anyway. In any event, Askia clearly belongs in any discussion of the Motley family's college experiences.

The family reunion group now turns to a favorite reminiscence about when Daddy and two of his friends went away to college. Daddy has told this story for fifty years to three generations of Motley children, including his own children, his grandchildren, and his great-grandchildren. All of us have been inspired by Daddy's and his friends' determination, charmed by their naiveté, and excited by their adventures en route to Lincoln University. "Daddy, tell us a story. Tell us about when you and your friends first went to Lincoln," we urge once again. We all listen as attentively as though we were hearing the story for the first time.

When Daddy Went to College

When we were growing up, Daddy used to entertain us with stories about his own childhood and youth, which we referred to as "the olden days." After a while, we knew the stories almost as well as he did. In the evenings we would ask him to tell us about his experiences, often requesting specific tales as we gathered around him.

"Daddy, tell us a story about when you were growing up."

"Yes, tell us about the olden days."

"Tell us about when . . ."

My favorite was about when he and two high school classmates, Willie Lee Gilchrist and O. D. Dunnigan, went away to Lincoln University. Willie Lee's and O. D.'s fathers were sharecroppers in Wyatt, Missouri, about eight miles east of Charleston, where Daddy lived. Grampa Henry Motley both worked for the Works Projects Administration (WPA), a New Deal program, and sharecropped. Daddy, O. D., and Willie Lee all attended Lincoln High School in Charleston, the only high school for blacks within a forty-mile radius.

Daddy and his companions walked the distance from their homes in Charleston and Wyatt to Lincoln University because they had no other transportation. That was my favorite part, the fact that they had walked. This was in 1939, during the Great Depression. They traveled north into Illinois, going through Cairo and Pinckneyville, and then westward to East St. Louis and Brooklyn. They crossed the Mississippi River into Missouri at St. Louis, and from there they proceeded to Jefferson City. This journey was nearly three times as long as it would have been if they had gone directly to Jefferson City. Their lack of familiarity with the state's geography prompted them to go to the St. Louis area first. That, and the fact that one of the group had planned to visit family in Brooklyn, near East St. Louis.

Daddy and his friends were inspired to go to Lincoln University, a black college founded by black Civil War veterans, by its president, Dr. Scruggs, and the director of the Department of Agriculture, Dr. Freeman. These two administrators had spoken at Lincoln High School in Charleston and had encouraged the students there to enroll in the college. Daddy and his two friends took this quite literally as an invitation to go to Lincoln University. Without even applying for admission, without any prospects for housing or knowledge of employment possibilities, and without transportation to Jefferson City, they set out for Lincoln University. They had only a few dollars in their pockets, their limited wardrobes, and a few personal possessions.

Grampa Motley was a man of few words, and he had said little to his son about higher education. According to Grandmommy, Grampa had received only four or five years of formal education. Nonetheless, my father reports that Grampa's prowess in being able to understand government documents and official jargon was legend. His neighbors, friends, and relatives would bring papers for him to read and explain. "I declare. I cain't make heads nor tails of this, Mr. Motley. I was hoping you'd look at this for me." Many years later, when he had retired and moved to Mounds, other blacks continued to ask for his assistance.

When Daddy told his father that he was going to Lincoln University, Grampa said little, but he reached into his pocket and took out all the money he had, about two dollars, and gave it to his son. Grampa spoke neither in favor of nor in opposition to the venture, but Daddy knew that with Grampa the old adage "Silence means consent" held true.

Daddy assumed that his mother would be supportive because he had heard her say often enough, "Once you rub your head on a college board, they can't take it away from you." Besides, he was her favorite and she was inclined to approve of anything he wanted to do, as long as it wasn't illegal or immoral. Further, she had told him since he was thirteen, "When you get grown, you're going to have to move up North. These white folks will kill you." At that time he had admonished a white insurance agent who had called his mother "Annie" that he should call her "Mrs. Motley." For Grandmommy, her son's pursuit of a college education may have been a way for him to get away from the South. With a college degree, he could get a job anywhere.

"On to College" read the sign one of the three college-bound young men put on his luggage. During their trek of several hundred miles, they were offered rides by strangers, which provided them welcome relief from walking. Not everyone was kind, however. One fellow drove alongside and called out, "You boys tired of walking?"

"Yes!" they shouted, anticipating another ride.

"Well, run then!" he responded with a laugh as he sped up his vehicle. They periodically stopped to eat the food that they had brought with them. Occasionally total strangers invited them into their homes, where they shared simple but delicious meals. They slept in fields along the highway.

Daddy, O. D., and Willie Lee all wanted to study agriculture at the university. Then they could go back home and buy their own farms, which they would run based on the new "scientific farming" techniques taught at the college. When Daddy and his younger brother Harry—who were very close—were children, they had planned to buy their own farms when they became adults. Black farmers in Missouri were generally sharecroppers rather than own-ers, so the two brothers had few role models for their venture. But they'd planned it carefully themselves. The nineteen-year-old John Motley must have smiled now as he thought of some of these plans: They would have adjoining farms. They would have matching Dodge trucks. Their foremen would be Mr. Lambert and his brother. Even their horses would be related to one other. Although some of these plans no doubt struck the college freshman as juvenile, Daddy's general plan to have his own farm was still very much alive.

Daddy and his friends had to keep a careful watch for trouble from belligerent young white men and boys throughout their trip. The economic woes of the Great Depression exacerbated white su-premacist sentiments, which had their roots in slave days in both southern Illinois and Missouri. Rural whites were apt to consider blacks, especially young black men, to be interlopers in their terri-tory. In Pinckneyville, a small, all-white town in south-central Illi-nois, the sheriff advised them to leave town before dark, observing that there was a "passenger" train that was scheduled to come through the town. He inquired, with friendly concern, whether they planned to be on it. "You boys are planning to catch the passenger train when it comes through, aren't you?"

"Oh, yes, sir!" they agreed, although they had no idea what the cost of train fare was. But since they could ill afford even a modest fare, that was beside the point. When the train came through Pinck-neyville, it proved to be a freight train. When it slowed or stopped, they decided to jump aboard. Just as they had stealthily gained entry to a cattle car, they turned around to see the smiling sheriff, who had hidden in nearby bushes, stand and wave good-bye to them. Each time the train stopped, Daddy, O. D., and Willie Lee jumped off, but the conductor always urged them to get back on board. When they thought they were close to East St. Louis, they disembarked for the final time. They walked and walked, ulti-mately realizing that they had been over ten miles away from that industrial river city.

In Brooklyn they visited O. D. Dunnigan's family, as planned.

These distant cousins of O. D.'s were so poor, though, that the three young men weren't sure whether they were better off there or on the road. They spent two or three days in this predominantly black town before continuing their journey. O. D.'s cousin offered to drive them to Jefferson City, so they set out in his car for the trip of about one hundred miles. They passed through the big city of St. Louis, about which they had all heard so much. A few miles outside of St. Louis and after they had spent most of their limited funds on gas, the car developed mechanical problems. They reassured O. D.'s cousin, who was embarrassed and full of apologies, that they would be fine, and they set out walking once again.

Several times they got rides from whites, who took them ten or twelve miles at a time. One man advised the three to be careful when passing through all-white areas of Missouri, which included most of the area between St. Louis and Jefferson City. One day they saw a car with four or five menacing young men heading in their direction. The white men stopped their vehicle, jumped out, and began to chase the black soon-to-be college students. After running for a long time, Daddy finally stopped. As Daddy now recalls, characteristically laughing heartily at the recollection, "They just about ran me to death. I had to stand my ground because I was too tired to run any more." O. D. and Willie Lee stopped running also, and the three began to advance on the white men. After a tense moment of indecision, the white men turned on their heels and ran.

When they were about twenty-five to thirty miles outside Jefferson City, they asked a man who was pumping water for a drink. As they drank their water, the man warned them about a white hangout that was approximately a quarter mile down the road. Young white men, who were apt to be openly hostile to blacks, frequented the place. The man suggested that they not pass by the place until after midnight, when it would be closed.

On the final leg of the young men's trip, a carload of professors from Lincoln University, returning to school early, gave them a ride all the way to the college. Jefferson City, the state capital, sat on the bluffs of the Missouri River. Lincoln University was on a hillside overlooking the pretty little city. At the time, their focus was not on the beauty of either the city or the college, however, but on the lovely, intelligent black coeds. Daddy recalls that, after having spent their last twenty cents on coffee cakes, they went to the office of Dr. Freeman, the director of the Department of Agriculture, but he hadn't returned from summer break. They then went to President Scruggs's office. There they were greeted by the receptionist, who was an upper classman at the school. Daddy describes her as the prettiest woman he had ever seen in his entire nineteen years. She was also very nice and helpful. And "she sort of took a special interest in the ole boy," he indicates now, although years ago, when we were children and when he was married to our mother, he very wisely omitted any discussion of this young woman. He and the young woman bantered back and forth briefly and then she stood up from her desk, perhaps to get information from a file cabinet. At that point he saw that she had the most unattractive figure he'd ever seen: she was very thin with a high derriere and little bird legs. Immediately his romantic interest in her was totally extinguished. He even had a difficult time continuing the casual, comfortable repartee they had established.

Meanwhile, Daddy and his friends had asked to speak with the president. Daddy, class valedictorian of his high school, had been chosen as spokesperson for the group. "Tell him we are here. He visited our high school a few months ago and he invited us to come here to his college. So here we are," he announced very politely, if a bit arrogantly, while the other two stood patiently in the background, "probably grinning and looking stupid," according to Daddy. The president immediately responded to their audacious and naive request. He invited them into his private office and listened patiently as these three country boys told him of their situation. They explained why they had come and that they had walked from Charleston to Pinckneyville, East St. Louis, Brooklyn, St. Louis, and then finally on to Jefferson City. They indicated that they had no jobs, nor any place to live. They knew nothing about the admission requirements or procedures, but they indicated that they were very eager to go to his college. They noted that they all planned to major in agriculture because they were from rural, sharecropping backgrounds. They presumed that Dr. Scruggs would help them with jobs and housing and all those things because he had, after all, invited them to his school.

"Don't worry about a thing," the president responded. Dr. Scruggs helped them to find jobs and accommodations, and to gain admission to the college.

The formerly private Lincoln University is now a state institution within the University of Missouri system. Once an all-black school, its current student body is predominantly white. The black Civil War veterans who founded the university had done so because they and other blacks were denied admission to the state-supported colleges and universities in Missouri, including the University of Missouri at Columbia, South East Missouri State Teachers' College at Cape Girardeau, and all others. South East Missouri State Teachers' College at Cape Girardeau was only about thirty miles from where Daddy lived. Thus, this is the school that he would likely have attended had it not been for the institutionalized racism that pervaded the state and the country at that time.

This story about my father's going to college is one that my five siblings and I have heard and have repeated many times over the years. We have shared it with our own children, our friends, and even our colleagues at work. I sometimes use this story in my own history classes at SIUE to illustrate many things: the importance of the oral tradition as a source of historical data, the institutionalized nature of racism, and the sacrifices many of our forebears made in order to gain a college education.

The Civil Rights Movement at Lovejoy Grade School

My own formal education began in 1951 in Springfield. I attended kindergarten at Isles School, which was racially integrated. Larry and June went there as well. The following year we moved back to Mounds, where we remained until 1959, when we returned to Springfield.

When we lived in Mounds, Larry, June, and I, and later Carol, attended Lovejoy Grade School, a segregated school in Villa Ridge.

Because the school was several miles from our home, we had to ride a school bus. We walked to the bus stop about one mile away from our home. Mr. Robinson, the bus driver and school custodian, claimed that he could not drive closer to our home because there was no suitable place to turn the bus around. In the warmer months, the walk was no problem, but in the winter it could be a very uncomfortable experience. We got cold as we walked, and even colder as we waited for the bus. It was not uncommon for Mr. Robinson to be very late. Sometimes we collected brush and twigs and made a fire to stay warm. More commonly, we huddled together and hoped that the bus would be on time.

Mr. Robinson was not a particularly nice man sometimes. Although he treated the Motley children well, he was unkind to the Rices, who were a large, very poor family. Buck, their father, was often unemployed. Miss Eddie Sue, their mother, was a pretty woman with flawless skin and beautiful light-brown eyes. Every year or two, or so it seemed, there was a new Rice who began catching the bus. The Rices lived a great distance from the bus stop—at least two or three miles, possibly farther. They were regularly late arriving at the bus stop. Often we could see them struggling to get there. They began running when they saw the bus, hoping to be at the designated stop before the bus reached the end of the line, one or two stops away, and circled for the return trip. Mr. Robinson usually waited for them, but he generally made a point of admonishing them in front of all the other children to be on time. Occasionally he was even more inconsiderate, taking off before they arrived, even though we could see them and even though waiting would have delayed us by only a few minutes. The children, myself included, laughed with glee as he closed the doors and drove away as though to leave them. Usually he would go only a few yards and then wait for them. At other times he simply left them. Then the Rices walked to school, which might take an hour or more. When they arrived at school, if it was winter they would be very cold. Their feet and fingers would be nearly numb, and the teachers would allow them to warm themselves by the heat vents.

The older Rice children were generally poor students. Their basic skills in reading, writing, and arithmetic were weak. Thus, they routinely repeated one or more grades. John Rice began school with June, three years ahead of me, but ended in my grade because I skipped one grade and John repeated two. John ended up in the same grade school graduating class with his younger sister, Edith, who had been held back at least one grade. Emma Rice began school with me, but was two or three grades behind me by the time I graduated from grade school. Two of the younger Rice children, Carrie and Ray, were very good students, largely due to the efforts of their older siblings. Edith, Emma, and John bought schoolbooks for the younger two and taught them to read before either had entered grade school. Carrie was one of the brightest students in her class.

Over the years I have thought about the Rices and other children similarly situated and have pondered why they did so poorly in school. Part of the problem was their home situation, perhaps, but I doubt that many students in Lovejoy had academically stimulating home environments. Parents probably saw academics as the purview of the teachers, rather than of the parents. Further, it is unlikely that most parents assisted their children with homework or even supervised its preparation. Even Mudeah and Daddy, who clearly valued education, did not take a role in reviewing our homework or even in making sure that we'd done it. Perhaps more significant with the Rices were their frequent absences, often due to having to work to help support the family. Chronic tardiness was also a problem for them. These factors caused them to miss a lot of classroom instruction.

A further constraint on the Rices' performances was the low expectations of them held by their teachers. Teachers in a small school like Lovejoy knew all the students and their families. They knew how well—or how poorly—siblings had performed, and they developed expectations of younger children in a given family in accordance with the past performances of older ones. In my own family, both Larry and June had distinguished themselves as excellent students, as did Carol and I. The Motleys developed a reputation as being "smart." The teachers often reminded me that Larry and June had been outstanding students and said that Carol and I were following in their academic footsteps. Conversely, the teachers expected Rices to be "dumb." The teachers' expectations were shared by other students, also. And probably by the Rices themselves. When I think of the Rices' experiences in school and compare them with my own and those of my siblings, I see the importance of teachers' attitudes and expectations. I see how important it is for teachers to communicate that they have confidence in each child's ability to achieve.

A further advantage that the Motleys had was our parents' high expectations of us. Mudeah and Daddy made it clear that we Motleys were smart people who would go on to college and become economically successful after we'd graduated. From early childhood we were socialized to go to college. The specific college and the exact major were left to our discretion, as was the means of paying for our education.

Lovejoy Grade School, and virtually the entire Illinois public school system south of Springfield in the central part of the state, was racially segregated. Years later, when I noted this in a discussion with my sister Carol, she stared at me and said, "It was a segregated school? I went to a segregated school?"

I said, "Yes. You don't remember that?"

"Well, now that I think about it, I don't remember seeing any whites there." As she thought still more, she recalled that Fay Wilkerson, the little white girl on the next farm, went to a different school. She also remembered that when Fay was with her white school friends, she would not speak to us or even look in our direction. We both recalled that the school bus system was segregated, also. We were bussed past the white school twice daily in order to maintain racial segregation.

Try as I might, I cannot recall any objections to bussing on the part of local whites. Privately blacks decried the unfairness of the "separate and unequal" education system, but I recall no public protests from them either. When the *Brown v. Board of Education* decision was handed down by the U.S. Supreme Court in 1954, I was eight years old and in third grade. Like other blacks, both adults and children, I was well aware of this decision, and we all over estimated its immediate impact upon our lives. We expected that our schools would be integrated immediately. Perhaps it would take until the following semester, or even until the next academic year at the very latest, our teachers said. The school board in Pulaski County delayed for many years, finally reluctantly integrating in 1966, twelve years after "separate but equal" schools were ruled unconstitutional. Pulaski County, like most newly integrated school districts in the country, fired all the black teachers and administrators.

Lovejoy and other Pulaski County schools were not only separate, but they were also distinctly unequal. In many respects these schools were very much like those in the South. This is not surprising in view of the district's location in extreme southern Illinois, across the Ohio River from Kentucky and across the Mississippi River from Missouri. Historically most migrants to southern Illinois have come from southern states. A relatively poor district, Pulaski County could ill afford to support a dual education system. Thus, the limited school funds were nearly exhausted on the education of whites. Black schools received what was left after the white schools had their choice of the meager resources.

The school buildings of the two schools exemplified the inequality of the dual system in Pulaski County. When I entered first grade in 1952, the Lovejoy Grade School was a four-room brick building. The only plumbing in the entire building consisted of a sink and a water faucet in the unfinished basement. There were no indoor toilets. We used outhouses, which were cold in winter and hot and fly infested in summer. All year they smelled of human waste. Nor was there a hot lunch program for black students; thus, we were obliged to bring lunches from home. The white school was much larger, with separate rooms for each of the eight grades. They also had teachers for each grade and additional ones for music and art. They had indoor plumbing, including toilets, as well as a cafeteria that served hot lunches daily.

Lovejoy had only two teachers for many years. Teachers taught four grades each. Corinne Hayes taught grades one through four; her older sister Flossie Buckley taught grades five through eight. Around 1957 our school was consolidated with another black school, which had burned. As a consequence, we then had four teachers, each of whom taught only two grades. One of the new teachers was Miss Lowry; I don't recall the other one's name.

The inequality in the schools extended to materials, including books, paper, and the like. We seldom had new books, because we generally received these only after the white teachers had selected what they wanted. Usually the white teachers took the new books and gave us their old ones. Further, it was very rare for all students in a given class to have the same edition of a book. More commonly, one or two students had the latest edition while the remainder had older ones.

Mrs. Buckley, our principal, periodically received a telephone call from the white principal indicating that he had books or other materials for us. Rather than going for them herself or having her sister Mrs. Hayes go in the car, Mrs. Buckley usually had several of the older boys walk over to the white school to retrieve the supplies and carry them to our school. At the time the boys were anxious to do this and the girls, myself included, felt cheated because we were rarely given the opportunity to spend time away from school during the middle of the day. In later years it occurred to me that, far from simply providing an opportunity for the boys to have a respite, the teachers were sparing themselves the embarrassment of going to the white school. Although usually the white principal and other adults were cordial enough, the white kids on the playground could be very cruel, calling the visiting blacks "Nigger!" and otherwise ridiculing them.

The poor condition of our school bus was another problem, but in the seven years that I attended Lovejoy we never got a reliable one. Several times a year it actually broke down on the road. Sometimes children were in the bus; at other times only the driver was on board. The school bus for the white students was newer than ours and in relatively good mechanical repair. One of the things I thought curious at the time was that the white school driver always put his "stop sign" out, reminding motorists that Illinois law required them to stop for a school bus that was either picking up or dropping off children. But Mr. Robinson, our driver, never did this. Nor did motorists stop of their own accord for the black schoolchildren. In fact we children stopped for the motorists. We once asked him why didn't he put out his sign, but Mr. Robinson just shrugged indifferently.

The schoolchildren liked to take a field trip to Fort Massac, in Metropolis, Illinois, each year. The old fort was now a lovely park overlooking the Ohio River. We'd play on the playground equipment, buy things at the refreshment stand and, finally, we'd have a picnic. After hours of fun, we'd return to the school and then make the trip home. The trip to Fort Massac presented a transportation problem, however, because our school bus was so unreliable. Thus, this trip that should have taken less than an hour might take several. In our childish excitement, we were willing to risk this inconvenience.

When we were on the way home from Fort Massac on one occasion, the teachers decided to stop to get us something to eat. We must have been delayed for a long time prior to this, probably due to mechanical problems with the bus. What stuck in my mind, however, was the fact that the little restaurant at which we'd stopped claimed that they would be unable to serve us. They claimed that they simply wouldn't have enough food. We hadn't even placed an order. We all understood what was going on: they were refusing to serve us because we were colored.

Students at Lovejoy Grade School were very politically aware, especially about issues relating to race. In many respects we could see repeated in our own lives the same segregated conditions against which southern blacks were fighting. We went to the Roxy Movie Theater in Mounds, where we were required to sit in the balcony, except on rare occasions when there was an overflow crowd of blacks. Then we were permitted to sit in a special, roped-off section on the main floor. Here the white folks made a big mistake because they allowed us to see that they had nice, plush seats that weren't ripped like many of the older ones in the balcony. Their toilets were nicer, too. Our restrooms contained only a toilet and a washbasin, but the white ladies room was very fancy. There were huge mirrors, a long vanity with little chairs where the women could sit while they put on their makeup—just like the movie stars did—and a sofa where they could relax. (Although I didn't see why anyone would go to the movie to sit on a sofa in the restroom.)

We also noticed that the drugstores and other businesses that had lunch counters or soda fountains served blacks, but we couldn't sit on the little stools or at the tables and booths. These were reserved for whites. In fact, while we waited for our order to be prepared, we were careful not to so much as lean against the stools, causing whites to eye us suspiciously. After we had received our ice cream cone, soda, or other food, we left the store and ate while walking along the sidewalk.

Perhaps inspired by the Civil Rights movement, my friends and I decided to resist these segregated facilities. Students at Lovejoy Grade School sometimes received permission to go into the village of Villa Ridge during the lunch period. We could have lunch there at a little black-owned restaurant where the chili was delicious. Or we could purchase cold cuts and other foods at one of the two general stores or order a soft drink or something else at the soda fountain of the local drugstore and drink it as we walked back to school.

One day some of us began to discuss the unfairness of our being able to buy things at the soda fountain but being expected to consume them outside the store. We noted that there was a booth or two in the store at which the white kids freely and leisurely drank their sodas or ate their ice cream. We decided that we would challenge this the next day. We would go into the drugstore, order something, and eat it at a booth. True to our plan, we did just that. I think the group numbered about five. Including me, there were Helen Stuckey, Mary Ellen Lloyd, her brother Dickie Lloyd, and possibly one other person. The owner was very nervous when we sat down, as were we. He said to Dickie, who had dropped crumbs on the countertop, "You're dropping something."

Dickie responded, "I'll clean it up." This infuriated me, as I had noticed that the white kids sometimes dropped crumbs, but they were not admonished for doing so, nor were they expected to clean the table. But I didn't say anything. The owner continued to stare at us the entire time. He didn't ask us to leave, however, probably because he was so surprised by our audacity that he was temporarily at a loss for what to do.

After our snack, we returned to school. By the time we got there, the owner had apparently recovered from his shock and called Mrs. Buckley, who was both the principal of Lovejoy and my teacher. She called us aside and asked us about what we had done at the drugstore. Upon hearing about our "sit-in," about which she obviously already knew, she told us that we knew that what we had done was inappropriate and dangerous. Then she punished us by refusing to allow any of us to go into Villa Ridge for a long time, probably for at least the rest of the semester if not the rest of the school year. Accustomed to my parents supporting the almost divine authority of the teacher, I thought it well advised not to tell them about this situation. On the one hand, I thought that they might understand and even approve of the sit-in. On the other, I thought that they might feel obliged to agree with the teacher. Years later, when I told Daddy about this, he said I should have told them, because he thought that Mrs. Buckley had not dealt with the situation in a fair manner. He felt that what we did was courageous, if ill-advised and dangerous, given the depth of the racism in the area. He also said that we should not have been punished.

I have always felt very proud about having challenged the racism of adults when I was but a child. I also take a pardonable pride in observing that civil rights sit-ins started long before those of the college students at Greensboro, North Carolina, in 1960, because our incident occurred in about 1957 or 1958. This incident also suggested to me that many similar protests have gone unheralded because no one publicized them. It raises questions about how many people, and under what sets of circumstances, protested the inequality of the institutionalized racism that has long permeated our country.

The teachers at Lovejoy Grade School did a remarkable job of educating their students, the limitations imposed by the segregated system notwithstanding. They were very committed to education, and they were very creative in their approach to it. They commonly had students help one another. Thus, as an older child listened, a younger one or even the entire class might read an assignment. Students helped one another with arithmetic by studying in a corner of the room or at the chalkboard.

Each student's progress was generally known by the student's peers. This had both advantages and disadvantages. Group pressure sometimes functioned in ways that were very embarrassing and discouraging to some students. Mrs. Hayes, an excellent artist, always drew a beautiful mural on the blackboard, on which she wrote the names of those students who had scored "100" on their spelling tests. In many respects the public acclaim of good spellers encouraged them and others to do well. But it probably had a negative impact, also, especially upon those who were not good spellers. The older Rice children, for example, virtually never had their names enshrined on the spelling mural. I sometimes wonder whether they eventually became too demoralized even to try to do well.

Mrs. Hayes also had a personal hygiene chart supplied by the manufacturers of Ivory soap. She wrote the name of each student on the chart. Beside each name were spaces for stickers indicating one's daily rating on personal cleanliness. Each day we underwent a personal inspection from head to toe as we stood in front of the class, all eyes riveted upon the student under scrutiny. Conducted by a favored student, such as me, the purpose was to note the student's level of cleanliness in a number of categories. Hair, ears, nails, teeth, and other parts of the body were carefully inspected. There were three ratings: an Ivory bar went to one adjudged to be very clean; a yellow sticker indicated that one needed improvement in one or two areas; and a red sticker denoted that one had extensive hygiene problems. The chart with the attendant stickers was in a prominent location on a wall of the classroom where anyone could see it. For those who received all Ivory bars, it was a source of tremendous pride. For others it was a badge of shame.

I had found this chart to be a wonderful idea for many years because I was frequently the inspector and I also had all Ivory bars. But one day I came to school with my hair not freshly combed. Mudeah had always taken great pride and had spent considerable time ensuring that all her children were properly groomed. She combed my hair and neatly braided it daily. But one day she had been unable to do so because of a problem on the farm. As a result, I had gone to school with my hair brushed rather than combed. For the first time, I dreaded the time when the health inspection, as we called it, was to occur. I hoped that perhaps we would not have time for it, as was the case on a few days a year. The inspector was Helen, my best friend and major rival. When it was my turn to proceed to the front of the room, I was mortified. Helen did to me just what I had done with anyone who had anything out of order. She gave me a yellow sticker. I was very embarrassed. Not just on that day, but for the remainder of the time that the chart was on the wall. I no longer took pride in the routine because students from other rooms came in to look at the chart. Everyone was shocked to see that Shirley Motley had gotten a yellow sticker.

I wish that I could say that this experience immediately rendered me more empathetic to others, but I don't recall it having had that impact. I do recall, however, that I vowed to see that Helen received at least one yellow sticker to mar her perfect "Ivory bar" record. In retrospect I can see the things teachers do, often inadvertently, to students that hurt them a great deal. Some students often received yellow and even red stickers, which was very humiliating to them.

A Good Time Was Had by All

Lovejoy Grade School brings to mind many pleasant experiences shared with the students and teachers. It was a very small school with never more than one hundred students in all of its eight grades. Everyone had known everyone else and their families for years in most cases. On rare occasion a new family moved into the area and sent their children to Lovejoy. We liked meeting these "new kids," and soon they were incorporated into both the school routine and the play periods.

I enjoy recalling the games we played during recess and lunchtime. A large cardboard box in the teachers' cloakroom held most of the few pieces of play equipment we had—a softball and bat, one or two jump ropes, and a few board games, such as checkers. On the playground was a swing set with perhaps six swings, but no other pieces like the jungle gym or slides at the white school. We had a baseball diamond, more or less. Actually it was the parking lot, but except for the teachers' cars and the school bus, there were few vehicles that came to our little school, so it was safe to play there. We didn't have real bases for the softball diamond, but the improvised ones that we fashioned served our purposes.

Jump rope was one of my favorite activities, especially if Katie May Fowler turned the rope. Katie May was a very tall, well-built girl who looked even older than she was. At fifteen she was several years behind her proper grade because she had flunked at least three times by the eighth grade. When she got pregnant at sixteen, she dropped out of school. This was very unusual for that time period, even for a high school girl; for a grade schooler, it was almost unimaginable. But, anyway, Katie May was really good at turning the rope. Katie May could always get it over a person's head, even if the girl at the other end wasn't very good at it. She could throw double Dutch, too, where two ropes were turned simultaneously but in opposite directions. And hot pepper, where you had to turn the rope really fast.

Swinging was fun, too, especially if there was no standing water under the swings. If there was, it was a little more tricky to get into and out of the seats. "Katie May, Katie May! Give me a push!" we'd yell. Katie May would give us a push and we'd soar way above the ground, sometimes causing the teacher to admonish us not to go so high.

We liked to shimmy up the supports of the swings, climbing all the way to the top, about ten or twelve feet high. If you spit on your hands, you could get a better grip on the poles, we soon discovered. Of course, then your hands smelled awful, and no one wanted you to touch them.

Katie May was also a good hitter when we played softball. If the pitcher gave her a decent shot at the ball, she would send it over the outdoor toilets into the field behind the school. This was likely to be a home run regardless of how far the ball went because the ball was apt to be lost in the high weeds in the private lot adjoining the schoolyard. Katie May was a good pitcher, too, although if she was angry she might throw really wildly, nearly knocking the batter down. And she could run. After she got a hit, she would sling the bat down, pull her long skirt above her knees, and take off, moving really fast. "Go, Katie May! Go, Katie May!" But if she was thrown out, she'd get angry. One of the worst things was when she would dramatically burst into tears. Then we stood around in horror as huge tears slid down her face and terrible sounds racked her body. It was an awful sight—this big girl who was so vulnerable.

When someone was injured on the playground or in the parking lot, one of the teachers or an older girl would get out the little first-aid kit and treat the injury. Soon the victim had not only a bandage but also a tale of the horrible sting of the alcohol as he or she proffered a scraped hand or skinned knee to all of us who gathered around to offer comfort.

During recess or lunch we might buy a soft drink from the machine in the wide hallway. At first sodas were a nickel; later they rose to six cents, and then to seven, and finally to a dime. For most of us even a nickel was too much, and a dime was out of the question. Occasionally I had money from doing farmwork or from Grampa or Grandma Bessie and Papa. Then I'd buy a soda pop. I'd debate over whether to get a strawberry, an orange, or a Coke.

Thinking about Cokes reminds me of a story about my Grandma Bessie, my maternal grandmother. She claimed that when Cokes were first produced, she'd really liked them, but "then they did something to them, and I haven't cared for them since." Whenever she said this, looking innocent about the entire matter, everyone else became rather amused, but no one ventured to say that what they had "done to them" was remove the cocaine.

A huge white cooler, similar in appearance to a chest-style freezer, sat alongside the soda machine at Lovejoy Grade School. This cooler contained milk, both white and chocolate, which the school sold to us at well below its market value. This was a state-subsidized program that allowed schoolchildren to buy milk for two or three cents for a half-pint carton. The milk in the cooler was always very cold, and sometimes it even had little crystals of ice in it. From time to time Mudeah gave me money to bring home cartons for the younger children and for her. This was against the rules, but occasionally we were able to do it anyway. Before we boarded the bus after school, someone might request to buy milk to drink on the trip home. If our supply was reasonably large, Mrs. Buckley, the principal, might agree. Then all who had a few extra pennies would gather around, clamoring to buy milk. I always got chocolate. Rushing home after getting off the bus, I would quickly cover the mile between the bus stop and home and triumphantly present the milk to Mudeah. "Mudeah, Mudeah! I've got you some chocolate milk!"

We had parties at school for special occasions, such as Valentine's Day, Christmas, and Easter. Everyone looked forward to these celebrations for weeks. We cut out paper, glued lace, drew pictures, and occasionally even sprinkled sequins or beads to make decorations for the windows and the classrooms. Mrs. Hayes drew beautiful pictures on her blackboard with her pretty colored chalk. When we were finished, the entire school looked very festive and appropriate to the season.

Refreshments for our parties were usually modest, perhaps cookies and Kool-Aid purchased from the meager funds we had raised selling candy, popcorn, and other things during the school year. Sometimes when we had a party at school, the teachers would buy sodas for us, allowing each student in turn to select the one wanted. Music was provided by recordings of square-dance music from the school library played on the phonograph that we had purchased ourselves from our fund-raisers. We begged to bring rock 'n' roll records from home, but the teachers usually objected to this type of music as "ungodly music." So we contented ourselves with the country music and learned to do the Virginia reel and other square dances. We cleared the desks away from the center of the room, making a dance floor for those who cared to dance—usually everyone wanted a turn. One of my favorite songs celebrated Sam Houston. I can still hear the music as we flew around the room, trying to remember the proper steps and never suspecting that Sam Houston had any part in anything like dispossessing the Indians or the Mexicans of their land. Nor in supporting the Texans in their demands to maintain our ancestors in slavery.

We usually had a Christmas program for which we practiced for weeks. Family and friends were invited to the final performance, which was usually held on the last evening before Christmas vacation. All the students had roles in it. There would be assorted speeches, many of them religious, and a play, which was usually about the first Christmas. We made the costumes ourselves, of course. The wise men wore towels secured with headbands around their heads, and the shepherds carried crooked sticks that someone had found on the way to school. Both the wise men and the shepherds wore bedsheets, as did the angel, who also wore wings made of cardboard.

The murder of Lowell Morris by Sam Fowler, Katie May's older brother, temporarily shattered our sense of well-being and became a subject of considerable discussion at Lovejoy Grade School. I recall Lowell as a handsome boy who looked really cute on the basketball court at Douglass High School in Mounds, where he was a star player. Sam, by contrast, was average looking. He struck me as a quiet, unassuming boy who tended to fade into the woodwork, even when he was a student at Lovejoy Grade School. According to Daddy, Lowell was something of a show-off who liked to pick on other, less-celebrated youths—such as Sam, who'd flunked several grades before finally dropping out of high school.

One evening after basketball practice at the high school, Lowell and some of the other guys were teasing Sam, as usual. But rather than laugh good-naturedly as he generally did, Sam got angry. Brandishing a gun, Sam fired at Lowell. Badly wounded, Lowell fell to the floor. By the time the word got afloat in Mounds, Lowell Morris was dead and Sam Fowler had been arrested for his murder.

At school we collected in the girls' cloakroom before class began to exchange news of this tragic event. Even Margaret Fowler, Sam's and Katie May's sister, crowded in as we looked about nervously, not wanting to hurt her feelings but not wanting to pretend that we had gathered for some other purpose. "I'm sorry, Margaret. Sorry, Margaret," we chorused.

But Margaret wanted to hear all the news too because she previously had not learned all the details. Daddy, a deputy sheriff of Pulaski County at the time, had been called to the scene, so I could provide a little information. I didn't really enjoy telling it, though, with Margaret there. Everyone really liked Margaret. She was a very nice person and a very good student.

After school was in session, we sat at our desks, listless. It was hard to believe that Lowell Morris was dead and that Sam Fowler had killed him! Eventually the excitement of this news subsided, and we returned to our schoolwork. Meanwhile Sam was convicted and sent to prison, becoming the first person that we knew personally who was incarcerated.

We had a very small school library, which probably did not exceed two or three hundred volumes, mainly books. There were a few magazines, such as *Life*, *Look*, and *National Geographic*. An avid reader, I read virtually every book there. I started with the ones I really wanted to read, moved on to others that were of less interest, and finally I just read whatever I could find. My brothers Larry and June had done the same thing, as the teachers noted with hearty approval. The only literature I didn't want to read was that about Africans. My reaction was shared by all, or virtually all, of my classmates. We were embarrassed by the scanty attire and the unfamiliar customs of these people to whom we were related in the yesteryear. Why did they wear those little cloths around their waists? Why did the women have bare breasts? Why did they dance about during those weird ceremonies? We had no appreciation of our African background. And the teachers provided no real insight into the customs and lifestyles of these people who looked so like us. One of my teachers once said that slavery had been a "blessing in disguise" for Negroes because it had brought us to America, where we had become civilized. Many years later, in the black cultural revolution of the 1960s and 1970s, I reassessed these biased views of Africans. I began to read about African history and culture. I met Africans. And I came to appreciate this aspect of my life.

During thunderstorms our teachers, looking anxious and afraid, insisted that we turn off the lights and sit quietly. Sometimes they even made us rest our heads on our desks. They would remove their jewelry and sit in quiet contemplation. They might even pace in the hallway, praying silently. I thought that this was really odd because I had always liked it when it stormed. In fact, I enjoyed the patter of the rain on the roof and the whooshing sound it made as the wind blew it against the windows. The cracks of thunder and bolts of lightning were frightening in a fun sort of way. I never feared that lightning would actually strike anything, although adults spoke of such things happening. When it stormed and I was at home, I'd run to the window and watch the rain coming down in sheets across the front yard. Soon the roof would begin to leak, and we would collect assorted utensils to set under the many drips. "Ping! Pong! Pang!" The rain fell like musical notes into pots and pans in every room of the house.

Observing no "separation of church and state" and committed to teaching morality, our teachers urged us to attend Sunday school and church. Periodically they would reward us by making homemade ice cream at school. The teachers brought the ingredients from home, and the bigger boys took turns cranking the freezer in the school basement. We could hardly concentrate on our studies, anticipating the moment when Donald Gene Robinson, John Rice, or Roland Paul would come up the stairs and quietly whisper to Mrs. Buckley that the ice cream was ready.

Students received varying serving sizes based upon the number of times we'd attended church and Sunday school. Although I was sometimes tempted to say that I had gone to both every Sunday, I was always very honest and admitted the actual number of times I had gone—usually about one-half to three-quarters of the time. The Rices always claimed to have attended every single Sunday, even though they belonged to a church in Mounds that was miles from their home and they didn't own a car. The teachers never questioned our reports, always accepting that we had attended however many times we claimed. They did admonish us, however, that the Lord knew the truth and would punish all wrongdoers at Judgment Day. I secretly feared that the Lord would not be quite so patient and might well strike down a liar on the spot, as some of the old folks claimed.

One time when the teachers had made ice cream, I acknowledged that I hadn't attended either church or Sunday school at all during the period under review, so I was prepared to busy myself reading while the others had ice cream. Oh, how I envied everyone who had gone to church. Then Mrs. Hayes, Carol's teacher, came into the room and, noticing that I sat apart from the group, asked why I wasn't having ice cream. She said that Carol had said that we had gone to church and Sunday school once, recounting some incident that reminded me that we had, indeed, attended. I was so happy I could have kissed my little sister. Mrs. Buckley seemed really happy, too, because she didn't like to deny anyone a treat. I noticed that when she gave me my serving, I got just as much as the others. At the time I didn't realize why, but later it occurred to me that she was probably rewarding my honesty in initially acknowledging that I hadn't deserved the ice cream.

One year the school district sponsored a Better Breakfast Contest. All schools were invited to apply by having one or several students make posters picturing a healthy breakfast. Donald Gene and Roland, both excellent artists, immediately decided to enter. Helen Stuckey, my best friend, also announced that she would enter the contest, as did a few others. Everyone, including the teachers, expected that I would also make a poster, but I wasn't really interested in doing so. I was a reasonably good artist and I knew what was considered to be a good breakfast, so I appeared to be a likely entrant. I just didn't want to do it.

Mrs. Buckley, my teacher, did not overtly object to my decision, but she did tell me to go to the store with the others and to bring back some drawing paper as they were going to do. The drawing paper was actually pieces of paper that the grocers used to wrap meats. They sold us huge pieces for five or ten cents each. Accustomed to obeying the teacher, I brought back the paper. "Now, draw a good breakfast," she said simply. So I dutifully prepared an entry. We drew the traditional healthful breakfast of that era—which now would be considered much too high in fat and cholesterol—tall glasses of whole milk, small glasses of fresh orange juice, bacon or sausage, eggs over easy, and buttered toast. Significantly, we depicted breakfasts that most of us never had, but we'd studied in health class what we were supposed to eat, so that's what we drew. Eventually six of us completed entries, which the principal sent to the county superintendent's office.

A few weeks later two or three white men came to our school to inform us that four out of the six entries had won prizes. One had won the county prize and would be entered in the state competition, and the other three had garnered second-place awards: Helen's, Donald Gene's, Roland's, and mine. Either Donald Gene's or Roland's had won the countywide competition. We were all so proud of our school. I think that there was only one winner from the white school across town, even though they had a full-time art teacher to supervise their work and they had lots of real art supplies, so they hadn't needed to buy wrapping paper from the grocer for their entries.

Askia Ammar at Howard University

"Askia Ammar, Washington, D.C." I looked with curiosity at the letter bearing this unfamiliar name in the return address, but in the familiar handwriting. It was addressed to me: "Shirley Carlson, 714 Leland Avenue, University City, Missouri."

A picture of Askia Ammar emerged as I read the letter. A pretty, black girl of seventeen, who looked several years younger. She was about five feet two inches tall, weighed perhaps ninety pounds, and wore a very large Afro hairstyle. Askia Ammar was my sister Carol Marie Motley, formerly known as "Carol," "Carol 'Ree," "Callyn," and "Curl."

It was fall 1969, and Carol had recently begun her first year at the prestigious, historically black Howard University. Here Carol, distinctly a "child of the sixties," was to become further radicalized. That is, beyond the radicalism of her high school days. Charlynn Spencer, Lynn, her best friend from high school in Springfield, was to share this experience with her as they had shared so many others. They had, for example, participated in civil rights activities one summer while visiting Lynn's grandmother in Mississippi. Back in Springfield the two of them were asked by a very nervous administration at Southeast High School whether they would like to graduate one year early. And, no, the fact that they lacked some high school credits, including in English, would not be a problem. More significant for the administration was the fact that Lynn and Carol had raised a lot of embarrassing questions. Why were there so few black teachers at Southeast High School and in the Springfield public schools? Why didn't the school include black history and other subjects pertaining to black life? Why did black people eat turkey and dressing for Thanksgiving dinner when they would have preferred greens and chitterlings? The future Askia Ammar had begun to emerge.

Carol had become a rebel on the home front as well. She had defied Mudeah on a number of occasions. Mudeah had imposed a strict curfew on her and had limited the number of times that Carol could go out in the evenings. This was not necessarily a reflection upon Carol, because Mudeah was very strict in her child rearing practices, especially when it came to her three daughters. Her three sons were granted somewhat more latitude, but even they had to abide by stringent rules or Mudeah would know the reason why! Any child under Mudeah's roof could still get a whuppin', she constantly reminded all of us. Unfazed by these restrictions, Carol found a way to avoid them. If Mudeah refused permission to go out, Carol simply climbed from the bedroom window and later returned in the same manner. One night as Carol climbed in the window, Mudeah waited patiently in the dark.

When Mildred and Calvin told me about Carol's forays and her defiance of Mudeah, I had to admire her. She seemed to me like one of those Japanese kamikaze pilots, who flew suicide missions into enemy territory. One had to admire their resolve, even as one questioned their wisdom. I also admired her courage when she challenged a longstanding practice of racism and black subordination in the school system of Springfield. Carol's self-confidence and commitment to principle were typical of many young blacks in the 1960s and 1970s, many of whom took part in similar challenges to a status quo that their predecessors had been unwilling or unable to change. The schools had been desegregated in 1871–72, but no black teacher had been hired until the 1950s. Nearly two decades later, black professionals and staff were still grossly underrepresented in the education system. Owing to the actions of Carol, Lynn, and others of their generation—and with support from other, older people—the situation began to change, however slowly.

The family was relieved that Carol was finally in college, because she had earlier demurred about attending. Eventually she had decided to go if two conditions were met. First, she had to go to Howard University because it was the most prestigious of the traditionally black colleges. And, second, she had to have a wardrobe befitting a Howard student. She specified a certain number of outfits—so many sweaters, skirts, slacks, and so on—because she had no intention of being around all those rich kids without the proper attire. An excellent seamstress, she set about making some of the requisite pieces. She announced that other pieces, sweaters for example, would have to be purchased. Because our parents could not afford these things, there seemed to be no solution. Mudeah said the little hussy could get a job and help her pay the bills. Then our brother John, who had recently returned from Vietnam, said he would take her shopping in Chicago, where he now lived, to buy the necessary attire. Having acquired the requisite wardrobe, Carol deigned to go to Howard University.

Askia Ammar. She had taken the name to symbolize her African heritage. "Askia," a title often bestowed upon ancient West African rulers, such as Askia Muhammed of Songhay. And "Ammar," to honor a specific African ruler. The name suited her—the consummate rebel.

As I thought about the new Askia Ammar, I recalled her "Curl" stage. She preferred to be called "Carol," spoken very distinctly, enunciated very carefully, but her family usually pronounced it "Curl." Except for her southern relatives, including Grandma Bessie, who called her "Cal" or even "Callyn." "Curl," with the pretty "turnaround dresses," who danced for family and visitors alike. "Curl," who ended her dance routine with a twirl and gracefully sat on the floor, her dress perfectly and evenly spread about her. "Curl," who cutely and prissily pursed her lips and smiled in such an engaging fashion. "Curl," who hesitated to work in the yard or to pick blackberries or strawberries because she might get dirty or stung by a bee. "Curl" was now Askia Ammar.

In the next few months, Askia Ammar sent other letters about her Howard University experiences. She wrote, for example, that she and Lynn were no longer roommates, although they remained best friends. Askia, now heavily involved in the "black revolution," had found it necessary to take a private room in the dormitory and to have a telephone installed—both very unusual luxuries for a college student at the time. She needed the solitude provided by the room and the communication link to the outside provided by the telephone. She became increasingly critical of "bourgeois society." She spoke of the transgressions of the "pigs," as the policemen were now called by the radical social activists.

My admiration of my younger sister soared, even as I noted certain inconsistencies in her views. The part about the chitterlings for Thanksgiving, for example. She didn't even eat chitterlings; I doubted that she had even tasted them. I could appreciate that because I had not tasted them either, but I wasn't urging blacks to eat them in preference to turkey and dressing. Also, it struck me that she needed quite a lot of luxury for someone who decried bourgeois advantages. The clothing, the telephone, the private room, and the private university one thousand miles from home all sounded distinctly bourgeois to me. But then, what did I know? I attended a state university, ate turkey and dressing on Thanksgiving, and was still intimidated by Mudeah.

As I read about Askia's growing radicalism in her letters, I wondered what she would do next. Ten years later, or twenty, or twenty-five—where would she be? What would she be doing? And what of her politics? Would she, in fact, remain Askia Ammar?

"Askia? She became a capitalist," someone is likely to respond at the family reunion when the name is mentioned. Currently a marketing professor, Askia no longer eschews capitalism and bourgeois values, nor does she advocate revolution. She can still deliver a darned good impromptu monologue on assorted social and political issues, however.

5

Remembering the Neighborhood

Family Reunion: From Patch to Patch

Picking blackberries and making jam and cobblers from them have been important features of the family reunion since 1991. That was the first year that we held the reunion at Johnny Cake Mountain Farm in Burlington, Connecticut. My brother John and his wife, Susan, had just built a beautiful new house on a seven-acre, heavily wooded lot.

Johnny Cake Mountain Farm is the perfect place for a get-away-from-it-all vacation. It is a combination of housing development and working farm, with turkeys, horses, and other farm animals. There is also wildlife, including deer, beaver, and the usual assortment of squirrels, opossums, and rabbits. Nicole, John and Susan's beautiful red-haired daughter, tells us about the horseback riding, offering to show those who ride the beaver dams, which only the children have seen thus far. A pond stocked with several varieties of fish is behind the home of the developer and general contractor, Dwight and his wife Liz. One of the neighbors even has llamas and once invited John and Susan and the other neighbors on a llama picnic. Tall white birch trees, ferns, and other greenery provide the perfect pastoral setting. Best of all, wild blackberries grow thick, juicy, and sweet in the woods. They are perfect for my blackberry cobblers, which have become a staple of the family reunion diet, and for the blackberry jam that Daddy makes each year.

We all pitch in to pick the berries. Daddy is the first to declare, "Well, I guess I'll go out there and pick a few berries." John eagerly grabs a plastic pitcher, which he rigs so that he can attach it to his belt, freeing both hands for picking. The expert manner in which he does this suggests that he has been practicing for this occasion. Harry, a first-time picker and city boy, heads out with pail in hand, ignoring warnings that his shorts are not the best choice of attire. Later he discovers why as he plunges into thick, thorny canes in pursuit of some good-looking berries and emerges with nasty scratches on his legs. But he returns two days later, wearing long pants. I have retained my berry-picking zeal of years past, so I'm eager to get out there. Carol and Mildred, dressed in cute, coordinated outfits, virtually have to be dynamited out of the house. They each pick a few berries the first day, but in the future they manage to stay out of sight when the berrying starts, as do Susan and Rent, our sisters-in-law. The children, Vanessa and little Susan—big Susan's best friend's daughter—eagerly run out to pick berries, also. It's their first experience at foraging and they really enjoy it, even though they pick few berries. The two girls run from cane to cane, picking a few berries at each before being distracted by another.

Daddy will make jam as soon as the picking is done. He and an assistant will remove the stems and wash the berries. Next Daddy will put the berries in a huge pot, adding sugar and Sure-Jell, and then cook the mixture, stirring almost constantly. When the jam is of the proper consistency—Daddy always knows this without timing it, the hallmark of an excellent country cook—he'll pour the jam into jars, screw on the lids, and turn them upside down on a fresh tea towel. They will remain in this position until they have sealed. We will each take home half-pint and pint jars of Daddy's blackberry jam, packing them carefully in our hand luggage. Meanwhile there is plenty of jam during the family reunion. Jam with oven toast has become a staple of the breakfast menu. Interestingly enough, assorted friends seem to appear right at breakfast time. Now that Daddy has started making jam again, none of us wants to buy any because "store-bought" jam simply doesn't compare to his. We rather selfishly try to keep the jam in the family because we don't want friends and acquaintances asking for it. As John says,

"As long as they don't know what they're missing, they won't expect to have any." He tells Susan, who likes to share the jam with friends, "Get them a bottle of wine; they'll never know the difference." A few people know about the annual rite of making homemade jam, however, and they do, indeed, expect jam every year.

After dinner I will make blackberry cobbler, the family's favorite dessert, which I have devised based on trial and error and my recollections of Mudeah's blackberry cobbler. I mysteriously claim to have a "secret ingredient." No one in the family cares what it is because, as they have made perfectly clear, no one intends to make the cobbler anyway. That's my job, as they've also made perfectly clear.

One of my favorite memories of making blackberry cobbler involves Larry. It was at the 1991 family reunion, I believe. I had wanted to make a small cobbler as a surprise for Vanessa and little Susan; Larry was helping me find an appropriate dish. After about five minutes, I gave up the search, but Larry continued to look. He searched every cabinet and spent at least twenty minutes in the process, but he came up with just what we needed. "Shirl, will this do?" he asked, holding up the perfect dish. Then he and I tried to keep Vanessa from looking into the oven and seeing the surprise prematurely. "Oh, Ness, stay away from the oven. It's very hot!" we warned. Later she and Susan were really happy when they saw the cobbler we'd made especially for them.

The berry picking brings back memories of our life on the farm in Mounds when, of necessity, we picked berries for food and to sell. We picked strawberries in May and blackberries in July. We grew the strawberries ourselves in the large truck garden across the little stream—actually, we called it "the big ditch"—that ran through our property. The blackberries grew wild on our own and on adjoining farms, so we had to forage for them. Whether it was strawberries or blackberries, I often volunteered to pick them because I enjoyed the activity so much. I also really liked the praise that went with bringing home a pail of strawberries or blackberries. Further, it was a way to gain solitude, so difficult to come by in a large family that lived in a very small house. If I went berry picking—especially for blackberries, where I might be obliged to wander some distance in order to gather enough—I could be away from home for hours without any questions being raised, as long as I was home before dark. I would pick berries, often pretending to be an orphan who lived off the land and the money earned from selling whatever I could scrounge. Or sometimes I pretended that I was the sole support for my family, who had nothing to eat, and I was thus obliged to forage for our meals. I had similar fantasies as I gathered black walnuts, pecans, and hickory nuts in the fall.

The only real hazard in picking berries was the snakes that were sometimes in the strawberry patch or under the blackberry canes, so we had to keep a watchful eye for them. Most snakes in our area weren't poisonous, but we were afraid of them anyway. Besides, there were rattlers in southern Illinois, we knew. Sometimes I became quite convinced that I had, in fact, seen a rattlesnake. Then I would abandon my picking and the bucket of berries. But I always returned after a few minutes because I didn't want all my efforts to go to waste.

Occasionally Carol would go with me, usually not entirely of her own volition because she didn't like to pick berries or anything else or to do any other farm chores. She would complain: "It's too hot." "I'm afraid of snakes." "A bee might sting me." "I want to play." Because she was "a baby"—only seven at the time we made our second move from Mounds to Springfield—Daddy and Mudeah tended to be very tolerant of her and seldom required her to work. Mildred says that there's where I made a mistake for which we all are paying now. She says that I should have whipped Carol's little butt then and dared her to tell it.

"But then she would have told on me, and I would have gotten a whuppin'," I object.

"Yes, that's right. But if you had beaten her up every time that she told off on you, she would have stopped tattling. It would have taken only about twice," Mildred quite reasonably observes. "Then we wouldn't have to put up with her whining now," she adds.

Anyway, back to the berrying. Many of the strawberries in our patch were half wild, so they were small but very sweet. With strawberries, often the smallest ones are the most delicious. Mudeah would slice or mash them, add sugar, and serve them for dessert. She also made jam and jelly. Whole strawberries didn't can well, so we saved few of them for the winter. The blackberries would be made into a cobbler, one of the family's favorite desserts at that time, as it is now. Or sometimes she would warm the berries a bit, add sugar, and serve them for breakfast with slices of oven toast or hot biscuits. This was my favorite breakfast, even though the teachers at school said that it was not a well-balanced meal. Indeed, seldom did we have a breakfast that would have been regarded as a "healthy breakfast" back then. If there were enough blackberries to make it worth her efforts, Mudeah made jam and jelly or canned them whole in their own juices.

When there were extra blackberries, we were permitted to sell them to the neighbors. Miss Patty McBee and Mr. Robert Green, both of whom were elderly blacks, were my two best customers. They paid well, and they also were very kind and attentive. I often sat and talked with them after the sale, as well as at other times. Occasionally I sold berries to white neighbors, but I wasn't eager to do that. The white folks would generally pay less than blacks and would also denigrate the quality of the harvest. The latter, I suppose, was a justification for the low price they offered. Interestingly, no customer ever proposed that I give them the berries and let them pay me later. If they had, I would have objected, whoever they were. Had I come home without my money, Mudeah would have been angry, and I would have sooner risked a lynching from the white folks than a whuppin' from Mudeah. A lynching was conjectural; a whuppin' was certain.

Daddy tells of similar experiences selling blackberries, pecans, walnuts, and eggs when he was growing up in Charleston during the Great Depression of the 1920s and 1930s. In Charleston Grampa Motley became a sharecropper. He grew cotton, which he paid his children fifty cents per one hundred pounds to pick, money that they used to buy clothes and other necessities. Even though it was not common to pay one's own children for their labor, Grampa insisted on doing so because he reasoned that this would teach them independence. Making a living was difficult all along, but it became even more so during the Depression years. As with many other economic woes, blacks were the first to feel the strain. Daddy says that they worked so hard that he sometimes envied the dog because he got to lie around in the shade while they worked in the hot sun. He admired the horses and worked as hard as they did. In Depression-era Charleston the Motleys needed all possible supplements to their income, so when it rained and they were unable to pick cotton, Daddy and his younger brothers, Harry and Vernon, gathered eggs, blackberries, nuts, and other things to sell in town. As the oldest brother, Daddy was the one who went into town to sell their goods. Their customers were generally white because blacks could not afford to buy these products. Through his contacts with his white customers, as well as with other whites, Daddy began to experience racism, which had been much less apparent in the Cairo–Future City area, where his associations had been mainly with other blacks.

Daddy would select a nice house, go around to the back door and knock, and then the lady of the house would answer. Her standard reply when asked if she wished to buy the berries would be, "Oh, no. I just bought some really nice ones yesterday." But then she would start to sort through those he offered. "Well, how much do you want for them? I guess I could use a few to make a pie." He would respond that it was up to her.

"Yes, ma'am. Pay me what you think they're worth." If he proposed a price, she would always object that it was too high. Much higher than for those she'd purchased just yesterday. And those were much better berries, she would remind him. Ultimately, it was left to her discretion, and she would propose a price that was unreasonably low, but because he needed the money, Daddy would accept. Besides, as Daddy recalls with a laugh, "I wasn't damn fool enough to argue with a white woman!" He had heard stories about black men and boys who'd been beaten or lynched for being disrespectful to white women, so he wasn't taking any chances. Meanwhile, the woman would have picked through the berries, selecting all the best ones. When she was done, he knew that no one else would want to buy the ones she'd left. I might as well take those home so Mama can make a pie, he would think.

One time Daddy had pecans for sale, which a white man whom Daddy called "Old Excuse" offered to buy. He told Daddy to go to his house and wait for him there. After about thirty minutes, the man came home and said he didn't have the money yet, but he would get it soon. Then "Old Excuse" left again. This continued for much of the day, until the man finally returned home with the money.

Generally the money his white customers paid was inadequate compensation, as Daddy well knew. He and his brothers had spent a lot of time picking the berries, walnuts, or pecans and walking the eight miles round-trip to town from their rural home. He knew also that his customers' ability to take advantage of him was in large part because he was black. But he had no viable alternative. Whites were his only likely customers, and he needed the money they provided, however inadequate the sum. After selling his products, he'd buy a penny sucker or a jawbreaker to eat on the walk home. Occasionally he'd buy a "washnut pie," a big, cheap dessert with a filling that "tasted terrible" but relieved his hunger considerably.

Blackberry picking for the 1994 reunion was, of necessity, a solitary affair. The reunion was to be held in Godfrey, Illinois, at Harry's and my house overlooking the Mississippi River. A neighbor who has a farm less than a mile away had berries for sale. They were tame berries: thornless, much larger than wild ones, and they grew in rows. It wasn't really the same as foraging for wild ones, but it was the best we could do because we didn't know where there were enough wild blackberries for our purposes. And they were delicious. The blackberry season would end barely a week before the family reunion, so the berries had to be harvested beforehand. Because no one else was available for this task, I picked thirty pounds of berries to freeze for the jam and cobblers at the reunion. Maybe I'll have a few frozen berries left for cobblers after the reunion, I thought.

Mildred technically was available to pick, but when I talked to her about it, she said, "I would help you, but . . . " and her voice trailed off, becoming inaudible.

"But what?" I asked rhetorically. I knew the answer.

"I can't help it if I didn't grow up in the country like the rest of you," she said, which we both knew was quite beside the point.

"Oh, yeah, that's right. You're a city girl," I conceded, still waiting for a rationale as to why this exempted her from picking the berries. Berry picking is a learned skill acquired in minutes. It doesn't require a lengthy apprenticeship.

"I've just never been the berry-picking type of person. I am the berry-eating kind, though," she concluded. I decided to accept that explanation because it was the only one I was likely to get. She is also the "decision-making type." When I told her later that I had picked thirty pounds of berries, hoping for amazement on her part, she fretted over whether that would be enough for jam and cobblers. "You'd better get some more. That's not going to be enough," she warned.

Krystle and Kraig, my grandchildren, nine and eight at the time, visited us before the family reunion. Eyes glazed with nostalgia, I decided to take them blackberry picking. I fantasized a fourth generation of Motleys as berry pickers. In a concession to the modern era, I immediately told them that I would pay them if they would help me pick berries.

"Okay!"

"How much do we have to pick?"

"How much will you pay us?"

We agreed that I would pay one dollar for every small pail—about one-half gallon. At first Kraig and Krystle were eager, especially because we found big, thick berries under a shade tree. But soon bees also discovered the shade, and they started buzzing around us. That did it for my grandchildren's enthusiasm. We moved out of the shade to avoid the bees, and then we were in the full sun, which beamed down, growing hotter and hotter. Meanwhile, each child had filled a pail, and both were ready to go.

Later I returned alone and picked more berries for the reunion.

Meanwhile, I thought about previous reunions and other reminiscences. I imagined tales that we would tell when we met. I wondered how much of my manuscript on family history I would share. What will please my siblings and their families? What will offend them? Who will play each role in the major motion picture? I wondered. I thought of our constant struggles to avoid talking about sex or swearing, especially saying the "f-word," around Daddy. Blackberry picking, making jam, and baking cobblers always reminded me of the farm in Mounds and of assorted friends and neighbors: Mr. Meeks. Mrs. King, who later became Sister Luke. Miss Pat and Mr. Robert. And many, many others.

I knew that as we ate the cobbler, we would continue our reminiscences about family history. Someone would comment, "This is good pie, Miss Shirley. It got sugar in it!" We would burst into laughter as we recalled Cheetah Riley's famous compliment to Mudeah about her blackberry cobbler. All the while that I picked berries, I was smiling, thinking about rushing home to the computer and writing additional vignettes about family history.

Cheetah Riley

Cheetah Riley was eight or ten years old, dark complected with close-cropped, peppercorn hair. He was usually barefoot and nearly naked, except for a pair of shorts that were holey and a bit soiled. He whined when he talked, and he scratched and swatted flies, gnats, or other insects—some real, some imagined—almost constantly. He sniffed regularly because his nose ran both in winter and summer, suggesting that he had numerous allergies. His name— nickname really, I don't even remember his real name—was appropriate. He could run fast, and jump high, and all that, like a cheetah. But he looked more like a little chimpanzee. Like "Cheetah," the chimp in the *Tarzan* movies. He had long, thin arms, which seemed perfect for swinging from a vine or reaching out to grab a banana. He had a small head and a slender, elongated torso.

Cheetah and his large family were our neighbors in Mounds.

They lived across the road and up the hill from us in the hired hand's rundown cabin on the Greens' farm. The Rileys had about seven or eight living children and several who had died at birth or in infancy. They were a particularly poor family, one of the poorest we knew. Only the Rices were as poor. Abject poverty could be seen in the sparse furnishings of their four-room house. There was only one bed, in the parents' bedroom, that had a bedstead. It had a feather tick with an opening down the middle. Every morning the Riley girl who made the bed had to reach inside and "stir" the feathers with her hands to reshape the mattress. In the other bedroom there were assorted feather pallets and rag quilts on the floor. The living room had a few straight-back dining chairs, which might be moved to the kitchen during meals or onto the porch at other times. A wood-burning cook stove, a crude wooden table, and a nearly barren cupboard were in the kitchen. A few tin plates and cups and some spoons were the only tableware.

The poverty of the Riley family could be further deduced by looking at their sparse diet: parched field corn, bread fried in a skillet atop the stove, apples from the orchard nearby, fat meat and occasionally bologna, and whatever they could grow in the garden or forage from the woods. Rarely did they serve a hearty meal; probably never did they have a well-balanced one. Sugar, purchased in small amounts, was used mainly to sweeten coffee. More commonly, the Rileys "borrowed" it from neighbors, who knew that they would never be able to return it. "Mama say, can she borro' a little sugar fo' huh coffee?" Cheetah or one of his siblings would ask, proffering a little tin cup. Neighbors took turns filling the cup or giving whatever amount they could spare.

"Say hello to yo' Mama for me," they would say as the child turned to leave. After he'd gotten a little coffee from another neighbor, he would go back home.

The Rileys could not afford Christmas presents for all of their children, so often the older ones received none. When other kids discussed what they had received or expected to receive for Christmas, the Rileys attempted to save face by saying, "I'm getting such and such for New Year's," anticipating that no one would inquire later about the elusive gift.

Cheetah's siblings were Sonny, Buddy, Gail, Martha, James, and the baby, Obadiah. Mudeah had delivered at least two of the children. Gail and Martha, Cheetah's older sisters, were two of my closest friends. Martha and I spent a lot of time playing together, but Gail, the older girl, was often too busy for children's games. She took on the role of surrogate mother to her siblings because their mother was often ill. Martha and I made mud pies and pottery, and played hopscotch, jump rope, and other games. If our older siblings—Gail, Larry, June, Sonny, and Buddy—were able to join us, we might also play crack-the-whip, red rover, or hide-and-seek.

The Rileys sometimes came to our house to play. If it happened to be around mealtime, we children would invite them to eat with us. After going through a round of "I'll eat if you eat" among the Riley siblings, it was almost always concluded that the group would join us for the meal. In the background, Mudeah often tried to warn us not to issue the invitation because it would mean two to four extra mouths to feed—very hungry mouths at that—and we could ill afford dinner guests. She was always very gracious, however, once the invitation had been extended and accepted. Mudeah dished up to all equal portions of beef stew or beans or whatever she had cooked. She very kindly and politely offered the platter of cornbread or biscuits to our guests first. When they very hungrily and rudely grabbed the biggest pieces, she signaled her own children not to object. She knew that the Rileys were always hungry and in need of a decent meal. And they were always so obviously appreciative as they noisily ate the meal, slurping and smacking, and cleaning their bowls or plates with their bread. They especially liked her desserts, usually peach or blackberry cobbler. After they had eaten, Cheetah would say in that whining voice that made him sound like he was on the verge of tears, "That sho' is good pie, Miss Cora. It got sugar in it! Can I have another piece?"

"Oh yes, baby," Mudeah always said. She had taught her own children that it was rude to ask for seconds. But clearly Cheetah was still hungry, and she could not refuse his rather modest request. After the meal was over, we might play a little longer, and then the Rileys went home. Sometimes Mudeah had served only part of the meal while we had company and later she would surprise us by calling us in to eat again. When this happened, we were so happy because we were always hungry after sharing our food with the Rileys.

Once we were playing at the Rileys and one of the children in the family offered to let us pick some apples from their landlord's orchard next to the Rileys' house. This we happily did. Later that night, two embarrassed Rileys appeared at the door and said, "Mama say we got to get the apples back." We were all stunned because they had offered us the apples and because we had fed them so often, for which they were never able to reciprocate. This had seemed to me a good way for us to get some apples and for them to have the "blessing" of giving. But Mudeah said that we had to return the apples. She said that was the kind of thing that happened when you "messed with people like that." At the time I was really angry because I was looking forward to eating the apples and maybe some of Mudeah's fried apple pies.

Cheetah had a crush on Carol, who did not return the feeling, as far as I know. Even so, we now tease her that the two of them had "courted" years ago. When we talk about living on the farm and about Cheetah and his family, inevitably someone says to her, "That was when you and Cheetah were going together." We reminisce about how he always favored her in the games we played. There was one game where everyone was to stand in a circle, holding hands. One child would be selected to be "it" and would be tossed about the ring, feigning illness, while the others sang:

Doctor. Doctor, can you tell?
What will make Mr. Cheetah Riley well?
He is sick and about to die,
That would make Miss ——— cry.

Here the one who was "it" was to call out the name of the one whose presence would restore him or her to health. Cheetah always shyly said "Carol." At this point the loved one was to step into the circle while everyone giggled, and then the loved one became the new patient and the game continued.

Mr. Riley worked in East St. Louis and came home only once or twice a month for the weekend. He often arrived on foot because the family's car was not reliable. In fact, I'm not sure that they even owned a car most of the time. When Mr. Riley was at home, his family treated him like royalty, which seemed to meet his expectations. The best food, the best chair, the best everything became his. Meanwhile, he often hollered and cursed so loud that he could be heard in the distance. A quarter of a mile away, we strained to hear what was going on as he bellowed his complaints. Mr. Riley found fault with everything: the way his two older sons—both teenagers—ran the farm or the way the garden had or had not been maintained. There was constant turmoil until he left a few days later.

Eventually the entire Riley family packed their meager possessions and moved back to East St. Louis, from which they had come only a few years earlier. Once, Gail visited me after they had moved, but after that we lost contact with them.

Cotton-Picking Neighbors

Larry, June, and I sometimes earned money by working for neighboring farmers picking string beans, cotton, strawberries, or whatever crops were ready to harvest. One neighbor even grew peanuts and pecans, which she picked on "halves"—the picker got half and the owner got half.

Everett Meeks was our most frequent employer. Mr. Meeks would come by our house in his old truck and honk until someone ran out to the road. Then he would holler, "I'm picking beans [or cotton, or whatever] today!" Then he'd continue down the road to inform others. He'd pick us up on the return trip. We would run out and jump into the back of the truck with the others he'd collected by then. Often the Rices were there, and sometimes the Rileys. Back at his farm, we would be joined by his son's family, which included his stepdaughter, and my best friend, Helen Stuckey. In fact, the first time I met Helen, we were preparing to pick something at Mr. Meeks's farm.

For years I thought that the Meekses—Everett and his wife, Grace, and the two grandchildren they were raising—were quite well-to-do. They had a relatively nice house, although it was sparsely furnished. I think they even had an indoor toilet, a very rare luxury in our area. They had a telephone and a television long before most people in our area had either. They had a truck and a huge tractor, both of which Mr. Meeks kept in good repair. Further, he was one of the few African American men who regularly employed others on his farm.

We picked string beans for Everett Meeks, and occasionally for other farmers, at fifty cents a bushel. Mr. Meeks kept a little bag full of half-dollars and paid on the spot for each bushel. Sometimes I earned several dollars in one day. I liked hearing the coins jangling together in my pocket. Every time I added a coin, I recounted all the coins, although I always knew perfectly well exactly how many I had. I just liked to count them all at once.

Mr. Meeks also raised cotton, paying several dollars per hundred weight for it. Each picker had a cotton sack, which was so long that it dragged on the ground. Adults had the longest sacks, which were about nine feet long. Children had shorter ones, about seven feet long, until they reached the point that they needed roomier sacks. Very small children sometimes had short crocus sacks, which were about two or three feet long. It was something of a humiliation to be required to have such a short sack, so children often liked to demonstrate that they needed longer ones. They did this by picking so much cotton that their parents constantly had to dump it into their own sacks. Besides, children preferred long sacks because they would not be emptied into the adults' sacks but would be weighed separately, and the amount could be recorded individually as well. We children took great pride in doing a lot of work. That was one of the few things that might win open praise from an adult: "That Shirley can sho' pick cotton!"

I could pick about one hundred pounds by the time I was ten or eleven years old. This was quite good for a child. Mrs. King—later Sister Luke, as she preferred to be called after she went down South and got herself a new husband—was often the best picker. Some claimed that she added weight to her sacks by putting unopened cotton bolls, leaves, and other things in it. I don't recall whether she actually did this, but I do know that she attempted to "fluff up" the beans she picked by pouring them from one bushel basket into another several times. Mrs. King was a hard worker. She would leave her own fields to work in someone else's, so that she could have the additional income. After the paid harvest was in, she returned to her own fields, which she usually worked alone until she married "Mr. J. Goo," as my brothers used to call her husband. (They claimed that, with his thick glasses, Mr. Luke looked like Mr. Magoo, the cartoon character.)

After the day's harvest, Mr. Meeks generally drove into either Mounds or Villa Ridge. He invited those who had worked for him to go along, but usually Larry, June, and I declined. Not that we didn't want to go, but we were trying to save our money. The trip into town was an opportunity to buy ice cream, candy, sodas, and other treats. We had been taught frugality and practicality by our parents, so we usually spent our money on school clothes and shoes. We kept a little for spending change. And we saved some. I recall being shocked to learn that some kids had to give most of their earnings to their parents, who needed this income to support the family. Sometimes Mudeah bought enough fabric with my money to make matching dresses for Carol and me. This usually infuriated me because I didn't want to spend my money on Carol. I thought she should earn money herself, even though she was only six or seven years old. Further, I didn't want to dress like my sister, who was six years younger than me. Taught to be respectful of my parents and other adults, and afraid of being slapped into tomorrow, I usually did not let on that I resented this. My mother's response would likely have been, "You're just being selfish. You should take care of your little sister." And Carol, a real little suck-up, would have smiled prettily at Mudeah, and later she would look cuter in our matching dresses than I did.

I did some chores for neighbors for free. For example, I sometimes fetched water or brought in firewood for Miss Patty McBee or for Mr. Robert Green because both were aged and infirm. And I also liked them both a lot. Like many of our neighbors, we carried water in two-and-one-half- or three-and-one-half-gallon buckets from the farm of Kenneth Wilkerson, a white man who lived about a quarter of a mile from us.

As a child I often enjoyed being around these older people. They were always very happy to have the company; thus, they were very attentive. We would sit on the front porch and talk for long periods of time about our families, my schoolwork, and other matters. This gave me an opportunity to talk about my excellent grades without instigating the discussion, so I didn't consider it bragging to go on at some length about my accomplishments. They seemed to enjoy hearing about them. Sometimes they gave me treats, such as peppermint or other hard candies. Occasionally the older people told wonderful ghost stories, which frightened me so badly that I had nightmares, but I loved these tales even so. The fact that adults told them convinced me that ghosts did, indeed, exist, even though Daddy and Mudeah always laughed and shook their heads and said that there were no such things as ghosts. I thought that they were trying to protect me from the knowledge that such frightful things as ghosts existed.

Mr. Robert had a severe case of asthma. When I saw him, I would say, "How're you doing, Mr. Robert?"

"Oh, I'm doing just fine. Just fine," he always responded. Two seconds later, he would begin to wheeze and cough and then he'd say, "Lord have mercy on po' me, Jesus, if you please." Then he'd continue wheezing and coughing until he was able to catch his breath properly. Some older people claimed, upon being asked, that they were doing "tolerable" or "tolerable fair." But with Mr. Robert it was always "fine." Sometimes I wondered why Mr. Robert, who claimed to be doing so well, appeared to be doing so much worse than those who claimed to be doing only "tolerable" or "tolerable fair."

Mr. Robert was very nice, and I visited him quite often—even though it did take him ten minutes to leave his porch, get a couple of pieces of candy, and return. I liked watching him eat the hard candies he provided because he had a lot of missing teeth. It was so interesting to watch the candy disappear and then reappear from behind one of his few remaining front teeth. Also, it made an interesting sound as the candy clicked around in his mouth.

Shopping Around

Sometimes, mainly on Saturdays, we made trips into Mounds, where my siblings and I could spend some of our earnings. After we moved into town in 1958, we were only a few blocks from the stores, but I had less money because we were too far away from the farms where children could find seasonal employment.

Our first stop was at the five-and-dime, where we bought school supplies. A cheap notebook was twenty-five cents; a nicer one that would probably last the entire school year without having to be taped together was fifty-nine cents. They had assorted boxes of crayons, but we usually contented ourselves with the smallest box, which had eight colors. I always coveted one of the huge boxes with forty-eight crayons, but unless Grampa happened to be visiting and went shopping with us, there was no point in asking for that, even though it was my own money. Two pencils, or maybe three if they hadn't run out of that kind, were five cents. A package of notebook paper for our two- or three-ring binders ranged from ten to twenty-five cents. We often got one large pack and divided it among all of us school-age children, saving a few sheets for those who were too young to go to school. New shoes and fabrics for clothing would usually wait until late in the summer, when we would make a trip into "the city"—Cairo—where there were more stores and a larger selection of goods, as well as lower prices.

We were now free to spend what money we had left as we liked, although Mudeah and Daddy always indicated certain things that they deemed either a waste of money or a wise use of it. At this point, our parents would probably go shopping at one of the two grocers in Mounds, where they might also sell some eggs from our hens. Meanwhile we children wandered about, trying to decide what was good enough to buy with our money.

The Whataburger Stand in Mounds had delicious food. Although I rarely actually went there, I frequently thought about it. It was a small stand with walk-up service at a little window, which was nice because if there had been indoor seating, blacks wouldn't have been allowed to use it anyway. Other places that served sit-down style permitted only their white customers to use their counters or tables.

The Whataburger Stand's hamburgers and french fries were outstanding. The hamburgers were much larger than those elsewhere. The meat was juicy and tasty—and just a little greasy. A hamburger came with "everything," including lettuce, tomato, pickle, ketchup, and mustard. I always had mine without mustard, which I detested, and I generally preferred to omit the ketchup as well. The french fries were freshly made: deep-fried, liberally sprinkled with salt, and served with ketchup on the side. They were almost as good as Larry's. They also sold milk shakes and malted milks, both of which were delicious. They made them in the now-old-fashioned metal canisters that were the norm at that time. Chocolate was my favorite, but vanilla and strawberry were nearly as good, I always thought. They were so thick that one could hardly sip them through the huge straws. I didn't mind that part, however, because it meant that I was forced to drink slowly, and it lasted longer that way.

When we lived on the farm, Daddy occasionally brought home several malts or milk shakes for us to share. It was usually rather late at night, after he'd gotten off from his job as deputy sheriff. Sometimes we were in bed when he came home. "Larry, June, Shirley, Carol, Calvin," Daddy or Mudeah would call. We knew that this meant Daddy had brought home malts, so we would quickly spring out of bed and run into the kitchen, where Mudeah had divided them into equal shares. There was no point in hoping that one would have a bigger portion than the rest. Mudeah was the best divider I've ever seen. Occasionally she permitted one of us to do the dividing. It was wise to be scrupulously fair when one had this responsibility because the one who'd done the dividing got the last choice. There were none of the "little piece for you; big piece for me" schemes in the Motley household. To this day when I divide something, I do so very carefully, halfway expecting Mudeah to say, "Let them pick first, Shirley."

The drugstore soda fountain was another very appealing place to go. They sold all kinds of ice cream treats—milk shakes, malts, ice cream cones, ice cream sodas. The three-dip ice cream cones pictured in the window always interested me, but they were ten cents, twice what I usually spent on a one-dip cone.

We went to the Roxy Movie Theater—or the show, as we called it—about once every month or two. Children up to age twelve paid fifteen cents, and everyone else paid thirty-five cents. Sometimes we would take our own popcorn, especially if it was in the winter when we wore heavy coats under which we could hide the little greasy bag. I always had some uneasiness when I did this, however, because I was sure that the ticket seller could smell the popcorn just as I could.

After purchasing our tickets, we went to the concession stand. Usually we bought candy for five cents, but on rare occasions we'd buy popcorn for ten cents. Then we would proceed up the long flight of steps to the balcony, where colored people were required to sit. From our perch, we could see the white people in the more modern first-floor section with the nice, comfortable seats. The seats in the balcony were often worn and sometimes ripped after many years of use. Whenever the downstairs area got new seats, the old ones would be moved upstairs.

Lovejoy Grade School took a field trip to the theater, which held special daytime viewings for schoolchildren, about once a year. I don't know why we did this, because the movies had absolutely no educational value in most cases. I recall, for example, having seen the movie *Them* during such a trip. *Them* was a horror movie about giant ants that destroyed property and captured human beings, dragging them underground where they were to be stored for food. I loved the movie and had nightmares about it for years. That was always the test of a good horror movie—how long I continued to dream about it, waking up in the middle of the night screaming. I also agonized over whether it was possible for ants to mutate to the point that they would grow so large. Even though both my parents assured me that the movie was strictly a fantasy, I kept my eyes on the ants in our area for any sign that they were getting larger than usual.

Gone with the Wind was another movie that I saw during a school field trip to the Roxy. Because I had no way of knowing otherwise, I took this movie based on the Margaret Mitchell novel to be an accurate portrayal of the South during the Civil War and Reconstruction eras. I even felt sorry for poor Miss Scarlet when she had reached such a low point that she didn't have a decent thing to wear and had to use the drapes to make a frock. I can't say as I sympathized all that much, though, when she had to work the fields with her own lily-white hands. All the women I knew—my mother, my sister, myself, my grandmother, and the neighbors—all had to do this, so it didn't seem all that horrifying of a prospect. And I thought that Prissy was a really stupid character even then. All of that running around like the proverbial "chicken with its head cut off" just didn't appeal to me.

The teen joint—around the corner from the Southern Illinois Nite Club, which was owned by a man named Memphis—also captured my attention. It rarely, however, captured my business because Daddy and Mudeah warned us to stay away from it due to its proximity to adult nightlife and the fact that it, too, was owned by Memphis. Adult disapproval made the place even more intriguing. Black teenagers and even younger children could go there to play records on the nickelodeon and dance. They could also buy soft drinks and snacks. Some teenagers hung around outside on the street corner, talking and flirting and watching people walk by on the sidewalks or drive by in their cars. From the outside, one could hear the music blaring popular tunes, such as "Stagger Lee" or "In the Still of the Night."

Calvin, just two years old at the time, used to sing and dance to "Stagger Lee," which he called "Stagger Leaf." Calvin's dance was an imitation of Elvis Presley, whom we'd seen on the Dorsey Brothers' television program and on the *Ed Sullivan Show*. We'd all clap and encourage his performance, in much the same fashion as we do now with my nephew Jason, who has liked to dance—especially for show—since he could stand up without assistance. Sometimes June would take Calvin places with him. He said that the girls would really hang around him then.

Inside the kids fast danced. The girls wore their cancan petticoats starched as stiff as possible, revealed beneath their twirling, fashionable dresses and skirts. Couples slow danced, their cheeks pressed against each other, causing the hot-combed hair of the girls to "go back" when they sweated.

After my Aunt Toots, only two years older than my brother Larry, came to live with us, she miraculously convinced Daddy that it was okay to go to the teen hangout occasionally. I'm not so sure that Mudeah was that convinced, but she insisted that if Toots went, she had to take me. So I would go along, promising Toots that I wouldn't tell Mudeah about how she laughed and flirted and danced with the many boys who "flocked around her like flies to honey." Luckily for Toots, she had "good hair," so she didn't have to worry about sweating. She had a whole string of admirers, but she soon fell in love with one: Eugene Hughes, who was a big basketball star at Douglass High School. His family was from North Mounds, the poorest section of the small town; thus, my mother was somewhat less than happy about the match. She didn't try to intervene, though, beyond contending that most people from North Mounds "never amounted to anything." In my family, that meant that they weren't college bound. My mother's way of reminding everyone that she had disdain for the Hughes family was to mispronounce Eugene's name. Thus, to her he became "Nugene Hugegess." Sometimes Mudeah even called him "Lugene," as though she could neither remember his name nor pronounce it properly. Toots and Eugene married shortly after their high school graduation, much to Mudeah's chagrin. Over forty years and three children later, they are still married.

The city library was another place I liked to visit. If I was sure that I'd be able to return the books within two weeks, thereby avoiding a fine that I could ill afford, I would check out several books. Larry, June, and Carol often did likewise. The library seemed so large and the selections so endless compared to the school library at the back of Mrs. Buckley's room. But I did recall that the Springfield Public Library was much larger and had lots of tables at which even the colored people could sit and read. We'd gone to the South Town branch regularly when we'd lived just a few blocks away from it. A few times we'd even gone to the Downtown branch.

Mudeah and Daddy, always frugal, used to save money by buying day-old bread and baked goods at a little shop in the back of a white woman's house in Mounds. When we'd lived on the farm, Mudeah or Daddy would stop by there in the car and pick up what we needed. But when we moved into town, it was often my job to go on foot to get bread, cakes, and other baked goods. One time I happened to arrive just at closing time, and the woman offered me a special price. I think she said I could have a whole sack full of snack cakes for just ten cents. They were usually three for a dime for the larger ones and two for a nickel for the smaller. After nervously demurring because I didn't want to boldly spend Mudeah's money without her permission, I decided to accept the offer. I could always pay Mudeah the ten cents out of my own money if she was mad. But she was really pleased and commented on what a good little bargain hunter I was. She'd even boasted to Daddy about what a good deal I'd made.

Making the trip to get the baked goods was very embarrassing to me because I didn't want the other kids to know that we ate day-old bread. We took our own paper bags because the woman usually didn't have any. Walking down the street with a couple of big empty paper bags stuck under my arm, I figured everyone knew that I was on the way to the day-old bread place. On the way back with huge loaves of bread protruding from the bags, it was even more obvious where I'd been. I quickly figured out a route that would make it possible to avoid face-to-face contact with anyone I knew personally, however. But it meant that I had to walk through the white areas, and here I ran the risk of white people, especially teenaged boys, making inappropriate comments and possibly even calling me "Nigger!" By carefully laying out a route where there were few young people, and by walking in a fast, no-nonsense, self-confident fashion, I usually managed to avoid this hazard as well. I'd entertain myself with thoughts of Daddy—who was no longer a deputy sheriff but who still owned a .38—shooting anyone who bothered me. I would picture Daddy, suitable armed, appearing from nowhere and striking fear into any offenders, who would im-mediately become contrite, begging for my forgiveness and com-passion. Besides, I had noticed Daddy really didn't like to go to the day-old bread place either.

6

Country Cooking and Soul Food

Family Reunion: In the Kitchen with the Motleys

The Motley clan sits around the kitchen table once again, laughing and talking as Larry prepares another of his excellent meals. We know that our chances of getting additional meals are enhanced greatly if we keep the cook company. Besides, Larry is very entertaining as both cook and comedian.

Food is very important at the family reunion. We spend a lot of time talking about and planning meals, shopping for the appropriate ingredients, cooking, and eating. We even take pictures of our favorite dishes for the reunion photograph album, which we have yet to complete or to start. And we've submitted our favorite recipes to Mildred, who is assembling a family cookbook.

We expect to overeat, so we don't worry about it for this one week. We focus on what tastes good, as opposed to what is healthy. We forget about restrictions on calories, cholesterol, fat, sugar, salt, and all of the other things that make food so delicious. And we fry everything: fried catfish, fried potatoes, fried bacon, fried green tomatoes. By the way, those tomatoes that caused such a sensation in the movie *Fried Green Tomatoes*, based on the Fannie Flagg novel, *Fried Green Tomatoes at the Whistle Stop Cafe*, would not have passed muster with us. Too firm. Further, one should not serve them in a little basket covered with a checked dinner napkin. Nor should one pick them up with one's fingers and nibble little bites. Fried green tomatoes should be soft enough to require eating them with a fork. And they should be served on a plate. They are not a cutesy-pie hors d'oeuvre. They are a country food. The latter, unlike the former, is acclaimed for its taste rather than for its appearance. No one makes little things on toothpicks, or anything that has tofu, or anything cut into little pieces. We prepare real food, like in the "good ole days."

The centrality of food at the reunion became clear from the first one in 1987 in West Goshen, Connecticut. The St. Louis contingent—Carol, Calvin, Mildred, Fae, Krystle, Kraig Jr., Ramirez, Ramirez's friend Derrick, and me—rented a huge van and drove the nearly twelve-hundred-mile trip. Larry, Rent, and Vanessa had flown in from San Francisco the previous evening. We arrived in the early morning, tired and hungry. We had stopped to eat at fast-food places several times, but eventually we had grown tired of that fare and were anxious to get to our destination. As soon as we got there, Susan asked, "Are you all hungry?"

No one responded because we didn't know who was going to cook. We weren't anxious to sample Susan's cooking because we'd all either actually experienced it or had heard tales about it. In all honesty, I must admit that I have told stories about her cooking. And Mildred has never forgiven me for allowing Susan to make the mashed potatoes one year for the Christmas dinner. Periodically Mildred still says to me, "So why did you do it? You knew she couldn't cook." Despite innumerable attempts to do so, I've never managed to give her a satisfactory answer. I really should quit trying.

While we were still deciding what to say, Larry and John also asked whether we were hungry, and Larry added, "John and I'll cook, if you're hungry."

"Yes, I'm starving!" a chorus of voices immediately responded. John and Larry then prepared the first of many delicious meals.

We share recipes at the reunion, often recalling ones that Mudeah made when we were children. We also recall the dishes that Daddy made. "Daddy, do you still remember your recipe for ———," we ask. He used to cook and can when we were children. Wearing one of Mudeah's aprons, he would make bread-and-butter pickles or bake cakes and rolls. His real baking specialty was a beautiful and delicious coconut cake, which he made each year for Christmas. Sometimes the neighbor women would brag on Daddy's cooking, as well as his lack of self-consciousness about it. They thought it was so nice that he would cook because their own husbands usually disdained this job as "woman's work." Daddy's attitude was, "I can do anything as good as any blamed woman!" As he cooked, he cleaned the kitchen so that when he was finished, everything was orderly and clean. At the family reunion Daddy makes two outstanding old recipes: blackberry jam and rolls.

The family tradition of both sexes sharing responsibility for meals is apparent at the family reunion as we take turns grocery shopping, cooking, and cleaning up the kitchen. Ideally, we would harvest the fruits and vegetables from our own gardens, but this is not possible. John and Susan don't have one. Harry and I have found that ours isn't particularly productive since we moved from Edwardsville to Godfrey. Thus, we must rely upon assorted open-air markets, specialty shops, and even the supermarket in search of the freshest ingredients. This calls to mind an oft-told tale: Rent and Susan were doing the shopping for the first reunion. They decided to get some fresh sweet corn, which they picked themselves. They selected large, full ears and proudly returned with their find. John and Larry took one look at the corn and said, "Where did you get this?"

"It was in a field," they responded, as Larry and John began to laugh. Two city girls, Rent and Susan didn't know the difference between field corn that one feeds to the animals and sweet corn for human consumption.

Everyone—or at least almost everyone—takes turns serving as chef. Usually one or two people prepare a meal while the others converse, play a card game called bid whist, watch videotapes, read, or whatever. There is always a group in the kitchen or breakfast room to keep the cooks company and to serve as tasters. None of us likes to cook without an audience of at least one; a whole group is preferable. The cooks entertain their audience by sharing recipes, tips on proper preparation of dishes, and other important information, whether related to the meal or not.

Larry is, by unanimous agreement, the principle chef. He is outstanding. A perfectionist when it comes to cooking, he is very exacting in the preparation of whatever he cooks. He makes test pieces and cooks in small quantities. For example, Larry tries his barbecue sauce on one piece of meat and then has one or two of us taste it and give commentary. He wants constructive criticism. If someone simply says that the food is excellent without offering further observations, he stops asking that person. The proper response is something like, "This is delicious. It could use a bit more lemon. Then it'll be perfect." Or "Excellent. How about more hot sauce?"

Larry has always been an excellent cook. When we lived in Mounds, he would sneak food out of the house, go into the woods—what we used to call the "canebrake"—and cook it. The canebrake had all kinds of huge old trees, lots of underbrush and, best of all, grapevines. We practiced our Tarzan routine there. We would swing from the vines and yell like Tarzan and, of course, beat our chests in victory. Larry kept a cache of salt and pepper and a few old cooking utensils stashed in a tree trunk. But he also cooked in the kitchen. He made the best french-fried potatoes I've ever tasted. If potatoes were in season, he would dig fresh new potatoes. Using a small paring knife or a pocketknife, he would slice them very thinly, so that one could almost see through them. Then he would deep-fry a few slices at a time. Finally, with a liberal sprinkling of salt and lots of Louisiana hot sauce—Durkee's preferably—they were ready to eat.

Larry is convinced that the real secret to good food is "Don't make enough." That way, everyone will want more. His wife, Rent, complains, "Girl, Larry never makes enough!"

Harry is the lobster cook in the family. Once you've had his tender, perfectly cooked, expertly seasoned lobster with drawn butter, it's very difficult to find ones elsewhere that suit you. For the non-lobster-eaters, he grills steaks, another of his specialties. As assistant cook, I am responsible for cooking the sweet corn, preparing a salad, and perhaps baking a peach or blackberry cobbler. Daddy's Lobsters on Route 6 in Woodbury, just down the road a piece from Mill House Antiques and about a forty-minute drive from Burlington, was the best place to get fresh lobster for the reunion in Connecticut. The owner, a fisherman, had fresh lobsters every day. His prices were excellent—three one-and-one-half-pound chicks for about nine dollars. Harry and I, and anyone who wanted to accompany us, would drive down one afternoon and pick up a dozen or so live lobsters for a lobster boil that evening. At the 1993 reunion we discovered that Daddy's Lobsters had gone out of business. Those we bought at the grocery store, even though they were live, just didn't compare with the ones from Daddy's Lobsters. So now we're trying to find another place near Burlington to get fresh lobsters.

Carol and Larry make fish and spaghetti, which is spectacular. They serve it with light bread, just like when we lived in Mounds. If there is any left the next day, we try to beat each other to it for lunch because it's delicious reheated, too. Mildred makes a delicious Italian dinner with lasagna, garlic bread, and salad with homemade dressing. She knows just the right combination of cheeses to put in the lasagna. She doesn't use ricotta, which most people in the family don't like and which most lasagna recipes specify. John and Larry make breakfast much of the time. Breakfast usually starts with John's sausage-cheese biscuits, which could be a whole meal in themselves. John also makes some kind of blended drink that has assorted fresh fruits mixed with wheat germ. The first time he served it at the family reunion, we all had to discontinue drinking it after one or two mornings because of the high fiber content. John also makes excellent banana bread from a composite recipe based on three or four cookbooks.

As we sit with the cook during the preparation of meals, while we eat, and when cleaning up the kitchen, we talk about family history, perhaps starting by recalling various members of the family noted for their cooking skills. In most cases they are noted for their good cooking, but a few have distinguished themselves by being really awful cooks.

We also talk about various food preferences of family members. My own aversions to mayonnaise and mustard still amuse my family. Occasionally someone attempts to "put one over on me" by adding just a tiny bit of one or the other in a prepared dish. After watching the cook smirk for a while, I comment—for example, "June, I know you put mustard in the salmon croquet." Despite his trying to feign innocence, he knows he's been caught.

"Wow! You really can tell."

"Yes, unlike some people who claim not to like certain dishes," I respond, turning my eyes on Carol, who knows we're getting ready for a round of "I don't eat pork" stories. Carol decided when she was thirty-something to discontinue consumption of pork because the pig, in her estimation, is a filthy creature. In consequence, she has taken considerable kidding from her pig-eating siblings. I guess she'd forgotten about witnessing, when we lived on the farm, how disgusting the chickens were when they pecked at each other's behinds.

Carol doesn't always know when she is being served pork. One time Calvin cooked pork roast, served with all the trimmings, and invited us—Carol, Mildred, Mudeah, and me—to dinner. Later, someone called, and we were describing what a delicious dinner Calvin had made. "He had a pork roast, potatoes . . ."

Carol overheard the discussion and exclaimed, "Pork! That was pork! I ate pork!"

"Yes, I thought you knew."

"I thought it was a standing rib roast," she replied. So now she has to endure all kinds of "standing-rib-roast" jokes.

Another opportunity to tease Carol about not eating pork presented itself as we were flying to Connecticut for the family reunion one year. Carol, Calvin, Mildred, and I were traveling together. Calvin, Mildred, and I were seated three abreast on one side of the aisle. Carol was across the aisle and a row ahead of us. The three of us seated together were served first. When we saw that the meal was pork, we started laughing in anticipation of Carol's response. We agreed that we would not respond to her inevitable inquiry about the menu.

"Shirley! Shirley!" Carol was quietly calling my name because I was the one closest to her. I ignored her, pretending to be absorbed in discussion with Calvin and Mildred.

"Shirley! Shirley!" she called a little louder, as I continued to ignore her. Now the three of us were laughing with our backs to her.

"Shirley! Shirley!" Carol was practically yelling. Everyone on the plane was looking in her direction, except her siblings. At about that time, the flight attendant plopped a ham sandwich in front of Carol. Carol looked at it in disgust, as though she were on the verge of becoming sick to her stomach. Then she placed her napkin over it and shoved it as far away as she could. At this point, Calvin, Mildred, and I started to laugh openly.

Stories of eating pork—or not eating pork, as the case may be— remind us of Mounds, where we had raised and slaughtered our own hogs.

Ice Cream in Summer

Mudeah canned during the summer. By fall she had filled the large kitchen pantry with jars of peaches, apples, pickles, green beans, blackberries, and other fruits and vegetables. Most came from our own farm, either raised in the garden or the truck patch or foraged from the wild; we bought a few things, including peaches and apples. Everything she canned had to look attractive. Mudeah carefully arranged peach halves in quart jars before covering them with a heavy syrup. She neatly placed whole cucumbers in pint and quart jars and then added a spicy vinegar mixture. Jars of jellies and jams—strawberry, blackberry, and grape—made a colorful array on the shelves. Everything looked so pretty and delicious that we kids could hardly wait until Mudeah and Daddy went for a rare visit to a friend's house or elsewhere so we could sample the goods. After they were safely out of sight, we opened a jar of something—pickles and peaches were two favorite choices. Everyone had to participate in opening the jar so we were all equally implicated, ensuring that no one would tell our parents about our misdeed. Afterward we washed away all traces of the evidence.

We made homemade ice cream from a custard that Mudeah cooked atop the stove and that Daddy and we children hardened in an old-fashioned, hand-cranked freezer with a wooden tub. Daddy and Mudeah claimed that some people had electric freezers, which required no turning by hand and which made delicious ice cream. When we looked skeptical, they pointed out that the cook at the high school in Mounds used an electric freezer when she made ice cream for lunch at the school or for sale during halftime at the basketball games. We had to admit that her lemon ice cream was indeed delicious, even though it had been made in some newfangled contraption.

We took turns cranking the freezer while we sat under the locust shade trees at the side of the house. When it was too hard to turn, Mudeah drained the salty water from the freezer, wiped the lid, and lifted the top from the canister in order to remove the dasher. Then she put the lid back on, added ice, covered it with heavy towels, and let it "ripen." Meanwhile, we each got to taste a little ice cream from the dasher. Delicious! We could hardly wait until Daddy or Mudeah declared that the ice cream was ready to be eaten.

Watermelons were another summer treat. Daddy sometimes grew them, but we usually purchased them from men who peddled their goods in town or along our road. "Watermelons! Watermelons! Missouri melons!" The melons from the boot-heel area of Missouri were reputed to be the best. One time Daddy got a melon that looked unremarkable on the outside, but when he cut it, it was golden yellow. None of us had ever seen this before, and our immediate assumption was that it was rotten, even though it smelled just like a regular watermelon. Although it turned out to be a delicious new variety, we didn't fully appreciate it. In our view, a ripe watermelon was supposed to be red. Later, when I saw golden yellow tomatoes, I had the same reaction to them.

Summers also provided opportunities to visit my friends Helen Stuckey, Emma and Edith Rice, and Gail and Martha Riley. "Mudeah, can I go, too?" Carol often asked and Mudeah, much to my chagrin, generally agreed.

"Take your little sister or stay at home!" was Mudeah's standard retort if I objected. So I'd take Carol.

Every now and then I tried to summon up the courage to say, "Okay, I'll just stay home," but I didn't want to risk Mudeah's wrath, nor did I want to stay home.

"Go on, and take your little sister with you. Take her by the hand. Now that looks real sweet. And you'd better have fun!" she'd say. She always urged Carol and me to hold hands, which I tolerated only until we got out of our mother's sight. She also wanted Carol to call me "sister," which she thought was so cute. She pointed out to me that our two schoolteachers, Corinne Hayes and Flossie Buckley, and their sister, Stevetta Harrell, called one another "sister." The two older ones even called Miss Harrell, who taught high school English at Douglass, "baby" or "baby sister." (That just about made me nauseous.) I didn't even like it when they pronounced "sister" properly, stressing the "i." Carol called me "susta'," which I found almost unbearable. She recently reminded me that one time when we were in public—I think we were at school—she had called me "susta'" and I had told her rather angrily that she'd better never call me that again.

My favorite place to visit was Helen's house. She was my best friend from the time we met when she and I were about nine until my family moved to Springfield four years later. In addition I liked being around Helen's mother, Pauline, a very pretty and friendly woman. If I'd been required to bring Carol along, Pauline would invite Carol to stay with her while Helen and I played. "Carol, would you stay here and help me? Let those big ole girls go on about their business," she would say. I don't know how they spent their time, but Carol always seemed to enjoy being with Pauline.

Pauline was also an excellent cook. When lunch or dinner was ready, she insisted that I eat with them, despite my good-mannered protestations. "I'll tell your mother I made you eat with us," she'd say kindly, no doubt recognizing the fact that I was virtually salivating. She made the best navy bean soup I have ever eaten. Originally from Missouri, she made delicious cornbread from white cornmeal in the southern fashion. Everyone, including Helen and her brother, called Pauline "Polly." Polly sometimes even played jacks with Helen and me. She was really good at it.

Mudeah and the other women were critical of Polly because she was a newcomer to the area and her behavior was somewhat unconventional for a woman in our community. Polly had borne two children out of wedlock prior to her marriage to Carl "Big Wind" Meeks. Further, she had compounded her indiscretion by giving each child the father's surname, and they had different fathers. Polly's marriage to Big Wind and her subsequent move to rural Mounds and Villa Ridge coincided with the coming of the telephone to many households, including our own. Mudeah spent untold hours talking on the telephone to our neighbors about "that gal," the derisive term she used for Polly and other women of whom she disapproved. Since we had a party line, there is no telling how many people heard her comments.

Polly also smoked, expertly exhaling smoke through her nostrils and casually flicking the ashes into an ashtray. Unlike the other women, who wore dresses regardless of the situation, she frequently wore jeans, not only when working in the field but also around the house and even when she went into town. And Polly liked to drink beer. She and her husband often had quart bottles of it in the refrigerator, just like Grandma Bessie and Uncle Curtis. Sometimes Polly and Big Wind even went to the Southern Illinois Nite Club in Mounds, a nightclub where they drank and danced. As big as Big Wind was, he was reputed to be a really good dancer. Real light on his feet, they said. Frequenting a bar was something that people in Mounds associated with men and street women. Nice women weren't even supposed to look into a bar. When they passed one, they were supposed to modestly avert their eyes. But Polly would get all gussied up in a pretty dress and sling-back shoes, put on makeup, and go out and "kick up her heels."

Sometimes I wondered whether Mudeah and the other women weren't critical of Polly because they were jealous of her. She was pretty, young, and vivacious, and she liked to have a good time. Although Mudeah was pretty herself and only ten years older than Polly, she seemed a lot older. Mudeah was also much more restrained in her physical appearance. She never wore flashy clothes or makeup—except for a little lipstick—or tossed her head back when she laughed. And she never, ever went into a bar, with or without Daddy.

After Mudeah got to know Polly, which didn't take long because both she and Polly were very gregarious, she really liked her. The two of them visited back and forth, but adult women had little time for socializing, so they didn't do this often. But Mudeah no longer referred to her as "that gal," and she no longer said anything about the children's paternity. Even during the period of initial disapproval, Mudeah didn't hold Polly's presumed transgressions against her children. That's how white folks did, we'd heard. They'd refuse to even acknowledge their own kin if they had been sufficiently shamed by them. Thus, Mudeah never indicated that I shouldn't be friends with Helen. Her point apparently was to admonish us that certain behavior was not acceptable. At this time in my life, she could have saved her breath, I thought, because I couldn't imagine doing anything as nasty as what people had to do in order to have a baby under any set of circumstances, much less with a man who wasn't even my husband! Larry and June had told me all about that in our whispered conversations in the barn. Later, I discovered that they hadn't exactly gotten all the facts straight, but at the time, since they were about twelve and thirteen, we all thought they knew about these things. We were all thoroughly disgusted when we found out what shocking things perfectly respectable people, like our own parents, had done. It was called "sex," Larry and June had said, admonishing me not to use the term around Daddy, Mudeah, or any other adult.

The most memorable visits to Helen's were the ones when I went alone. Those were the times when I could do things that weren't allowed at home because I didn't have anyone to tell off on me. That was in all likelihood the reason Mudeah permitted Carol to tag along with me.

One time when I visited Helen, her cute brother Lionel, whom we also called Lonnie, was riding bareback on a horse, just like the Indians in the westerns. Helen and I begged him to let us ride, too. When he objected that we didn't know how to ride without a saddle, we both lied and insisted that we did. "You'll fall off and hurt yourself," he warned.

"Oh, no. I've ridden bareback lots of times," we both claimed. We eventually wore down his resistance, so he let us take turns climbing on the horse behind him. Helen went first and acquitted herself very nicely. Indeed, I began to wonder whether perhaps she had ridden bareback lots of times. Then it was my turn. With a bit of difficulty, I finally climbed onto the horse and firmly held onto Lionel. He walked the horse slowly around the pasture. Everything went fine at first. Suddenly the animal made a rather sharp turn, perhaps to avoid stepping in a rut, and I began to lean to one side. Although Lionel tried to help me to remain upright, I slid off the horse and with a solid "Thud!" I hit the ground hard. The impact practically knocked the wind out of me, but I didn't want to admit that I was in pain. I'd already shamed myself miserably by falling, so I didn't want to make matters worse. Besides, I was afraid that Lonnie would never again allow me to ride with him. I bought a little extra time for myself by pretending that I'd found the whole experience very funny. Laughing heartily, I lay on the ground as though too tickled to stand. After initial skepticism on Helen's and Lonnie's parts, they began to laugh also. Then I jumped up energetically, claiming that I wanted to get back on the horse. Mercifully Lonnie said it was time to take the horse back to his grandfather. I tried not to limp or to look relieved as Helen and I walked back to her house, probably to play something less taxing like jump rope or jacks.

During another visit to Helen's, she and I and Lonnie went for a swim in their pond. Lonnie was the only one of the three of us who knew how to swim. Helen and I both claimed that we could swim "a little," but neither of us knew the first thing about it. Since colored people were usually not allowed in public pools and we didn't know of any private ones, we'd never even seen anyone swim. Only in the movies and on television. We bravely and fool-ishly went into the pond, wading deeper and deeper into the murky water until it reached nearly to our chins. My only real fear was of getting my hair wet, thereby alerting Mudeah to the fact that I'd been swimming. We played in the water for a long time, finally emerging when it was time for me to go home.

Sometimes I marvel at the fact that I never sustained serious in-jury or that I didn't inadvertently kill myself during these danger-ous escapades. Even more miraculous was the fact that Mudeah and Daddy never found out about most of them. Their wrath and the inevitable whuppin' were more to be feared than any other con-sequences of our actions.

Other less dangerous summer recreation included chasing but-terflies during the day and lightning bugs after dark. We could spend hours at either activity. For some reason, Larry and June liked catching the lightning bugs, which some people called "fireflies," but not the butterflies. The latter they apparently thought of as a "girl" activity, so Carol and I were on our own. When we caught butterflies Carol and I would tie one end of a piece of string around them and hold on to the other end, similar to flying a kite or hold-ing a helium-filled toy balloon. After a while we'd untie the but-terflies and, somewhat the worse for wear, they would fly away high over our heads as we waved good-bye. We'd put the lightning bugs into a jar and watch them light up the night. Sometimes we would cruelly rip their iridescent hind ends away and smear them on our arms and legs, admiring ourselves as we too glowed in the dark.

Softball was a favorite summertime sport, even though we usu-ally didn't have a ball. The best substitute we could provide most times was an old sock stuffed with rags. A stick served as the bat. With a sock-ball hit by a stick, it was difficult to get more than a base hit; a home run was virtually impossible. Sometimes the "ball" would come apart, and we had to call a time-out in order to repair it. Bases were whatever was available—a bare spot in the grass, a piece of cardboard, or a tree. We were very skilled at improvising.

Larry and June made stilts of old lumber. The stilts consisted of a pair of long pole-like sticks that were perhaps five or six feet in length. My brothers made a little wedge or foothold about one and one-half to two feet from the bottom of each pole, permitting us to add that amount to our heights. Each of us in turn would grab hold of the top of the stilts, place our feet at the appropriate places, and walk around until we lost our balance and fell.

We also made walkie-talkies from old tin cans connected by string. Two people many yards apart were supposed to be able to communicate by means of this device, just like in the spy movies. We generally started out a good distance apart, but slowly we had to get closer and closer together before we could hear each other. "I can hear you!" one would cry triumphantly. Usually this was when the two were so close that they could have heard each other without benefit of the walkie-talkie.

The carnival came to town once a year, and we began begging Mudeah and Daddy well in advance to take us. The entire family would pile into the car and drive into Mounds. Daddy and Mudeah would stroll around together, usually with the youngest children in tow. Or sometimes they would drop us off at the carnival and return later for us. Meanwhile they'd visit the Griggsbys, Brookses, or other friends who lived in or near Mounds. Larry, June, Carol, and I were permitted to walk around without adult supervision for a couple of hours. I, of course, had to keep up with Carol. Sometimes we ran into friends and wandered around with them.

We each had a little money saved from our summer farmwork to spend at the carnival. I recall trying to decide what was worthy of my hard-earned money. There were many good things to eat—candy apples, ice cream, peanuts, popcorn, cotton candy, hot dogs, and occasionally saltwater taffy, my favorite. The rides were lots of fun, and I usually went on two or three of them—more if I could afford it. The games of chance interested me a lot, but I had noticed that people rarely won the large stuffed animals and other items prominently displayed in the booths. The winner usually got a small item kept inconspicuously under the counter and scarcely larger than the palm of one's hand. A few people meandered about proudly carrying their huge prizes, but that was a rare sight.

The tent with the "freaks" both attracted and repelled me. They advertised human anomalies, such as the alligator boy, the tattooed man, the bearded lady, the five-hundred-pound laughing woman, the dog-faced boy, and the two-headed baby. Although often tempted to go inside, I never did due to the high price of admission, the fear of what I might see, and my parents' hints that it was both a waste of money and an exploitation of unfortunate people.

The item I coveted most—for years it was the same one—was a string of colorful glass beads that looked like large bugle beads alternated with round ones. The beads were given as prizes for a number of games, including one where steel claws on little steam shovels were cranked high above a field of lavish prizes: diamond watches and rings, gold bracelets and necklaces, fountain pens on silver chains, and many other prizes. The player tried to maneuver the claw to pick up one of the items and then place it into a small tray, but one usually got either nothing at all or a cheap little toy. Although occasionally I attempted to win the glass beads, I never was successful in my efforts. It seemed as though every girl I knew at Lovejoy Grade School had a strand of those beads. Mudeah said that the beads were tacky and cheap and that only a floozy would wear them in public. Sometimes she made it seem as though the floozies had all the fun. They hung out in nightclubs drinking beer and highballs, danced with men who were not their husbands, smoked cigarettes, and wore bright nail polish and lipstick, flashy clothes, and beautiful glass beads! Although that's what I thought, I knew better than to say anything like that to Mudeah.

Although summers could be a lot of fun, they were also the time when our work was most intense: hoeing, harvesting, canning, and many other seasonal chores commanded our attention, leaving limited time for recreation. Everyone's participation was essential to the family's survival, so for the most part we children did our share without a lot of complaints.

Chitterlings in Winter

Daddy and our neighbors slaughtered hogs in winter. They killed the hog by first knocking it in the head to stun it and then slitting its throat. Then they stuck it in a big barrel full of scalding water to loosen the hair so they could remove it. Next they hung it up by its hind legs as the blood drained into a huge tub. After the hog was secured in this position, they cut its belly from its neck to its hind legs. With a gurgling sound, the internal organs fell out of the body cavity and into the tub. The tub full of entrails was taken inside where Mudeah and the women waited to process them.

The part that I recall most vividly is the cleaning of the intestines for chitterlings. The women removed most of the waste by squishing it out of one end. Then they cut the intestine lengthwise with a knife and removed the remaining residue. The combination of the sight and smell of all this was nauseating. Yet, the women laughed and talked as they worked. They discussed ways of cooking the chitterlings so that the smell could be contained. Impossible, I thought, convinced that chitterlings would smell terrible no matter what a person did to try to prevent it. They talked about making sausage, pickled pigs' feet, smoked jowl, crackling bread, and other pork dishes. Hams, shoulders, and other large pieces would be sugar cured and hung in the smokehouse.

By this time, Carol and I were thoroughly disgusted. We always felt sorry for the animal that had been slaughtered, and we were revolted by the smell. We wore folded handkerchiefs tied over our noses in the fashion of cowboys, and we breathed through our mouths to avoid smelling the chitterlings and other organ meats. Then we begged to be permitted to go visit friends. This request was usually honored, with the usual admonition to "be home before dark." Our experience and revulsion in witnessing the slaughter of the hogs and the cleaning of the chitterlings may explain why to this day neither of us has ever ventured to taste chitterlings, the preeminent soul food.

Winters were fun, also. Winter meant frozen ponds where we could go ice skating with our friends. The pond across the road on the Greens' place was the most frequent site for such forays. Larry, June, and I, as well as several Rileys or Rices, would climb over the fence into the cow pasture where the pond was located. Usually it didn't get cold enough to freeze the water very solidly, so it was rarely more than a few inches thick. But that didn't restrain us any more than did our parents' repeated warnings about the dangers of skating on thin ice. As soon as the pond appeared to be frozen, we would be out there on it, several of us at a time. After only a few minutes, ten or fifteen at most, we would hear a loud "Crack!" as the ice started to break. Giggling and running, we quickly scrambled to the side of the pond. Miraculously none of us ever fell through the ice. In fact, I don't even recall anyone as much as getting wet feet.

Winter also meant that we could select a tree for Christmas from among the many evergreens growing wild on our own and neighboring farms. When Daddy went with us, he insisted that we pick one of our own trees, but when we children were old enough to go alone, we chose whichever tree we liked regardless of where it was growing. Before the holidays we'd stake out several trees as possibilities and then return a week or so before Christmas to bring one home, hoping that no one had beaten us to our favorite. That our choice was usually asymmetrical or thin on one side didn't matter. The bad part wouldn't show. We had to put it in the corner, due to limited space. Besides, we didn't have enough decorations for an entire tree, so we could only decorate about two-thirds of it. Once we brought it home, Daddy put it in a stand and then we were ready to decorate. We used ornaments and lights that Mudeah stored away from one Christmas to the next. It was fun to watch each year as she brought them out and we saw the familiar pieces once again.

The Christmas tree lights were old sets purchased in the post–World War II era, when they were wired in a series. This meant that if one bulb in a string burned out, the entire set failed to light up when it was plugged into the outlet. Then Daddy would have to figure out which bulb or bulbs were inoperative. It might take anywhere from a few minutes to an hour or more to get all of the lights working. Even so, we knew that others would burn out before we took the tree down after New Year's Day. Despite the frustration of trying to keep the lights on, we enjoyed the way they illuminated the tree so beautifully. Next we would add the popcorn we had strung in garlands, carefully draping them around the tree. Sometimes we made paper chains of construction paper, like the teachers at school had taught us to do. Next came the ornaments, and finally the tinsel icicles.

Now we were ready to wrap the presents. Mudeah routinely saved the wrapping paper and bows—both new and used—from one year to the next. Presents were usually inexpensive or practical things, such as clothing, shoes, and school supplies. Sometimes Santa Claus added presents on Christmas Eve, but his contributions were often modest, also.

On Christmas Eve Daddy and Mudeah made us go to bed early "so Santa can come," they said. I sometimes worried that Santa would attempt to come down our chimney and end up in one of the two stoves attached to it; there was no fireplace from which he could emerge safely as in the movies. Daddy reassured me that Santa would know better.

"But how will he get in?" I'd insist.

"He'll come in the door," Daddy replied. Come in through the door? I thought. It didn't seem quite right for Santa to do that, but then again it was better than ending up in the stove.

Before we went to bed, we made sure that Santa had a big piece of cake waiting for him. We wanted to leave him a glass of milk, too, but Daddy and Mudeah said we could leave it in the refrigerator and Santa could pour himself a glassful. On Christmas morning we children got up early, quietly creeping into the living room to see what Santa had left. Mudeah and Daddy must have heard us because their bedroom was next to the living room, with only a curtain strung across the doorway to provide privacy and to muffle the sound. They never objected to the early Christmas morning preview of gifts, however. We didn't open wrapped presents, however; we only looked at those that Santa had left unwrapped under the tree. Usually we knew in advance what our presents were, having found them when Daddy and Mudeah were away from home. But we always hoped that Santa had left something that we hadn't discovered before Christmas. One year I got a six-shooter and a doll, two very appropriate gifts because I liked both traditional boys' and traditional girls' toys. Another year I got a nurse's kit. Still another year I got a wristwatch with a dial that glowed in the dark. We didn't get the more expensive presents like bicycles, or the frivolous ones like walkie-talkies. We usually didn't ask Santa for these things, although we wanted them, because we'd heard that Santa brought things depending upon your parents' ability to pay for them. At least that's what Larry and June said. That news didn't upset me nearly as much as when they announced a year or so later that there was no Santa Claus!

Santa always left oranges and apples, as well as assorted nuts and hard candies. We each had little bowls of these special treats, which we got to hoard in our room. Some of us could make our Christmas fruits, nuts, and candy last for a week or more, while others ate them within a day or two. Christmas dinner was a real feast: baked chicken with cornbread dressing, mashed potatoes, gravy, candied sweet potatoes, homemade rolls. There were two or three desserts, such as sweet potato pie and coconut cake. Daddy usually made the latter because it was one of his specialties. After Christmas dinner, we might go visiting friends and neighbors or they would visit us. It was customary for people to share food and little treats with "company" during these visits.

Another special treat that we had, especially in winter, was sassafras tea. This was made from the roots of a tree that grew wild and abundantly on the farm. Larry and June would dig the roots in the fall, dry them, and store them for later use. Some people claimed that sassafras tea had curative powers, especially for colds. Occasionally Daddy and Mudeah would give it to us when we had a cold, but I'm not sure that either of them was convinced that it was medicinal. They probably just knew that we all liked it a lot. During illness was one of the few times that our parents were apt to be a bit indulgent with us.

When it snowed, we sometimes had our favorite winter treat: snow ice cream. We children would start to beg Mudeah to make it as soon as we spotted the first snowflake. "Mudeah, will you make snow ice cream?" we'd ask. The answer was always the same. "Let me see if I have the ingredients." Usually she did, but there was also the cautionary note, "We'll have to see if it snows enough." She liked for the snow to be several inches deep so that we could scoop it up carefully with a large spoon, without scraping the car or whatever we collected it from. On those times when Mudeah made snow ice cream, we got to eat as much of it as we wanted.

Winter had its hazards, too. Winter meant half-frozen fingers for Mudeah and Daddy, and later Larry and June, when they milked the cows. They would come into the house afterward and warm their hands and bodies by the fire, turning first their fronts and then their backs to the fire. Winter also meant that we had to take our baths—usually weekly affairs—beside the fire because it was too cold to do so in the bedroom where we normally bathed. Once Daddy got the job as deputy sheriff, he started taking baths two or three times a week, sometimes every other day. We kids thought this was rather wasteful because preparing to take a bath was quite a time-consuming production. First, Daddy and the boys had to haul water from a neighboring well, spring, or ditch. Sometimes we had collected enough rainwater and could avoid hauling it. Once it was collected, Mudeah poured the water into a huge cast-iron pot outside and built a fire under it. Finally, it was brought into the house and poured into a large, round metal tub, which usually hung on the side of the smokehouse.

Sometimes we shared bathwater, if the supply was low. Then the first person—usually one of the younger children, such as Carol or

Calvin—would take a bath first, saving the water when done. The next person would add a little additional hot water to warm it up a bit and then climb into the tub. We didn't like to do this because the second user's water was not very warm. Further it was rather dirty, with a residue of curdled soap around the edges. It was difficult to work up a good lather in this water; thus, the second person never felt quite clean. When I had to bathe after someone else, I'd sometimes think about how it would be when I "got big." I'd have running water—hot and cold—and I'd take long, luxurious baths in water that covered my body up to my shoulders, and I'd have lots of nice bubbles, just like the glamorous movie stars did. I'd imagine myself washing with a big, fluffy sponge and drying with a huge towel large enough to wrap all around my entire body. Then I'd put on a beautiful terry-cloth bathrobe and sit at the vanity and brush my hair with a fancy brush, which I kept on a pretty silver tray alongside a matching comb that had all its teeth.

Doing the laundry was difficult in winter, also. The hauling and heating of the water was the same as with that for bathing, but then we filled the electric washing machine with it. In the earlier days, before we had a washing machine, Mudeah used the same round tub that we bathed in and a washboard to do laundry. She also used homemade lye soap to help get things really clean the way she liked them. She considered it an embarrassment and a sign of laziness to hang laundry out to dry unless it was spotlessly clean. After washing clothes, linens, and other items, we hand-fed them though the wringer attached to the washer. A few items were starched with a concoction Mudeah made atop the gas range. Then Mudeah and I took the clothes outside and hung them on the clothesline. This was the really cold part during the winter. With bare hands we picked up each piece and secured it on the line with wooden clothespins. Our fingers would get so cold that they would turn red, and then they'd start to ache, and finally they would go numb and we could hardly feel them at all. If we were lucky, it would then be time to go back inside and prepare the next load. Sometimes when we went outside to collect the dry laundry, it would be stiff and frozen.

The Spies Who Came In from the Cold

"It's late now. You kids go on to bed," Daddy said. It was about 9:00 or 9:30, not that late in my estimation, but I didn't dare say so. Carol, the youngest, was already asleep. Larry, June, and I left the cozy living room, lingering a moment in the warm kitchen before going into the unheated bedroom that the three of us shared.

The bedroom was small—perhaps ten feet square. Four large pieces of furniture jammed inside dominated the room. Larry and June's double bed and my twin-sized one took up most of one wall, leaving barely enough room to walk between the two. My bed was the one closest to the door. At its foot was a desk with an ancient typewriter on the end with a kneehole. We used the other end for the little enameled washbasin, where we took our morning washups. For many years, Grandmommy's old chifforobe containing some of her personal possessions stood at the end of Larry and June's bed.

In one corner of the bedroom was a closet of sorts. Although the closet was tiny, our small wardrobes weren't crowded. By day, at least, this little nook was a closet. I knew because I could see the blouses, skirts, dresses, slacks, and shirts. By night, however, it became the home of assorted ghosts who sprang to life after dark—usually when I was trying to get to sleep or when I awakened in the middle of the night. Then I covered my head with my favorite red-and-blue quilt, taking comfort from its familiar soft folds, and tried not to scream for Daddy to come to my rescue. Once the boys were asleep, I could forget about any help from them. They both slept like they were dead, no doubt from having been enchanted by some supernatural being.

The wind whistled between gaps and knotholes in the floorboards. The brick siding helped to make the walls fairly airtight, but the cold air found its way through the small gaps around the windows and doors. Usually Daddy and Larry and June put plastic over the windows during the winter, which helped a lot. Of course, then we could barely see out of the windows.

Larry, June, and I quickly undressed and put on our nightclothes, modestly keeping our backs to each other in the dark, cold room. We pulled off our shoes and socks last, trying to avoid contact with the splintery wood floor as long as possible. Only the linoleum floor in the kitchen was colder than this one. Sometimes I left my socks on in bed, but Mudeah seemed to know the very nights to come in and look at the neatly stacked pile of dirty clothing and to demand, "Shirley, where are your socks? You know you're not supposed to sleep in them. They'll make your feet get all sweaty and stinky." The last thing I worried about during the winter was having sweaty feet, stinky or not, but talking back to Mudeah was not prudent. In fact, it was downright stupid!

Hopping into bed, we slipped between icy covers and pulled the quilts securely up to our chins, farther if it was particularly cold. Each bed had several quilts, mostly handmade by Mudeah. In really cold weather these were supplemented by as many others as we had. We even got to use the pretty new quilts Mudeah had just made then. During the coldest nights, coats would be heaped atop the quilts. The latter addition was apt to make it all but impossible to rest comfortably as one struggled in vain to keep all body parts under the assorted layers. Our torsos were reasonably warm, but a leg or arm carelessly extended could get cold very quickly. Thus we slept in the fetal position with knees drawn up virtually to our chins, trying not to move out of the small warm spot each of us had created. As the night wore on, the coats might begin to shift due either to their own weight or to a movement on our part, and then suddenly all the covers would slip off the bed and onto the floor. The big problem here was that it was virtually impossible to cover oneself without assistance. So we'd have to help each other or, as a last resort, summon Mudeah or Daddy, neither of whom was happy to go through the entire covering-the-kids scenario again.

A final problem was the need to make a late-night trip to the outhouse. Mudeah never permitted chamber pots, or what some folks called "slop jars," in the house, regarding them as old-fashioned and disgusting—which they were, but they were sure convenient on a cold winter's night. Thus, we'd have to go outside if we felt the call of nature. We were supposed to go all the way to the little toilet, fifteen to twenty yards behind the house, but we often went only to the side of the house. More than once a car coming over the little hill or pulling into the driveway caught me unaware and I scrambled away, trying to avoid detection. It was a very tricky feat to walk while squatting, without getting anything on either my clothing or my shoes.

Sometimes when we were in bed, the boys and I could hear Mudeah and Daddy talking. We listened carefully, trying to make out what they were saying. If it wasn't too cold in the room, one of us might lurk near the bedroom door and then report back to the other two. But if it was cold, practicality outweighed curiosity and we stayed in bed trying to keep warm.

Daddy and Mudeah often talked about the farm. The addition of more cows and expanding into a major dairy operation was a favorite topic. They talked about enlarging the barn, building more stalls for the milking, and even purchasing milking machines. Mudeah would no longer have to help with the milking and the other outdoor chores. She would spend her time doing things in the house: sewing, which was her favorite; canning; and freezing stuff in the new deep freezer they talked about getting. She'd probably get a new sewing machine, too, one with a lot of fancy attachments, even more than Virgie Wilkerson's had. She'd get a Singer, no doubt.

The farm they had in mind was bigger than anything we'd seen in Mounds or thereabouts. Or at least my mental picture of it was. It was like a picture book: We'd have a real nice house, with a white picket fence all around it. There would be a swing set and a sliding board in the back yard. And we'd each get a new bicycle. Larry and June wouldn't even have to share one. Carol could get one of those cute little ones with the training wheels. And when Calvin got big enough, he could have a fancy tricycle with a horn and streamers on the handlebars.

As I lay in bed thinking about the farm we would have some day, my plans became more and more elaborate. We'd have indoor plumbing, especially a bathroom like we'd had in Springfield. I'd have my own room. I wanted a canopy bed and a fancy vanity with little drawers and a triple-fold mirror and an upholstered chair, too, but all that seemed too much to expect. Besides, I didn't want to be greedy or selfish. My present bed with a nice linen chest or a dresser would be just fine. With the money I saved from picking beans, cotton, strawberries, and other things, maybe I could buy one of those little dressing tables I'd seen in the Sears catalog. Perhaps Mudeah would make me one of those ruffled skirts to go around it if I bought the material for it myself. And maybe I could get matching curtains. I didn't really need a mirror for it immediately. I could save my money and get that later.

Maybe we'd even get a horse. Not one of those ill-tempered, clunky workhorses, but a nice, gentle horse for riding. Then we could stop trying to ride the cows, which never worked particularly well anyway. It was a lot of fun, but cows really didn't take to it very well. Just as we had gotten on one, the darned cow would take off running and we'd try to get her to stop before it spoiled her milk. Then, too, we were always afraid that Daddy would catch us, and then we'd be in big trouble. He might even whup the boys. And he'd probably yell at me that he was going to wring my "scrawny little neck." Although my scrawny little neck stayed intact, I was always afraid that this would be the time that he would make good on this threat. I had never seen a little girl who'd had her neck wrung, only chickens.

Mudeah was the first to get up in the mornings. She put on an old housecoat and then built a fire in the potbellied stove in the kitchen. The living room stove would be lit later, perhaps when Mudeah sat down at the quilting frame to work on her latest quilt. When we became more affluent, we got gas stoves in the living room and the kitchen, but the two bedrooms remained unheated. If it had been particularly cold during the night, the water in the bucket on the kitchen sink might have a shell of ice over it. Or worse, it might be frozen nearly solid.

Mudeah made coffee on the gas range, which had replaced the wood cookstove soon after we had moved to Mounds from Springfield. I often awakened to the delicious aroma and the faint, comfortable sound of coffee percolating. Children generally were not given coffee in our family. Occasionally we were allowed a sip or two with lots of sugar and cream, which rendered it scarcely recognizable as coffee. The old folks admonished us that, "Coffee will make kids black inside." Although we sometimes wondered whether it would have this effect on adults too, or why we should care if we were black inside, we didn't dare raise questions. To have done so would have meant that we were questioning adult authority and wisdom, which was not tolerated in our household, nor in any others with which we were familiar. I'd lie in bed and think about how when I got big I'd have a cup of coffee in the morning. I'd pour it into a saucer, blow on it to cool it, and then slurp it—just like the old folks did. For some reason, Daddy and Mudeah never did it that way. They simply drank their coffee directly out of a cup. Both were pretty good slurpers, though. Years later when I tried coffee, I was so disappointed because it didn't taste nearly as good as it smelled.

Daddy was the next to get out of bed. Then he and Mudeah would get dressed and go to the barn to milk the cows. Later, when Larry and June were older, they took over this task. I never learned to milk a cow because I was afraid that I would accidentally hurt the cow's teats. Besides, I was disgusted by how soft the teats felt. We had an assortment of dairy cattle, some with calves. I recall a Jersey, a Guernsey, and a white-faced cow, but there were others as well. Once one of the cows had a beautiful fawn-colored calf with a white star on her forehead and big beautiful eyes. She reminded me of Bambi in the Disney movie that we had seen at the theater in Mounds, so I named her Bambi. I used to pet her, feed her hay, and talk to her. One day Daddy sold Bambi. I understood why. The little cow was a purebred Jersey, soon to be both a good milk cow and a good breeder—and we needed the money. Nonetheless, I was devastated. I can still picture them leading Bambi out to the road to take her away on a truck. After that, I never wanted a pet calf again, nor would I give one a name, nor did I pay any special attention to any other farm animal. Except for our dog, Boy Scout.

After the milking, Daddy took the milk to the smokehouse to separate the cream from the milk, placing both cream and milk in huge five- and ten-gallon milk cans when he was done. Later he would set the cans from both the previous night's and the current morning's milking out by the road or take them down to "the corner," where the milkman picked them up and took them to the dairy company in Carbondale. Although modest, the money from the milk and cream was one of the few sources of regular income that we had until Daddy got the job as deputy sheriff.

Meanwhile Mudeah had returned to the house to prepare breakfast. It was now time for us kids to get out of bed, wash up, get dressed, and brush our teeth. By the time we were ready for school, a hot meal was on the table: oatmeal and prunes; fried potatoes with onions and ham, sausage, or bacon; scrambled eggs and biscuits; occasionally cold cornflakes, every now and then with bananas; rice with gravy, maybe even with some kind of meat. Warm, sweetened blackberries in their own juices with oven toast was my favorite. Mudeah could make even the plainest of dishes very tasty. Thus, breakfast was usually delicious.

After breakfast Mudeah combed my hair and later Carol's, when she got big enough to go to school. This was always a traumatic experience because Mudeah didn't play when it came to combing hair. Mudeah didn't play, period. She pulled the comb straight through our long hair, scarcely slowing down when it snagged a kink or a piece of lint. Not surprisingly, our combs usually lost most of their teeth within a few months, and my sister and I lost a lot of hair. Mudeah brushed vigorously, often with the stiff bristles of the brush raking across our foreheads and ears. The occasional "Ouch!" that escaped our lips was apt to be greeted with a cold, "Shut up! I'm not hurting you!" Continual protestation, which Mudeah interpreted as disrespect for her, was likely to be rewarded with a crack across the head from the comb or the brush. Our only salvation came when Daddy was in the room. Then Carol or I played the situation for all it was worth.

"Ow," we would whimper, just loudly enough to be heard.

"What's the matter, gal?" Daddy would ask gruffly, though rather sympathetically.

"She's hurting me," would come the response from a now pouting daughter. Sometimes we would even burst into tears at this point. This really got Daddy's sympathy. He never could stand to see one of his daughters crying.

"You're hurting that gal! Don't be so rough!" he'd snap at Mudeah. This was a mixed blessing. While she was likely to be more gentle at this point, Mudeah would also be angry at both father and daughter. She rarely vented her ire directly at Daddy, but when he left the house, she was sure to retaliate against Carol or me. We hoped she'd be done with our hair and we'd be on our way to school at this point. Between clenched teeth she would deliver her routine threat.

"You'd better stop clowning in front of your Daddy. I'm going to whip your little butt next time!" That was enough to bring a person back to reality. Mudeah didn't make a lot of idle threats, we knew. A second transgression in a short period of time was a fairly sure ticket to getting a whuppin', complete with her constant preaching about the error of our ways. Further, she'd recall every other transgression since the last whuppin', laying it on for that as well.

"Go get me a switch. I'm going to whip your ass!" This was the point of no return. At that juncture the best thing a person could do was to go out and quickly find her a good switch—one large enough that she wouldn't think we had "taken her for a Goddamned fool," yet small enough that she couldn't kill us with it. One time Carol had to get her own switch, and she returned with a huge locust stick. It was so big and full of thorns that I was afraid Mudeah would really hurt her. With true sisterly love, I carefully grabbed the stick with one hand and Carol with the other and yanked her around to the side of the house.

"This is too big. And it's got thorns," I said, tossing the stick into some tall weeds. Meanwhile, Mudeah had witnessed the entire scene and had been touched by it. Or perhaps she just wasn't in the mood any longer to administer a whuppin'. Sometimes she seemed content merely to scare the hell out of us. "Gal, you'd better go on to school," she'd said to me as Carol scrambled into the house.

On weekends Larry did a lot of practice shooting with his BB gun, using birds as targets. After killing the birds, he hid them under bricks, piles of debris, or in other places in the hope that Carol and I wouldn't find them. Having seen *Bambi*, I objected to hunting in general, but especially to the killing of the really cute animals, such as deer, birds, squirrels, or rabbits. Sometimes Carol or I found Larry's kills. When we discovered a little dead bird, Carol and I had a funeral to give the deceased a proper send-off to its afterlife. Looking very solemn, the two of us buried the bird in the yard and decorated the grave with wildflowers. Then we sang songs, and sometimes we even cried.

7

With a Child's Heart

Family Reunion: The Children and the Children's Children

The children enjoy the family reunion as much as the adults do. In fact, in some cases our children are adults. Michael, Fae, Nicole, and Ramirez are all over twenty-one. The Motley siblings have few children: Larry has one child, Vanessa; John has two, Michael and Nicole; I have a daughter, Fae; Carol's son is Ramirez; Calvin has Damon and Aaron; and Mildred has a fictive son, Jason. In addition, Fae has two children, Krystle and Kraig. Ramirez became a father on November 14, 1995, to Akilah. Each of these children and grandchildren has attended the family reunion.

The children really like to hear stories about people whom they know personally—themselves, their cousins, their parents, and others. Further, these vignettes make them aware that their experiences are a part of family history, too. They are connected to the extended family. Perhaps they will tell these same stories, as well as others based on their own experiences, to their children and their grandchildren.

The children sometimes take advantage of the family gatherings to find out about their parents' earlier transgressions. "Aunt Shirley," Vanessa says sweetly, "would you tell us a story?" She listens attentively and appreciatively to one or two short vignettes, and then she moves in to address her real issue. "Tell us about Daddy." She likes the story about his sneaking food and going into the woods to cook it. "Daddy!" she says, sharply reproaching him as though he'd just yesterday committed the misdeed. Larry looks at me with the

"Oh, you're telling her about that again!" look. But neither he nor the other parents mind these stories—they tell them, too.

We Motleys take a good deal of pride in our children, believing them all to be extraordinarily intelligent, good-looking, and witty. They are also generally well behaved, even though most of us do not use the technique of whuppin' that we experienced as children and that we all hated so much. "When I have children, I'm not going to whup them," we'd each pledged years ago. We are also proud that our children are free to ask questions, make comments, and otherwise participate in adult conversation. That's the way kids learn, we all agree. When we assemble at the family reunion, the children participate in most activities, including playing cards, storytelling, and general discussion. They are rarely shooed out of the room while we talk about "adult" things.

One evening we are gathered in the kitchen, the usual assembly spot for the cardplayers who meet each day to play bid whist and to laugh and talk. The mood is festive. Everyone is having a wonderful time. Vanessa looks curiously from one family member to another. Finally she speaks. Accustomed to children talking freely, we smilingly encourage her, giving her our undivided attention. "Daddy, Aunt Shirley, Uncle John, and Grandpa . . . all have big noses," she observes. The smiles quickly fade from our faces, as we stare at her in embarrassment, especially those of us who have big noses. She continues, "Aunt Mildred and I have little noses!" For a moment we are all quiet, stunned into silence.

"You must have put her up to that shit!" Larry exclaims, looking accusingly at Mildred. Finally, others speak, laughing about our noses and about Vanessa's outspokenness. We tease each other about the shocked expressions on each of our faces.

The next day some of us decide to go shopping. We go to one of our favorite off-price stores, Marshall's. Vanessa accompanies me into the dressing area as I try on various garments. Perhaps I am looking for something to camouflage my big nose. As I step from the dressing room into the waiting area immediately outside the door, Vanessa is waiting to give me her opinion of my attire. A three-way mirror is there as well, so I survey myself critically as she looks at me intently.

"Aunt Shirley, you don't have a big nose," my niece declares very sincerely, even sweetly. She speaks as though someone other than herself has indicated that I do, in fact, have a big nose. There is no recognition that she was the only person who had said, just the night before, that I had a big nose! I glance around the dressing area. None of our other relatives are around to hear Vanessa declare, in contrast to her earlier observation, that I don't have a big nose. Where is everyone else? Why don't I have any witnesses to Vanessa's change of heart?

It reminds me of an earlier incident years ago when my daughter, Fae, had said to me, "Mom, you would look like Dihann Carol, if you didn't have such a big nose." Years later, when I was still whining about her comment, she claimed that she did not mean that I have an unusually large nose, only that Dihann Carol has a particularly small one.

The children request other stories about clever things they each said or did. Because Vanessa was the first one to ask, we tell another story about her. We recall that when Vanessa was first learning to talk, we were rather concerned as to whether she would know that some of the things her father said privately were not properly repeated in public. He swears profusely, often punctuating his words with "motherfucker." Yet Vanessa has generally not used this term or other profanities.

One day, Aunt Mildred asked Vanessa, who was about two years old, where her tape recorder was. Vanessa replied, in a very deadpan fashion, "I broke the motherfucker." Everyone was stunned and a little embarrassed. Never before had Vanessa said "motherfucker."

Larry was proud. Grinning, he said, "You know, she used the word so appropriately."

We turn our attention to Kraig, repeating one of his favorite tales. I recall that Kraig, usually an affable child, was angry once with his sister, Krystle, for something she had done. She apologized, "Sorry, Kraig."

"Sorry, sorry," he mimicked. "I'm tired of that sorry bullshit!"

"Grandma, did you hear what he said? He shouldn't say that, should he?" Krystle responded, looking at me with horror.

"No, he shouldn't say that," I responded reproachfully to Kraig, while trying not to burst into laughter. He was always so tolerant of her that I was as surprised by his negative response as by his profanity. Since he didn't normally use expletives, I thought it best not to make a big deal of it.

We talk about the other children and grandchildren, recalling clever stories about them, also. "Mildred, do you remember the time you hung up on John?" someone asks.

"I knew one of you was going to mention that," Mildred responds as we all begin to think of that story.

Someone answered the telephone, no doubt waiting with one hand on it until the second ring so as not to seem overly anxious. It was John, calling from Chicago. We passed the telephone around, each spending a few minutes chatting excitedly with him. Then it was Mildred's turn to talk.

"Hello," she said.

"No, I don't know who you are," she continued after a pause.

"Don't you know?" she concluded after another pause.

We all stood around, smiling expectantly. Then Mildred did the unexpected. She hung up the telephone.

"Why did you hang up?" someone asked.

"Well, *I* didn't know who he was and *he* didn't know who he was, so I hung up," she said emphatically. We all laughed. Mildred had no patience with the "Do you know who this is?" routine of her older brother.

I like to tease Mildred about the recurring dream she had when she was about four. She was constantly pursued by an old, evil witch. It ended with her saving herself in the same way each time. "I flew to Shirley." Sometimes I say to her now, "Fly on over here to me, Mil."

Now it is Ramirez's turn to be teased about his childhood escapades. Since childhood, Ramirez has had a chauvinistic streak—

or perhaps it's self-confidence. When he was only eight or nine, he and I had a discussion about the chronology of Christmas and New Year's Day. He maintained that New Year's Day came a week before Christmas, while I contended that Christmas was before New Year's. He recalled assorted personal experiences that proved his point. I produced a calendar and showed him the dates of each of the holidays. After studying the calendar for a moment, he said, "Well, they must have changed it."

A few years later this chauvinism—or self-confidence—was revealed in another situation. I offered to teach him to play racquetball, which I had played for several months. His response clearly indicated that he expected to win. Puzzled, I inquired, "Do you already know how to play?"

He simply answered, "No." Obviously, then, he expected to win even though he knew nothing about the game. I resolved that I had to win for the sake of my sex.

When Fae Was a Little Girl

"Who picked all those flowers!" I demanded, looking at the beautiful heap of flowers mixed with sand lying in the entry. A mound of red and yellow with bright green accents had been dumped on the floor. I looked angrily at the two four-year-olds, Fae and her friend Steven. A quick glance between the two of them revealed my daughter as the culprit and Steven as her loving accomplice. She opened her mouth to speak and then pointed accusingly at Steven.

"Steven!" she shouted, hoping to save herself. His eyes widened in surprise and horror. He stared at her in disbelief, but he didn't protest his innocence. He simply looked at her, disappointed that she would betray him, yet unwilling to reveal the truth. But I knew the truth nonetheless. I turned to my daughter.

"Fae, you picked the flowers," I said. My voice was calmer, perhaps because I had been touched by Steven's loyalty. Fae didn't protest her innocence either. "Where did you get them?" I asked.

They acknowledged what I had already come to realize: the flowers were from the yard next door, where the little white house was ringed with beautiful spring flowers. Or rather, was ringed with tulips until rather recently. I'd never met this next-door neighbor, although we did have a nodding acquaintance. I had seen her from time to time as I crossed my front lawn. Often she was working in the yard, minding her tulips. She had taken such obvious pride in them.

I wondered whether she was aware of her loss yet. Had she walked out into her yard today, planning to admire her flowers? I imagined the look of horror on her face as she discovered that she hadn't a single tulip left in her entire yard.

"You must go to the lady next door and tell her that you've picked her flowers and apologize to her," I said to Fae.

"Okay," she responded, hanging her head in shame. Why is it that children manage to look so adorable when they've done something wrong? She stood there, a picture of loveliness in her play outfit, with her long braids hanging down her back and little curls encircling her face. "I'll go with you, but you'll have to do the talking," I added softly.

Moments later we rang the doorbell of the house next door, and an elderly woman came to the door and greeted us pleasantly. I introduced myself and my erring daughter and indicated that Fae had something to tell her. We both turned to Fae.

"I picked your flowers. And I'm sorry," Fae said, managing to look entirely lovely and thoroughly innocent. She gazed up at the woman, not knowing what to expect from her.

"Oh, that's alright," the woman said very quickly and nonchalantly. She had no idea that my daughter had picked all of her flowers. She was no doubt thinking of a small bouquet. Or perhaps a large bouquet.

"I'm so sorry," I added. In all fairness, I thought, I had to tell her the extent of the matter. "I . . . I think she picked them all," I confessed. But the woman was looking at the miserable four-year-old on her doorstep. I'm not sure she even heard me.

"Oh, that's alright," she said once again. At this point, I figured that I had done my motherly duty, so I thanked the woman for her kindness and Fae and I left.

When Fae was almost six, Allan, Fae, and I moved to the new family housing complex on the beautiful, nearly three-thousand-acre campus of Southern Illinois University at Edwardsville (SIUE), about twenty miles northeast of St. Louis. Called Tower Lake Apartments, the housing site overlooked a beautiful lake with swimming and boating. It was surrounded by dense woods and rolling hills, where we periodically spotted deer, red foxes, and other wild animals. The woods were a forager's delight, with an abundance of black walnuts, blackberries, apples, and other fruits and nuts. The apartment was within walking distance of the central campus, where I was to begin graduate school in history in September. We remained there for two years, until June 1972, when we moved into an apartment in Edwardsville. In August 1972 I began my teaching career at Forest Park Community College in St. Louis, later renamed St. Louis Community College at Forest Park. After nine years there, I returned to SIUE, where I joined the history faculty.

Shortly after our move, the University held an official open house and dedication of the Tower Lake Apartments. The administration requested that student residents volunteer to host area dignitaries in their homes as a part of the festivities, so we volunteered to entertain guests.

We really liked our new three-bedroom apartment with its central air conditioning. We had chosen a furnished apartment, paying only $10 more a month—a total of $135, including utilities—for the use of the sparse but attractive and durable furniture. The apartment had a large, very long living room with a dining area at one end, a kitchen, and one bathroom. The bedrooms were small, but nice. Fae's bedroom window offered a view of the lake. Because our apartment was on the ground floor, it also afforded her considerable opportunity to talk with her friends, who—we were soon to discover—sometimes stationed themselves outside her window.

An Illinois state senator-elect from East St. Louis was our guest on the day of the open house. A former Illinois assemblyman, the

Senator had recently been elected to the State Senate, but he had not yet taken his seat. He was an attractive man, affable if somewhat self-absorbed. He was a brown-skinned African American of medium height, with a stocky build. Perhaps his most striking feature was his black hair, graying at the temples and worn slicked back with "greasy kid-stuff." His head reminded me of the old witticism, "If a fly landed on it, it would slip and break its neck in three places."

The day of the open house was beautiful, sunny, and warm, though not uncomfortably so. The preparations for the visit had gone well. I felt particularly confident and comfortable, partly because I thought that I looked really fine. I wore a short navy-and-brown dress, which looked really pretty, and I also wore a stylish new Afro-wig, which made me look a bit like Askia Ammar, my militant younger sister, known in earlier days as Carol. The meal, catered by the university, was excellent. Our visit with the senator had been very pleasant, even though he had done almost all of the talking.

Fae, who had turned six on August 17, had been a perfect child that day. Very pretty, tall and willowy with long, thick braids, she had an engaging personality and impeccable manners. She liked to read a book on etiquette called *White Gloves and Party Manners*, given to her by her Grandma Carlson, and to observe its edicts from time to time. She had made charming conversation during the senator's entire visit. When she came over to me and began to whisper, I encouraged her to speak aloud. In a nice, clear voice she announced, "Mom, why don't you take off your wig and let the senator see your real hair?"

Mortified, I gave her the universal black woman's "evil eye," a very nasty look signaling her to "Be quiet!" Does she think I'm going to take my wig off my head and say, "Oh, Senator, would you like to see my real hair?" I wondered. The senator graciously pretended not to hear and went on with another anecdote or a point of his own. After that fiasco, I was almost afraid to allow Fae to speak, lest she say something to further humiliate me.

Fae was puzzled by my angry response. Years later, she told me that she had thought that I would be pleased at her suggestion and that the senator would enjoy my demonstration. She thought it was a "neat trick" that I could transform my hairstyle from its usual soft curls into a huge Afro. In fact, she had believed that I might profusely compliment her for having made such a good suggestion.

"Someone Throwed Water on Me"

"Daddy! I didn't like it! I didn't like it at all!" Krystle angrily said to her father. She was recalling a ride she and her mother had taken at Knott's Berry Farm amusement park. The ride was a roller coaster that went inside a mountain. Its most unique feature was that at one point it plunged through water, which splashed upon the riders. Fae had really liked this part, but Krystle hadn't.

"Someone threwed water on me," Krystle told her father. He listened intently and lovingly, and successfully stifled a smile. "Daddy, would you throw water back at them?" she inquired, still angry.

"Yes," her father said earnestly, as though he were indeed going to go to Knott's Berry Farm, demand entrance to the ride, and throw water at the culprit who had offended his daughter. Comforted by this, Krystle's anger subsided and she hugged her father.

Krystle, Kraig Jr., Fae, and I had gone to Knott's Berry Farm that day. Both Fae and Krystle had really looked forward to the very ride that later had angered Krystle. We had seen an advertisement for it on television, and it had looked as if it would be fun. Kraig had dropped the four of us off at the amusement park on his way to work.

The park wasn't open yet, so we went for breakfast at a Pancake House restaurant across the street. Kraig ordered a stack of pancakes for breakfast, insisting that he could eat a full order, rather than the child's portion that the waitress had recommended. And he did. He ate every single bite and asked for more. His mother very wisely said that he shouldn't have more because then he would not have an appetite for the treats at Knott's Berry Farm.

At the park the four of us rode many rides, including the ferris wheel. Kraig and Krystle, two and three years old respectively, also rode ones for the smaller children. Finally, we came to the aforementioned water ride. Kraig did not meet the minimum height requirements for this ride, so I volunteered to stay with him. Secretly I was relieved that I had a good reason not to go on the ride. I'd had about enough fun on rides by that time. Krystle and Fae, smiling and holding hands, hurried away to line up for the ride. Later, the two returned, drenched. A smiling Fae was carrying an angry Krystle, who immediately said to me:

"Grandma, I didn't like it! I didn't like it at all! Someone throwed water on me!" I sympathized with Krystle as Fae explained what had happened, but Krystle remained furious. It was not until she told her father about the incident that she felt better about it. After all, he was going to throw water back at them.

Kraig and Matthew

When Kraig was about two years old, he liked to wear two pairs of sunglasses—one on top of the other.

"Kraig, you only need one pair of glasses," I said the first time I saw him do this. He was sitting in his infant car seat in the back of my car.

"I'm Wayne Wayne Wayne!" he protested. He'd seen Dwayne Wayne, a character on the Bill Cosby Show, wear a pair of eyeglasses with a flip-up sun visor over them, and Kraig had thought that he was wearing two pairs of glasses.

This was at about the same time that Kraig sometimes claimed to be Matthew, "a bad little boy." Most of the time Kraig was sweet and loving, but he sometimes became unpleasant and demanding. Then, he said he was Matthew.

One time Matthew became angry with me—I don't remember the reason for it—and started to flail and kick at me. I grabbed him firmly by his shoulders, held him at arm's length, and said sharply, "Calm down, Kraig!"

"You are the meanest grandma in the whole world," Krystle,

who was standing close by the two of us, said angrily as I continued to hold a frustrated Kraig.

"The meanest one in the whole world?" I repeated, somewhat amused.

"Yes!" she confirmed, still angry.

"In the whole world?" I said once again, looking solicitous. "In the whole world?" Meanwhile, Kraig had calmed down and was watching the interaction between his sister and his grandmother.

"Yes!" she said sharply, but then a little smile began to turn up the corners of her lips. "But I still love you," she said, offering me solace. It seems that she still thought that I was the meanest grandmother in the whole world, but owing to her own powers to love even the meanest of grandmothers, she still loved me.

"I love you, Grandma!" Kraig said, as though he hadn't been the center of the storm in the first place.

Rismos, the Baby, and Other Family Friends

Many of the Motley children have had imaginary friends and favorite toys. Some of the children have even had imaginary friends that have become real. My imaginary friends were Rismos and the Baby. When I was about five or six, I would call them at mealtimes. To do this I always went to the same place—the old tractor-pulled mower. Standing atop the mower, I would yell at the top of my voice, "Rismos and the Baby, come home!" Daddy and Mudeah often encouraged me to call them. I thought at the time it was because they didn't want Rismos and the Baby to miss dinner. In retrospect I sometimes picture how funny and cute it must have been for my parents to witness my earnest commitment to my imaginary friends.

I don't know Rismos's exact family situation, but she seems to have been a single mother. Whether she was widowed, divorced, or never married, I don't know, but I don't ever recall her husband or any other man having been a part of my thoughts and plans. Nor did I ever call a third person to dinner. Sometimes I wonder why I had two imaginary friends, neither of whom was even remotely close to me in age or in social status.

Years later, my sister Carol had three imaginary friends: twins Mercasene and Kerkasene, and their older sister, Jany B. Sometimes Carol referred to them by their diminutives; thus, they became "Merc, Kerk, and Jany." One always had to say their names in that order. Neither Carol nor I remember anything else about those constant companions of hers.

Calvin's imaginary friend was Dammy Bear. Dammy began as an imaginary bear, but ultimately Calvin was given a small teddy bear, which he named Dammy Bear. Someone once suggested that the bear's name was actually "Danny Bear" and that Calvin could not pronounce it distinctly, but Calvin promptly pointed out that the bear's name was Dammy.

Damon's imaginary friend was Mr. Bee, a huge bumblebee, the prototype of which was on the box of "Bee cereals," — Damon's favorite, of course. When Calvin and Damon came to live with me in Edwardsville in the winter of 1983, I asked what Damon would like for breakfast. He replied simply, "Bee cereals," his own name for them. I said I would get them. When I went to the store, I found that there were literally dozens of cereals. Cereals filled a whole aisle of the National Store in Glen Carbon where I had gone shopping. So I wandered slowly down the aisle, reading the boxes and looking for a bee on one, which I presumed had been responsible for the name Damon chose to call them. After looking at dozens of boxes, or so it seemed, I found one that had a bumblebee on it—Honey Nut Cheerios. When I got home Damon, who was about three or four years old, was very happy and exclaimed, "Bee cereals!" So I knew I had found the right one. Then he proceeded to play games with Mr. Bee, not the one on the box but the imaginary one. Mr. Bee would fly over our heads and Damon would yell at him, "Mr. Bee! Mr. Bee! Come here, Mr. Bee." I think he eventually did get a real "Mr. Bee" doll by sending in a coupon from the back of the "Bee cereals."

Kraig's constant companion since he was a tiny baby has been

Bear. Bear was originally Krystle's teddy, but she never developed the attachment to him that her younger brother has. Kraig has cuddled Bear, talked to him, and slept with him for his entire life. Whenever Kraig travels, he takes Bear.

Bear becomes more handsome as he grows older. His pink-and-white coat is now graying; his fuzzy nap is thin in some places. And Bear is somewhat asymmetrical, due to many trips in the washing machine. Bear has even undergone surgery with needle and thread several times. Bear reminds me of Margery Williams's story of the *Velveteen Rabbit*, the toy rabbit who was transformed into a real bunny because he was loved by the little boy. Bear is so real that Harry and I have a framed picture of him alongside those of other family members.

I once asked Kraig what Bear's name was. He replied "Bear."

"But what is his other name?" I persisted.

"Bear," Kraig replied once again.

Krystle, who was standing close by said impatiently, "It's Bear. It's just Bear."

There are many stories about Bear. When Kraig was about two or three, he said to me. "Grandma, Bear is sick."

"Oh, no. Bear is fine," I reassured him.

"He's dying, Grandma. Help Bear, Grandma. Help Bear!" Kraig persisted, handing Bear to me.

So I held Bear gently, talking softly to him, and encouraging him that he would live. "Oh, Bear, poor Bear. You'll be fine."

When I had restored Bear to good health, Kraig grabbed him, said, "Okay. Bear is fine now," and walked away with Bear in tow — and probably with his index finger in his mouth.

When Kraig was seven, Bear was accidentally left behind at the Nashville, Tennessee, home of Stacey, who has been a friend of his mother since their junior high school days. Kraig's mother, Fae, did not know that Bear was missing until they had returned to the hotel where they were staying for the night. Because it was too late to return for Bear and they had to leave early the next morning, Bear remained in Nashville. But Fae is a "good Mom," as Kraig once told me. She knew how important Bear was to Kraig, so she made elaborate plans for his journey home when Stacey did not send him promptly. Fae sent Stacey a stamped, self-addressed box for Bear's return.

Bear has had many other adventures. Once when I was visiting in California, Kraig said to me, "Grandma, I'm going to go upstairs and get Bear."

"Oh, that's nice," I replied.

"Then I'm going to bring him downstairs," he continued.

"Oh good," I responded.

"And then, I'm going to hit you with him," he concluded.

"Kraig, it is not nice to hit anyone with Bear," I said firmly.

"Okay. I won't hit you. I won't," he said kindly.

Krystle has had a number of favorite toys, unlike Kraig, who has had just one. At one time, when she was almost three years old, Krystle's favorite was the Velveteen Rabbit, and she liked to watch the movie about him on videotape. Later she got a stuffed Velveteen Rabbit for Christmas. His framed picture sits alongside that of Bear in my guest bedroom. As I look at the two photographs of stuffed animals, I think about when I'd first gotten the video for her. Kraig and Krystle were visiting me for a week or so, and I'd bought some tapes that I hoped would interest them.

Krystle, two years and ten months old, was perched on the edge of the bed, watching *The Velveteen Rabbit* on videotape for at least the third time that day. Tarik Carr, my girlfriend Hameedah's ten-year-old son, sat beside her, at her insistence, but Tarik didn't mind because he liked Krystle as much as she liked him.

Krystle had a routine response to what she called the "Belbateen Wabbit." She had watched it several times a day every day that she had been with me.

"He's got a carrot!"

"He's got a hat!"

She repeated phrases and even whole sentences from the children's story. And when the Velveteen Rabbit turned into a real rabbit and hopped away, she had a routine response for that also: she burst into tears. Tarik hugged and comforted her as she cried pathetically. We are not exactly sure why she cried. Perhaps it was because the little rabbit leaves the little boy who loves him and goes away with his new rabbit friends. Maybe it was because the story was about to end. In any case, she cried at the same point every time—several times a day.

Her brother Kraig rushed into the room when he heard his sister crying. He misunderstood the situation and thought that Tarik had made her cry. Pointing to Tarik, he said protectively, "You! Leave her alone!"

"Kraig," I said. "It's okay. Krystle is crying because of the Velveteen Rabbit. Tarik didn't make her cry."

"It's okay, Krystle. It's okay," Kraig said then, comforting his sister.

"Don't cry, Krystle," I interjected. I had a routine there, too. "We can see the Velveteen Rabbit again," I promised. I rewound the videotape and started it again, and then Krystle commenced her routine.

"He's got a carrot!"

"He's got a hat!"

When Shirley Met Harry

"Shirley, there's someone I'd like you to meet. He works with Brent at the Consortium," my sister Carol is talking on the telephone.

"Oh, really?" is my less than enthusiastic response. "So tell me about him."

"He lives in California. Works for Hewlett-Packard. Nice house. Six-figure income. Pretty nice personality." It sounds like a vita, rather than a personal introduction. I also notice that she has said nothing about his appearance.

"What's the matter with him? Is he a funny-looking motherfucker or something?" I ask.

"Oh, no. He's nice looking. He's fifty-two. Good hair. Dresses well," she responds, but I'm not convinced because she has shown considerably less enthusiasm for this than for the vita material. I also recall that once I had been a party to setting her up with a guy who was not very attractive. I wonder how I can make her believe that disastrous date really wasn't my fault. I hadn't met the guy in advance; I'd taken Allan's word for it when he'd reassured us both that Carol's prospective date was "cute." He'd been very tall and thin with a mound of hair that was at least six inches long—this was long before the Afro became popular. He'd looked at Carol, smiling happily, and then he'd actually licked his "soup-cooler" lips. I just hope my sister isn't holding a grudge. Besides that had been a long time ago—over twenty years.

"Hm-m-m, I don't know," I demur.

"Well. Look at it like this. What else do you have to do on Saturday?" Carol does have a way of cutting to the chase. In fact, I don't have plans for Saturday. So I agree to meet this six-figure-income man with the good hair.

Meanwhile, I develop a mental picture of him, which I don't find appealing. He will be overdressed, wearing expensive, tasteful clothing that make him look as though he is preparing to go to a country club. He will be at least six feet tall and well built. He will be reasonably good-looking, with one feature that is strikingly unattractive—perhaps a wart (it might have hair growing out of it) or maybe a big nose. His defect notwithstanding, he will imagine himself to be almost irresistible in personal appearance. He will be self-confident to the point of arrogance. This will reveal itself in his total domination of the conversation. His speaking voice will be slightly affected, almost as though he has taken elocution lessons.

The more I think about this "blind date," I become convinced that it is a mistake. Several days later, I call my sister. "Carol, I'm not sure I'll be very good company with the news about Mudeah's health." We have just been told that our mother has cancer.

"Well, he told Brent that he's really looking forward to meeting you. He's even delayed his Christmas trip to California so he can meet you," Carol replies. I find this rather appealing—the fact that he has shown sufficient interest to change his travel plans and to confess it to Brent. "But if you're going to act like an ass, you can just stay home." Carol is cold!

"Well, okay. Like you said before, what else do I have to do on Saturday?" The date is still on my schedule.

The plan is that Carol and Brent, Brent's friend Harry, and I will get together at Brent's. Brent has promised to make his famous chicken wings, and we will play bid whist. Sounds good, except that with only four people it will be obvious that the funny-looking guy and I are supposed to be a couple. I try to induce my sister Mildred and my brother Calvin to join us. Mildred says she has other plans. Calvin says, "Okay, Shirl, I'll stop by." Which means he probably won't. But I'm so anxious for additional company that I convince myself that he will show up at Brent's.

The night before the big evening, Mildred has the opportunity to meet Harry. She calls me to give a report. "He's cute," she says, somewhat defensively. It makes me feel a little better because Mildred is very candid and would tell me about the wart or the nose, or whatever.

On the appointed evening, I dress carefully. I am attempting to achieve a certain effect—casually fine, as though I've not attempted to be devastating but I am anyway simply because I can't help it. I select an emerald green, wool turtleneck and a slim black skirt with a split to the knee. It does have the desired effect. Then I discover that a thread in the sweater is beginning to unravel, so I have to wear something else. This time I select a bright tangerine knit dress, mid-calf length with a drop waist and full skirt. Again I achieve the desired effect. My hair turns out perfectly. It is long, a little past my shoulders, and curly.

I drive to Brent's apartment. As I round the corner one block from his residence, I see a new Ford Taurus. For some reason, I have a premonition that this is Harry's car. Later I discover that I am right. Still later, he informs me that his "car of choice" is a Rolls Corniche. I think, and whose isn't? Meanwhile, I park my car, walk to Brent's apartment building, and ring the bell. Brent greets me at the door, smiling pleasantly, and I see Carol in the living room behind him. And there is Harry. He looks quite different than I had anticipated. He is attractive, with no strikingly funny-looking features. He is wearing a little baseball cap, which I don't find particularly appealing, especially indoors. It matches his outfit at least. He is wearing very casual attire—a red-and-blue jean outfit. I notice that it is carefully ironed; the jeans have creases. He does have nice hair, wavy and black with some gray. He has a full beard and a mustache. He is about five feet nine inches tall, and is slender. He also looks considerably younger than his fifty-two years. All in all his appearance is quite a pleasant surprise.

Brent introduces us, and the four of us sit in the living room and talk. Harry and Brent talk about music. Harry has made some audiotapes for Brent and has brought them with him tonight. That strikes me as very nice and thoughtful. I also like the way the two of them banter back and forth in lively repartee. They have a very comfortable friendship. Harry teases Brent about his shoes. "Man, is that the only pair of shoes you've got? You wear them all the time!" Harry says. Brent's shoes do look rather odd.

The evening is nice, but Harry and I don't seem to have a love match. In fact, he spends much of the time talking to Brent and with his back turned to me. Later, both Carol's and Brent's surprised reactions mirror my own when I tell them that Harry has invited me out to dinner for the next night. "Really?" Carol asks incredulously. "But he hardly looked at you all evening, until we all started playing cards."

"I didn't think you two had a love connection," Brent adds.

Harry and I go out the following evening, and he is very attentive this time. He has even brought me a flower and a darling little book by Alex Haley called *My Christmas Treasure*. We go to dinner at Rusty's Restaurant in Edwardsville. The two of us seem quite compatible as we discuss the kinds of activities we enjoy—such as racquetball and antiquing—and the ones we don't care for—such as professional sports and eating tofu. With the Super Bowl coming up in about one month, he isn't even interested in it. Even so, I tell Mildred later that we had a wonderful date, "but it's not the big one."

Two months later, I have a totally different response. Suddenly I am madly in love. At this point, Mildred likes to tease me, "I won't tell Harry what you said when you first met him."

The Wedding Guests

We drive along Route 55 North to Chicago. We are headed to John's condo on the Gold Coast. Nicole, John's daughter, is getting married tomorrow to Joseph Phillips. Her fiancé is an actor who is currently on the soap opera *General Hospital*. Several years ago he was a regular on the situation comedy *The Cosby Show*.

A few hours earlier, Mil, Cal, Ramirez, and Jason—the St. Louis contingent—had stopped in Godfrey where Fae, Krystle, Kraig, and I waited. The eight of us later stopped in Springfield to get Daddy.

"We'll take all the kids, if you'll take Mil," Cal had said when Krystle, Kraig, and Jason had wanted to ride with him and Ramirez in Mil's car. That left Fae, Mil, Daddy, and me in Fae's rental.

"Don't mess up my car!" Mildred had yelled as we took off on the next leg of our journey. We didn't see them again until they passed us several hours later as they took an exit to get gas.

"They're all smoking cigarettes and eating candy!" Mil laughed. We looked over at the group, all of them smiling happily and paying no attention to us. They did all seem to be smoking cigarettes. The next time we saw them, we were all in Chicago and they were still smiling. Mil's car was littered with all kinds of wrappers and half-eaten treats—doughnuts, candy, bubble gum. Small wonder that on the return trip all three kids had announced, "We're going to ride with Uncle Calvin and Ramirez!"

As we drive to Chicago, we recall stories about the children. They have always really loved Calvin and Ramirez. Both are easygoing and soft-spoken, have a high tolerance for noise and incessant activity, and buy lots of candy. Damon had been the first of the younger ones to brag on Ramirez. "He can do anything," Damon had said. "He's a good driver, too," he'd also announced, startling everyone. Ramirez was not yet sixteen and didn't have a driver's license, nor did his mother know that when she was away Ramirez took the car for a drive.

Vanessa was Ramirez's next admirer. "I want to be with the tousins," she would cry, hanging onto Ramirez and begging to stay with him rather than going with her parents.

Kraig and Krystle liked to spend time with Ramirez as well. Whenever he sat down, they would sit next to him, one on either side. When Kraig and Krystle had moved to California from Illinois, they'd really missed their cousin. They asked me about him whenever I visited them in their new home.

One time when I visited them in California, Kraig sat on the bottom step of the first-floor stairway, obviously thinking about something very important. When he saw me, he said, "Grandma, where's Bamirez?"

I responded, "He's at his house."

"At his house?" Kraig had responded, resting his head on his hand a moment. Then he shook his head thoughtfully and said, "I love Bamirez."

Krystle, who was standing nearby, cheerfully added, "I love Bamirez, too!"

One of the family's favorite recollections of Ramirez and Krystle occurred when we had gathered for a holiday dinner. "I'll take you to the hospital," two-year-old Krystle had comforted her fourteen-year-old cousin Ramirez. She'd grabbed her Aunt Carol's purse and a set of car keys and headed for the front door. "Don't worry. You'll be okay," Krystle continually had reassured him, patting him lovingly and speaking softly.

Kraig and Krystle, as usual, had chosen to be with Ramirez while everyone else sat around laughing, talking, playing bid whist, and teasing each other. And also as usual, he was very pleasant to them, but he talked very little to them or to anyone else, which was also as usual. Because he was so quiet, Krystle thought he was ill and decided to take him to the hospital.

When we finally arrive at John's building on the day before Nicole's and Joseph's wedding, the doorman seems to be expecting us. We assume it's because John has alerted him, but maybe it's because there are so few blacks in the building that he's happy to see others like himself. He immediately tells us the apartment number and rings ahead for us, smilingly directing us to an elevator. We get in with an assortment of suitcases, garment bags, stuffed animals, and children. He probably wonders whether we're moving in permanently, rather than for the weekend as we've claimed.

Within minutes we are standing in John's living room, which overlooks Lake Michigan. What a spectacular view, we all comment. Huge windows on two sides of the room give a panoramic view of Chicago. John's collections of African American military history and literature occupy huge bookcases in both the master suite and the living room and fill one entire bedroom. African American art is arranged on tables and lines the walls. We all take such pride and pleasure in these collections, as though they are a family project.

The wedding and reception are beautiful. Susan, Nicole's mother and John's former wife, knows how to entertain. Both the wedding and the reception are held in a stately old mansion on Chicago's South Side. The wedding is held in what was once someone's front parlor. The parlor is large, with big bay windows. The floral arrangements are spectacular; huge centerpieces are on each of the dinner tables, and even larger ones are stationed throughout the three downstairs rooms and the large foyer.

Calvin has created quite a sensation with a woman who sits at the table with Mildred, Fae, Kraig, Krystle, Elise, and me. Elise is the daughter of a friend of John's and Susan's. Although Calvin has said nothing to the woman other than "hello," she is now in hot pursuit. She tries to be subtle about it, but before long it is clear that she is very interested in him.

"So, are you on the bride's side or the groom's?" she asks me, volunteering that she works with Susan. "So, you're here with your family. This is your daughter, and . . ." she politely asks about everyone else at both our table and Calvin's before getting to the real question. "The man over there," she finally says, pointing to Calvin, who has just gotten up to get another plate of food. "Is he your brother?" Mildred looks at me curiously. Why is she quizzing you about the family! her look says. "So, is . . . he . . . ah . . . married?" She's almost afraid to hear the answer, but she smiles happily when I reply that he is single. She eyes him carefully when he returns a few minutes later. Calvin is a handsome young man in his navy pin-striped suit, white shirt, and tie. All coordinated by Mildred, right down to his socks.

I sit musing over the scene before me, no doubt imputing to this woman ideas and motives that she doesn't even have. I imagine that she is struck by the sound of her own biological clock ticking, because she appears to be in her late thirties. The wedding itself may have prompted such stirrings because she'd watched Nicole and Joseph pledge to share the rest of their lives. The two of them have had a beautiful ceremony in which they exchanged vows and also jumped the broom, the latter in the tradition of our slave ancestors. Nicole had been absolutely stunning in her white wedding gown, and Joseph was handsome in his tuxedo.

Perhaps this woman is imagining how lovely she and Calvin would look standing there before the assemblage, pledging their troth. Little does she know that Calvin has no thoughts of marriage. Well, he may have thoughts about it, but he is distinctly disinclined actually to do it. In fact, he has been married once, but he didn't even bother to tell any of his family about the marriage either beforehand or after it had taken place. It was his wife, Esther, before she'd become Nanyamke, who had made us aware of the marriage. She'd taken a trip one night to Mildred's and then to Carol's. Finding neither of them at home, she'd stuffed copies of the marriage certificate in each of their mailboxes. Then she had come over to my house. Because I had been at home, she'd told me about the marriage, brandishing a copy of the marriage certificate. I wasn't really sure what the point was. But she was very defensive, as though she thought I'd have some objection to the marriage. Or perhaps even more curiously, that I wouldn't believe her without proof. It was one of those "truth is stranger than fiction deals." Mainly, I was anxious for her to speak her piece and leave because it was quite late and my granddaughter, Krystle, an infant at the time, was visiting and I had just about gotten her to sleep when Esther had rung the doorbell. By the time Esther had left, Krystle—a real night owl— had been wide awake and good for another two hours of gurgling and cooing. Not that all of this wasn't precious and music to my ears, but I was tired after a long day.

While at this wedding, I think of other family weddings, also. Harry's and mine two and one-half years ago, Michael and Karen's three years earlier, and Fae and Kraig's eight years ago. Harry and I had been married on March 14, 1992, at Pere Marquette Lodge in Grafton, Illinois, overlooking the Illinois River, just upstream from its confluence with the Mississippi. We had first gone to the lodge, located in the Pere Marquette State Park, for dinner one evening shortly after we'd decided to get married. As we'd driven along the river road, we had discussed where we would like to live, allowing our imaginations free range. About halfway between Alton and Grafton, we had noticed perched on the bluffs above the Mississippi River a large house with about a million windows. "There! That's the perfect place!" we'd said at the same time. Later we ended up buying a one-acre lot on the bluffs of Godfrey, only to discover that it was right next door to the house we had seen that night.

On the day of our wedding—in fact only hours before—I had hurried to the hotel room of Hameedah, my matron of honor, to get dressed. Passing by the place where the ceremony was to be held, I had almost had a stroke because the decorated arch that was to be there was nowhere to be seen. Nor were there any of the floral arrangements I had ordered—or the florist either, for that matter.

Mildred saved the day. She came running up to me, "Shirley! Did you want the chess set sitting in the middle of your wedding?" When I said absolutely not, she assured me that she had taken care of the problem and the management was sending someone to remove it immediately. Further, she knew that I'd ordered them to set up chairs, which had not been done yet either, but she'd taken care of that as well. And she had cornered the florist who had been late arriving, and told her where to arrange the flowers. The cake had been delivered and assembled earlier, right on schedule and without her having to give instructions on that at least. As she instructed me to go on upstairs, I was delighted that Mildred had taken charge.

Otherwise, I would have had to do all those things just at the point that I was beginning to feel a bit nervous and frazzled.

Our wedding was perfect. It was small with just our immediate families present, except for the matron of honor and the best man. Krystle had asked her mother to ask me if she could be the flower girl. I hadn't originally planned to have a flower girl—I really hadn't thought about it in fact, but once she'd asked it sounded like a really good idea. I was also relieved that Krystle was reconciled to the marriage. She had liked Harry from the first time she'd met him, yet she'd had an objection to the union. I recalled her response several years earlier when I'd first told her and Kraig that Harry and I were to be married.

"You should marry Grandpa," my four-year-old granddaughter had said.

"So, was Grandpa mad at you?" she continued, after a long silence. I was still trying to think of what to say to her.

"For what?" I responded, still in a state of shock.

"For marrying Harry."

"No, Grandpa said that Harry is a nice guy." I had finally managed to put together a complete sentence at least.

"They're both nice guys," she observed, clearly indicating that this was not the issue. Once again, I couldn't think of an appropriate response.

"I like Harry," Kraig had interjected. For him the matter was very simple. He liked Harry. So if I wanted to marry him, it was fine with Kraig. For him, there were no other issues.

Krystle had also suggested that perhaps her brother Kraig could be the "ring boy." So I had asked Kraig if he'd be the ring bearer. Knowing nothing of weddings at his tender age of six, he'd responded, "Ring bear? What's a ring bear?" Krystle had helped me to explain the role of ring bearer, after which Kraig had agreed to it. But once we were poised at the head of the steps, ready to descend, he had panicked. "Nope. I'm not going to do it," he had announced. When I'd said what a wonderful job he'd done the previous night at rehearsal, he'd replied that at that time there hadn't been a bunch of people staring at him. I assured him that they were only looking because they could see how handsome he looked in his gray suit with the black cummerbund and matching bow tie. He finally agreed to proceed. "So I go and stand next to the guys, right?" Later he had enjoyed revealing to everyone that the ring he carried on the little satin pillow was really one of my loop earrings.

Krystle had agreed to wear—as a special favor to me—the sort of "girlie, girlie dress" that she usually disdained. It was a light pink party dress with bows and lace. She had fresh flowers in her hair— she liked that part, at least—and lace-trimmed socks. And a touch of lipstick. As she and her mother had put the finishing touches on her wardrobe, Hameedah had said to Krystle, "Krystle, you look so pretty. You're the prettiest one."

"Oh, no," my seven-year-old granddaughter had replied emphatically. "Grandma is the prettiest one!" When yet another person said that she was the prettiest, Krystle had repeated her earlier comment, a bit huffily this time. Earlier she had told her mother that it was rude for a wedding guest to look prettier than the bride, so to Krystle it was a supreme insult to suggest that she had been so rude as to be the prettiest at a wedding.

I wore a floor-length gown of ecru satin, with a skirt that draped in front in a manner later described by my new husband as "like a tulip." It had bell sleeves—actually, they too resembled inverted tulips—and a fitted bodice with a V neck worn off the shoulders. My headpiece was a garland of fresh flowers, which I'd feared might make me appear to be a "Mother Nature" look-alike. Daddy, looking very distinguished in his black tuxedo with matching silk cummerbund and bow tie, escorted me down the long flight of stairs of the lodge and into the main lounge before the huge stone fireplace that was the site of the ceremony. There stood my handsome husband-to-be, bedecked in a black tuxedo with black cummerbund and white bow tie. We both stood before the minister and smiled happily, like a couple of love-struck teenagers.

The Bosman Twins, an excellent jazz band from St. Louis, played for both the wedding and the reception. We had chosen "You Are

So Beautiful" as our theme, which the band played as we stood before the minister, Rev. Steve Jackson. I'd had a difficult time holding back my tears as Harry and I gazed at each other. It was also the first time I'd ever seen tears swimming in Harry's eyes. When they played the same song at the reception, we officially began the dancing. Harry and I left the next day for a honeymoon in Amsterdam.

Michael and Karen are at Nicole and Joseph's wedding, and seeing them brings me back to the present for a few minutes at least. I exchange pleasantries with them briefly, but the two of them are on the move, sharing the host and hostess role with Susan and John. As they walk away, I think about their wedding slightly more than three years earlier.

Michael and Karen had been married at John and Susan's new home in Burlington, Connecticut, in June 1991. The wedding had been held on the large stone patio overlooking Johnny Cake Mountain. The reception had been under a huge tent in the side yard, beneath a beautiful stand of white birch trees. The truth of the matter is that what I found most memorable about Michael and Karen's wedding was a very trivial incident, which has become enshrined in family lore. As the ushers were seating the guests, Mildred, Larry, and I had taken our seats two rows behind the places reserved for the parents of the newlyweds. Next three large women were seated in front of us. Suddenly Mildred, Larry, and I had the same thought: we looked down at the women's shoes and saw that earlier each of them had sunk into the new lawn by several inches, as evidenced by the mud on their stiletto heels. Looking at each other conspiratorially, we tried not to laugh. "Man, those were some big women," Larry commented later as Mildred and I laughed appreciatively.

Fae and Kraig's wedding in August 1986 had been at the Collinsville, Illinois, Hilton, about five miles from our home in Edwardsville. All preparations had gone well. The photographer was taking his final before-the-ceremony shots. The mood was light, and the bride didn't appear the least bit nervous. Minutes before the ceremony was to have started, the soloist had called to ask directions to the hotel. She and the pianist were in St. Louis at another engagement, and they would be there in about half an hour or so. "What! You're still in St. Louis?" the bride had wailed.

"Weddings never start on time," I reassured her. I really couldn't recall one that had started on time, but realistically, I had to admit to myself, I did think it was possible. I also made a mental note to strangle both musicians after the ceremony. One hour later, Fae had decided, upon Carol's urging, to go ahead with the wedding using recorded music. At that point the tardy musicians finally arrived, and Fae was able to walk down the aisle to live music. Their performance was outstanding. That and the desire not to get blood on my dress convinced me to let them live after all.

Fae was stunning as she walked down the aisle on her father's arm. Tall and thin, she looked like a fashion model descending a runway. Kraig was appropriately handsome and slightly nervous waiting for his bride. The champagne reception was held in the ballroom of the hotel. Everyone, including the bride and groom, danced for hours. Later my two grandchildren went home with me, where they remained until their parents returned from their one-week honeymoon. Ramirez had agreed to stay with me also, to help with the children.

My attention is once again drawn to the current wedding as someone announces that the dancing is about to commence. Joseph and Nicole are the proverbial lovely couple, as we all note. Soon they are joined by others, including Krystle, Kraig, Jason, and Elise. Krystle and Elise remain on the dance floor until their mothers announce that it is time to leave. Krystle is the star of the show. She looks as if she should be on stage or in a movie. She has all the latest moves. And she's serious about this dancing thing. She acts as if its her job or something, she's so dedicated. Later she says to me, "I've never danced like that before. I learned how to do it by watching television."

Their dancing calls to mind that of Jason, only three years old at the time, who danced to "Whoop! There It Is!" at the family reunion one year. I had never paid attention to the lyrics until he began singing and dancing. Jason got into the spirit of things as he twirled around the family room. He got down on the floor on his derriere and spun around like the big boys on television and in the videos. We kept time with the music with our hands and encouraged him. "Go, Jason! Whoop! There it is!" He loved it. He concluded his performance by "working the room," going around to each person in turn and dancing in front of them as he pretended to sing into a microphone.

"Remember your turnaround dress, Carol, and the way you used to dance?" someone reminded Carol.

"Oh, yes, that Carol 'Ree was quite a dancer," Daddy interjected as Carol flashed her demure, Carol 'Ree smile.

After dancing at Nicole's and Joseph's wedding for hours, Kraig and Krystle are so tired that they don't even ask me to tell them stories when they are in bed. Both drop off to sleep immediately. They had asked if Jason could spend the night with us. Kraig had added, "I'll sleep on the floor if he can." It was tempting, but I recalled that the night before, Krystle had said the same thing in order to induce me to have both Kraig and herself spend the night. I'd gone for it that time, but when it came to be bedtime, both had hopped into bed with nary a thought of either sleeping on the floor.

8

Bridging the Generations

Seven Generations of Motleys

It is bedtime for Krystle and Kraig, my grandchildren. We've already watched two videotapes, which we'd borrowed in an earlier visit to the Alton Public Library, where we'd also gotten books. We've had ice cream with assorted sugar sprinkles with the first feature, and popcorn with lots of butter during the second. We've even played "Monster of the Mississippi," a game that the three of us created for our own entertainment. We pretend that the barges going up and down the river are the clandestine voyages of a monster who likes to burst into the room, grab children, and drag them away to his secret place. The monster lives across the river in a castle, which appears as a power plant to those who don't know better. One can gain access to the castle by stepping into the wardrobe in the hallway of our very own family room, just like in *The Lion, the Witch, and the Wardrobe*, the videotape we'd seen that is based on the C. S. Lewis novel by the same name. Sometimes Grandpa Harry or the children's mom, Fae, plays the game with us and comes up with new ideas. Harry once unexpectedly whisked away the cover under which they were hiding, causing Kraig and Krystle to squeal with delight. Later they said that he was the very best one at playing "Monster of the Mississippi"—much to my chagrin.

Telling stories about family history and lore is the final bedtime ritual. We start with several of their favorites. After I've exhausted my usual repertoire of stories, I'm ready to go to sleep, but Kraig and Krystle want to hear more. Recalling something one of them had said earlier about having studied history in school, I start a discussion about what they are learning in history.

"Did you hear about the Indians?" Kraig asks.

Wondering if he has a specific incident in mind, I reply. "I'm not sure. What do you mean?"

"You know, how they took all their land and made them live on reservations?" he responds.

"That was really mean, wasn't it, Grandma?" Krystle adds. I agree that the Indians were treated very badly. I also tell them about my recent visit to Arizona and about some of the things I learned there about Native American history. I describe the irrigation system of the Hohokam Indians. Built one thousand years ago, some of their canals are still in use today. We talk about the style of housing that they built, as well as about other architectural developments of these ancient Indians of the Southwest. I want them to be aware of the oppression and victimization of the Native Americans, but I also want them to know about the rich culture and society that they developed as well.

Eventually we end up on the topic of African American slavery, and I consider telling them about their own slave ancestors, whose history I have been researching. I'm not sure how they will respond to this information. I wonder if they will be ashamed as some blacks are. Or perhaps they will be so troubled by it that they might burst into tears. Indeed, it has been only a short time ago that Krystle had cried every time she had seen the videotape *The Velveteen Rabbit*. And Kraig had cried when he had feared for the safety of the little animal who was half-dog and half-wolf in *White Fang*.

"Our ancestors were slaves, too," I begin. "Your great-great-great-grandfather was a slave. He was a baby—less than one year old—when the slaves were freed," I add, waiting for their response.

"Neat!" they both exclaim. They are now wide awake, and they want to know more about their Great-Great-Great-Grandfather Henry Motley, who was born a slave, and their Great-Great-Great-Grandmother Emma Motley, who was born shortly after slavery.

I begin with rudimentary information, expecting that they will not be interested in the many details I have unearthed. Soon it becomes clear that both want to hear everything I can tell them about their slave ancestors. Both comment that black history is their favorite subject in school. For the first time, I tell my grandchildren about the family history research that their Great-Uncle John and I have done, which has enabled us to discover the slave roots of our family.

In Search of My Great-Great-Grandparents

My brother John and I drove the eighty-five miles northeast of Memphis to Humboldt in Gibson County, Tennessee, where our great-great-grandparents Buck and Harriet Motley, had lived in the antebellum through the postbellum period. For many years we had wanted to research our family's history. Daddy had entertained us since we were children with stories about the family's experiences in Charleston, Missouri, and Future City, Illinois. Interviews with him and various family members had enhanced greatly our knowledge of family history. Most recently we had talked with our Great-Uncle Odell, our paternal grandfather's brother—who was also our oldest living Motley relative—and his wife, Louise, and daughter, Ida. He had provided important details about our history, including the fact that the family had lived in Humboldt, Tennessee, and later in Mississippi, before migrating to Wynne, Arkansas. After leaving Uncle Odell's house in Colt, Arkansas, John and I had made two very productive trips—one to Little Rock and another to Memphis—to sift through state records and other data.

This trip had taken place in September 1982, shortly after my daughter, Fae, had started college at Southern Illinois University in Carbondale. I had visited her and then continued on to Memphis, where I had met my brother John, who had flown into the city from New York. John was an executive with Chemical Bank, but his avocation was history. John and I had always had a strong bond, both as children and as adults, but we had never shared a research project. I was prepared to address potential problems here, however. As

I drove to Memphis, I thought of diplomatic but firm ways to establish my own primacy in this matter. Number one, I thought, we'll just have to make it clear from the outset that I will be project director. After all, I am the one with the doctorate in history. So I am the one who knows how to do historical research. My concern here proved misguided because my brother proved to be an excellent research assistant, very knowledgeable in the collection of historical data and appropriately deferential to the project director.

What neither of us had anticipated was that this trip would be a very emotional one because of the way we would both feel about the information we found. We had both anticipated that members of our family were slaves in the antebellum era, and we thought that we had come to terms with this. Later we would discover that an academic understanding of a family history of slavery and a personal confrontation with the evidence are two very different things. We experienced joy, sadness, rage, hostility, pride, shame—our emotions ran the gamut. Yet we were always very happy that we had undertaken this project. Our only regret about the research venture was that we could not devote additional time to the project.

On the trip to Humboldt, John and I talked about what we had already learned about the family history extending back for six generations from our own children to our slave great-great-grandparents born in the 1830s and 1840s. The births of Krystle and Kraig, in 1985 and 1986 respectively, and of Akilah Roberts, my nephew's daughter, in 1995 added a seventh generation.

Buck and Harriet Motley were the parents of four children when slavery was ended by the Thirteenth Amendment in 1865. Their children were George, Jacob, Elizabeth, and Henry, who were eight, six, one, and less than one year, respectively, when the family gained its freedom. Henry was my great-grandfather. A fifth child, Mattie, was born in 1868, and a sixth, Emma, in 1870.

Buck was a farmer and Harriet a housewife, according to the 1870 manuscript census of the United States. The black Motleys were enumerated with the household of William Motley, their former master. Although the two groups of Motleys—black and white—were listed as though they resided in the same domicile, they probably had separate houses. William Motley's household also included his wife, Margaret, whom he had married in 1867, and four children, one by Margaret and three by his first wife. A man of some means, William owned $6,000 in real estate and $1,000 in personal property in 1870. His personal property, most of it in slaves, had declined since 1860, when he had reported $4,500 in personal assets. William Motley also had $3,000 in real estate at that time. The $3,500 difference between his personal property holdings in 1860 and in 1870 could be accounted for by the loss of ownership of six slaves, the family of Buck and Harriet Motley. John and I took great joy in noting this financial loss because it had meant the freedom of our own family.

John and I wondered why Buck and Harriet had remained at the site of their enslavement. Aware that this was common in the postbellum period, we nonetheless puzzled over their individual motivation. We were both disappointed that our relatives had not chosen to leave. We joked about Great-Great-Grandfather Buck as an "Uncle Tom" who continued to live with the "massa." Our levity poorly masked our disappointment. We both knew that we had hoped for more radical figures, such as a "Nat Turner Motley," a "Harriett Tubman Motley," or a "Frederick Douglass Motley."

Previously given to philosophizing about the injustices committed by slaves who had killed whites while revolting against their enslavement, I finally understood Nat Turner, Denmark Vesey, Gabriel Prosser, and a host of others who had planned slave revolts. Why had not Great-Great-Grandfather Buck revolted? Or, at least, why hadn't he escaped with his family? Indeed, why had not our Great-Great-Grandmother Harriet led the family to freedom? It would take some time and considerable reflection before I could be proud of what these slave ancestors had done: they had managed to keep their family intact throughout the horrible ordeal of slavery. And that deserved both my respect and my love. They did not deserve my misguided, presentist, and judgmental observations.

In the 1880 census the black Motleys were no longer listed with the white Motleys. Buck was still a farmer, but Harriet was no longer there. She had in all likelihood died between 1870 and 1880, probably during or shortly after the birth of Emma in 1870. In 1880 Buck Motley's household included his children Elizabeth, Henry, Matt(ie), and Emer (Emma), and his grandson George.

We began the next phase of our investigation at the Gibson County courthouse, located on a typical southern town square and surrounded by the small town of Trenton, about five miles north of Humboldt. Inside we quickly found the county records center, neatly maintained by a very efficient and accommodating staff. They helped us locate the record groups we had requested and then left us to examine these and other materials. John and I hunkered down for hours, poring through hundreds of documents and sharing the most interesting and unusual ones with each other. We both eagerly examined any data that might have related directly to our family. Our excitement increased as we searched for any clue to our family's life in Humboldt.

A picture of antebellum Gibson County began to emerge as we read the numerous documents: marriage, birth, and death records; deeds and other land records; wills; tax assessment rolls; and others. Little of this information contained specific references to blacks because virtually all of them had been slaves in Gibson County before 1865. African Americans in Gibson County rarely lived as free persons. Only one free black family—headed by a female with five children—was listed in the last antebellum manuscript census. If others had become free, they had left the county.

Most blacks in the county lived on family farms, where they worked in the fields for their white masters. County slaveholders held one or two slaves in most cases. An occasional slaveholder had more than this; very few owned as many as eight slaves. Some owners employed overseers to supervise their slave laborers. These slaves' lives were in all probability like those of millions of blacks who worked in the South producing cotton, tobacco, rice, and other crops. Slaves here, as elsewhere in the United States, could be born, marry, give birth, and die without ever being noted in the public domain. Slaveowners kept whatever records they chose about their chattel. Some owners were illiterate, so their record keeping suffered for this reason, also. Births were often recorded, although not necessarily with the exact birth dates. Slave marriages, although not legally binding, might be noted by the master. Deaths were likely to receive comment, often in the same books with births. After slavery these records usually remained with the owners, leaving millions of African Americans without written documentation of their births, marriages, and deaths.

Because of the paucity of race-specific data on African Americans, we had to study the whites with whom our family had been associated. Thus, the white Motleys, some of whom had owned Buck and Harriet and from whom they had received their surname, became crucial to our research. The white Motleys included a large extended family, members of which had begun to move into Gibson County during the period between 1836 and 1840.

The white Motleys were migrants from rural North Carolina. William, John, Harrison, and James Motley were names that we ran across many times because a succession of fathers, sons, nephews, and other relatives gave these names to their children. Public records—such as wills, marriage certificates, bonds, and guardianship papers—make numerous references to these Motleys. Their wives, daughters, and other female relatives appear in the public records, also, although much less often than do the males. The Motleys were farmers who had purchased slaves and numerous tracts of land in Gibson County in the antebellum era.

We found additional information about the white Motleys at the Trenton library. Carefully sorted and cataloged private papers, local newspapers, and copies of public records were included in these collections. Except for a few doctors' bills for slaves, we noted few explicit references to blacks. For example, an 1852 bill from C. Sharp to James Motley—who was either the brother or the cousin of the aforementioned William Motley—had twelve entries for medical treatment. Seven were for visits to his mother Mary, his sister Nancy, and other family members; five were to an unidentified

"Negro man." Sharp had charged $1.50 for each visit and an additional fifty cents for a "blister plaster." Other bills were for articles that slaves might have used, such as food and farm utensils.

Wills occasionally made references to slaves. The will of the aforementioned James Motley, who died in February 1855, indicated that his slaves, including a man noted only as "Wash" and others whose names he did not specify, might be freed after James's death and after they had served "his mother during her natural life and after her death to be freed if he could free them without an additional expence [sic]. . . ." If James's heirs were unable to free them, the slaves were to go to his three younger siblings, John R., Harrison, and Nancy. As with many such provisions, this one was dependent upon the good graces of the heirs, especially of John R. and Harrison, to whom James entrusted the responsibility for attending to the possible emancipation. John and Harrison apparently chose to retain their human property, numbering three in 1855 according to county tax records, because there is no evidence of their manumission at this time. In March 1862 John R. Motley volunteered for the Army of the Confederacy. Although he survived the wartime experience, he died two and one-half years later, possibly due to an injury or disease contracted during the war. Upon John's death, his brother Harrison inherited all of his property, in accordance with John's will.

My brother John and I had very emotional responses to our research. We felt a certain exhilaration over being able to locate information on over 150 years and six generations of family history. Every piece of data was a key to our own past, and we treasured that aspect of the search. But we also felt hostility as we perused the many documents. We read about our own family and other slaves whose liberty had been denied them by a succession of white owners. This information was far more poignant to me—a professional historian and university history professor for many years—than any I had read previously about slavery. These were my family members. They were my great-great-grandparents and their children. I was at once enchanted by my growing knowledge of them and sickened by the bondage in which they had lived.

When we initially had read James Motley's will, my brother and I had mistakenly believed that this Motley had been the master of our great-great-grandparents and their children. Thus, we had hoped that our family had gained their freedom before 1865, in accordance with the terms of the will. But we had also been angered by the fact that they had been held as chattel. We noted that slaves had been listed alongside other personal property, such as household furnishings, farm implements, and horses and buggies.

We also recalled the many secondary and primary works we had read about slavery, and now we saw them as directly relevant to our own family's lives. John talked about a set of leg chains that he had recently added to his collection of African American memorabilia. "I can't stand to look at them!" he had declared emphatically. "I don't display them with the rest of my collection," he had added. Several years later when he showed them to the family as we gathered for our annual reunion, I understood his response to the chains. John had plunked them on the kitchen table. The Motleys, typically a noisy group that has something to say about everything, fell totally silent. It was only later, after he had returned them to storage, that we could say even one word about those horrible symbols of African American bondage. Although we never explicitly spoke of our own family wearing these chains, I know that is what was in each of our thoughts.

Great-Grandfather Henry Motley was born a slave in June 1864 in Humboldt, where his family continued to live for at least sixteen years after his birth. Emma Holloman Motley, my great-grandmother, was born in post-emancipation Humboldt in September 1872. By 1887 Henry Motley and Emma Holloman had married and moved to Mississippi. In our attempt to retrace our family's migration, the next research venue for John and me was Mississippi.

We had discovered through both oral history sources and census materials that both sides of our family had lived in Mississippi in the late nineteenth century. The Joneses, our mother's family, had lived in DeSoto County, in the northwest portion of the state. Erroneously believing that the Motleys also had lived in this county and that we could, therefore, simultaneously research both sides of the family, we set out for Hernando, the county seat, about an hour's drive from Memphis.

Even in 1982, we could see signs of a segregated social order in Hernando. John parked on the town square, and we both got out of the car, ready to proceed to the courthouse across the street. In moments several people passed by the car, cautiously greeted us, and eyed the front wheel on the driver's side. After this had happened a number of times, John and I looked at the tire, trying to determine what had sparked such interest. Finally, a black man said, very kindly but emphatically, "You'd better move that car," and quickly hurried past. He apparently did not want to be held responsible for our misdeed, whatever it was.

A second man stepped forward moments later and ventured an opinion, "Your car is parked over the line. You'll get a ticket." He too rushed away without further explanation. We looked critically at the car. The wheel was barely touching the white line that divided ours from the parking space beside it. But we decided that we were well advised to move it nonetheless. Why were all of these black people so concerned about this? And why were they seemingly afraid to talk to us?

We proceeded to the DeSoto County Clerk's office, where we asked for birth, death, and marriage records. The clerk looked at us warily and asked us to repeat our request. Seeking to allay her suspicion, I indicated that our family had lived in Hernando during the late nineteenth century, and we were hoping to find information about them. "Oh," she said, sounding rather relieved. Perhaps she had mistaken two unfamiliar blacks, who were obviously not from the area, for troublemakers. She showed us into a small, well-kept vault lined with official record books and then hurriedly left the room. I found myself imagining that she had gone for the county sheriff and perhaps the local lynch team. But we remained there for hours without interruption.

After inspecting these public records, we found that there were two sets of books: one was marked "colored" and the other "white." This dual system had been discontinued only in the modern era. We carefully examined marriage records, land records, wills, and other official documents, but we found no information about either the Motleys, the Joneses, the Rankins, or any other relative. We worked there until closing time but found no relevant data. A trip to the local library had proved fruitless as well. Yet we both had the feeling that there was relevant data there, even though we did not know how to access it.

John and I had felt so uncomfortable in Hernando that we declined even to have dinner there, preferring to return to Memphis, where we were staying at the Drake Hotel. As we left this small town, we noted that blacks were on one side of the town square, while whites remained on the other. The atmosphere seemed strained and uncomfortable.

Later research revealed the problem with our attempt to follow the Motley family's migration pattern: Grampa's Veterans Administration records indicated that his family had lived in Corinth, Mississippi, rather than in Hernando. It would take another fifteen years, until May 1997, before I would return to Mississippi to pursue the appropriate itinerary. Harry Portwood, my husband and new research assistant, accompanied me on this trip, which proved to be a very productive one.

New information from Grampa's Veterans Administration records allowed us to interpret the census data more accurately. The 1900 census had indicated that Emma and Henry Motley had at least three children while living in Mississippi. Mary was born in 1887, Pearl in 1892, and Jim H. in 1894. Emma had borne four others who were deceased. The couple had two other living children, both of whom had been born in Wynne, Arkansas: Bessie in 1896 and Benny in 1899. Thus, the family seems to have lived in Corinth for at least seven years, from about 1887 to 1894. County reports to the Mississippi State Superintendent of Schools further suggest that Emma and Henry Motley and their family had left Corinth before 1896. Their son Odell, of Colt, indicated that after 1900 my great-grandparents had four additional sons: Wesley, Irving, Odell, and Essex.

Born on September 10, 1894, the person noted above as "Jim H." was later called "Henry Motley" and is my grandfather. This can be deduced from comparing the date and place of birth given in the census with the same information from other sources. The discrepancy in the names is a mystery. The census taker might have erroneously recorded the name. Or perhaps another son named "Henry" had died, and this was a way of preserving the name "Henry" as that of the oldest son. Yet another possibility is that his name was "Jim Henry," and they merely dropped the first name.

The naming patterns in my family recall those of many other African Americans and Africans who retain a given name over many generations. For example, my great-grandfather Henry Motley's name has survived for four generations. His son, my grandfather, was also named Henry Motley. My father's name is John Henry Motley Sr., and my brother's name is John Henry Motley Jr.

"Buck and George Motley lived in Corinth!" I exclaimed. Harry and I were at the Corinth branch of the Northeast Regional Library. Great-Great-Grandfather Buck Motley and his grandson George had lived in Corinth during the late 1890s and at the turn of the century, according to an Alcorn County Assessor's Report to the Mississippi Superintendent of Schools. Both grandfather and grandson were listed in a county report for 1896, George as an "educable" child and Buck as his parent or guardian. "Educable" only indicated that George was of school age; it did not indicate whether he had actually attended school. Another report indicated that Mary "Modley" was an educable child, and that Emma "Modley" was her parent or guardian. Yet another indicated that Mary "Modley" was an educable child, and Henry "Modley" was her parent or guardian. Despite the misspelling of the surname, it was clear by the ages and names of the children, as well as by the names of the parents, that these were our relatives.

"Records in Alcorn County were kept separately by race until the 1960s or 1970s," a clerk at the circuit clerk's office informed us after we had requested marriage and other county records. "They aren't now, of course," she added as she pointed out the old records that we had requested. She showed us stacks of records and then directed us to a back room, where she invited us to examine them. "Stay as long as you like," she added pleasantly. Harry and I began to search the oldest "colored" marriage registers. We found that the records had been kept separately until May 1974.

"George Motley," Harry said teasingly. "Does the name George Motley mean anything to you?"

"George Motley! That was my great-great-grandfather's grandson! My cousin!" I responded. George and Mary Johnson had married on May 1, 1901. We noted that George had been unable to write because he had made his mark. The license did not require a signature by the bride, so we could determine nothing about her literacy.

"Buck Motley was married here, too," Harry announced moments later. My great-great-grandfather and Fronia Buckhannon had married on August 3, 1896, in Corinth. He, like his grandson, made his mark. After decades of widowhood, Buck, now over sixty years of age, had finally remarried. His new wife was apparently a much younger woman. Referred to in the public record as "Miss Fronia Buckhannon," she had not married previously.

"It looks like Buck and Fronia had a couple of kids," Harry noted within minutes of beginning to examine the first of a set of record books that we had found in a visit to the office of the Alcorn County Superintendent of Schools. These were the originals of the reports on educable children that corresponded to the copies we had seen at the Corinth branch of the Northeast Regional Library. By 1900 Buck was the father, or perhaps the stepfather, of six-year-old Retta Motley and five-year-old Beatrice Motley.

By 1900 Henry and Emma Motley, my great-grandparents, had migrated to Cross County, Arkansas. Henry was a farmer. No occupation was given for Emma in the census, as was commonly the case with women, but she was probably a homemaker. Both could read and write. Further, their school-age children attended school.

This fragmentary evidence suggested the high value that the Motleys had placed on education one hundred years ago. Significantly, Henry's most recent slave master had remained illiterate throughout his life.

My grandmother, Anna Barnes Motley, was born in 1893 in Arkansas, the state of birth for both of her parents. Her family, according to interviews with family members, was related on her mother's side to the Starks who developed the Stark delicious apples. Temmie Barnes, Anna's mother, was a beautiful woman with very fair skin and long, wavy black hair that bespoke her racially mixed heritage.

Henry Motley and Anna Barnes married on April 8, 1917, in Wynne, where they resided for the first years of their marriage. Anna Barnes had one child, Gertie, previous to her marriage to Henry Motley. She and Henry had five additional children: Senina, Savannah, John, Vernon, and Harry. All except Senina, their first-born, survived into adulthood. Savannah later choose the name "Shirley." I am named after this aunt.

Henry Motley briefly served in the U.S. Army during World War I. He was a private in the 67th Company, 17th Receiving Battalion, 162 Depot Brigade, from June 21, 1918, until his honorable discharge on December 21, 1918. After he left the service, Grampa worked alternately as a factory operative, railroad man, sharecropper, and farmer, while Grandmommy was a homemaker. During World War II, Grampa worked for the Work Projects Administration (WPA). Still later, he moved to Peoria, Illinois, where he worked for Caterpillar. When he retired in 1959, both he and Grandmommy returned to the family farm in Mounds.

Grandmommy and Grampa both died in 1978, within months of each other. Grandmommy died in Mounds, about six months before Grampa's death on October 21, 1978, in Chicago.

Conclusion:
The Next Generations

When I have finished telling Krystle and Kraig about their slave ancestors, they are full of questions about them. How did I know this information? Where did I find it? They actually enjoy hearing about the various documents I have read and about the others I plan to study.

Kraig and Krystle finally drift off to sleep. As I watch their beautiful faces and listen to their quiet breathing, I think about seven generations of Motleys—from my Great-Great-Grandfather Buck and Great-Great-Grandmother Harriet through Krystle and Kraig, my own grandchildren. One hundred seventy years of Motleys. I wonder about the ones who came before Buck and Harriet—in Tennessee, in Africa. Where did they live? What were their lives like? Will I ever be able to wind my way through the maze of years and incomplete records to find them? Maybe Krystle, Kraig, or some other relative will take up the search where my own research ends.

I wonder about the generations to come. In perhaps twenty years, Krystle, Kraig, or both might well have children of their own. And their children will have children, and so on. . . . How will all these new additions affect the family history? What will change? What will remain the same? What stories will they tell?

Shirley Motley Portwood is a professor in the Department of Historical Studies at Southern Illinois University Edwardsville. She grew up in rural Mounds and Springfield, Illinois, and lives in Godfrey.